BOARDS OF DIRECTORS
AND THE
PRIVATELY OWNED FIRM

BOARDS OF DIRECTORS
AND THE
PRIVATELY OWNED FIRM

A Guide for Owners,
Officers, and Directors

ROGER H. FORD

QUORUM BOOKS
New York • Westport, Connecticut • London

Library of Congress Cataloging-in-Publication Data

Ford, Roger H.
    Boards of directors and the privately owned firm : a guide for
owners, officers, and directors / Roger H. Ford.
        p.   cm.
    Includes bibliographical references and index.
    ISBN 0-89930-567-9
    1. Directors of corporations.   2. Private companies.   I. Title.
HD2745.F49   1992
658.4′22—dc20   91-24854

British Library Cataloguing in Publication Data is available.

Library of Congress Catalog Card Number: 91-24854
ISBN: 0-89930-567-9

First published in 1992

Quorum Books, One Madison Avenue, New York, NY 10010
An imprint of Greenwood Publishing Group, Inc.

Printed in the United States of America

The paper used in this book complies with the
Permanent Paper Standard issued by the National
Information Standards Organization (Z39.48-1984).

10 9 8 7 6 5 4 3 2 1

This book is dedicated to my father,
Herald H. Ford,
my first, and best, business teacher

Contents

Illustrations

Preface

When I reached the end of this project, I was left with a combination of relief and indebtedness. The relief comes from a realization that I now have some free time to spend with my family. The indebtedness comes from a realization that this book would not have been possible without an awful lot of encouragement and help along the way. I would like to take just a moment to thank some of those people now.

First, the book is the result of a long journey that began with my doctoral dissertation at Syracuse University. That project began as an idea in 1984, and was concluded in 1986 under the leadership of Professors David L. Wilemon and Donald N. DeSalvia (co-chairmen) and committee members Professors L. Richard Oliker, James N. Vedder, and Elizabeth C. Wesman. The real contribution of a dissertation committee is often overlooked during the struggle to ''get finished'' with a doctoral program. I realized how much its constant pushing and challenging really was worth, however, once the study was completed. This realization came in the form of a flurry of inquiries from both national and international media as well as business leaders from around the country who were interested in learning what I had to say about boards of directors. This book is, in fact, the result of a call from Quorum acquisitions editor Tom Gannon after he had read about my study in *The Wall Street Journal*. Dave, Don, Dick, Jim, and Betsey, let me tell you publicly that this exposure would not have occurred had you let me get away with the superficial board study I initially proposed to you.

I also had a great deal of help during the actual eighteen months of writing from a number of people. First, I wish to thank my secretary Mary Beth Board for her extensive help. I especially appreciated her patience for all the times I asked for help with projects that I could not explain because I did not know what I wanted myself. Next, I wish to acknowledge my graduate assistant Jim Dieterle for his extensive research help. His running to the library and reviewing articles saved me countless hours of work. I would also like to thank the James Madison University Entrepreneurship Center Secretary Marsha Shenk and JMU Management Department Secretary Bernie Click for their many contributions, as well as student assistant Lisa Eaton.

Many faculty encouraged me with the project, most notably Professor Charles D. Pringle and Professor Emeritus Lester R. Bittel. I also greatly appreciated the advice and encouragement of Professor Emeritus Stanley C. Vance of the University of Tennessee. Three individuals made very special contributions to the book in the form of cases. These appear in Chapter 10, and I wish to thank Warren Braun, Bill Judge, and Joe Rosenstein for taking the time from their busy schedules to prepare the cases. A biographical sketch on these contributors can be found at the beginning of the case chapter.

I also wish to thank Tom Gannon at Quorum for approaching me with the idea for the book. Without his encouragement that I might have something useful to say on the subject of boards of directors I doubt if I would ever have attempted the book. I appreciate all that he and the rest of the staff did to make the book a reality. I am especially indebted to my wife Holly, our daughter Cassandra, and son Ryan for putting up with me during the last year and a half while I juggled this project along with all the other demands on my schedule. Finally, I am grateful to God for giving me the skills and good health necessary to work, think, learn, write, and, hopefully, contribute!

Roger H. Ford

James Madison University
Harrisonburg, Virginia

BOARDS OF DIRECTORS
AND THE
PRIVATELY OWNED FIRM

Introduction and Background

INTRODUCTION

I became interested in the subject of privately held corporations at a fairly young age. When I was a teenager, my father bought out his partner of twenty-five years and reorganized his real estate development firm as a corporation. Either at his or the family attorney's wishes, my brother, sister, and I each became owner of a share of stock—one percent of the equity in the business. Although my understanding of all this was somewhat fuzzy, my interest was firmly hooked. From this point on, buzzwords such as corporate governance, board of directors, and shareholders had a special fascination for me.

A few years later I became more actively involved in the affairs of the family enterprise in ways ranging from building maintenance, minor office tasks, construction work, and, occasionally, as a principal in an investment. As early as my college days, I began participating in real estate projects that included partnerships and joint ventures, as well as projects handled by the family's basic corporation. During my first few years out of college, I also began a partnership with my wife, and later opened a restaurant with my brother. These experiences all helped to deepen my interest in small and entrepreneurial firms—particularly with regard to management and governance issues.

Starting in 1979, I had the opportunity to be involved in the creation of a new corporation from the ground level. Although there was nothing particularly unique about this small corporation (there were roughly a half million of them formed that year), the fact that it was part mine and that I had played a major role in getting it started made it very special to me. I read and reread the boilerplate material in the corporate minute book, and was particularly intrigued with the sections concerning the board of directors. Was there really something to this board concept that could benefit small corporations, or was it just legalese designed by lawyers to give small firms an appearance of respectability and legitimacy?

I happened to be a part-time MBA student during most of the five or six years that I was heavily involved with the small- and family-business activities. While doing some graduate research, I happened to stumble upon several articles and books on the subject of boards of directors. A few of these specifically addressed the topic of boards as they apply to small or privately held companies. Now I had an academic literature base to ground my interest in boards, and my inquiry began to get serious. In particular, I recall reading a book by Leon Danco, *Outside Directors in the Family Owned Business*, and an article by Bruce Posner in *Inc.*, "A Board Even an Entrepreneur Could Love." These publications strongly advocated the use of boards of directors by small businesses. In effect, they argued that the board, and outside directors in particular, could help the business owner in many ways, especially by compensating for human resources that the firm lacked, such as a big staff, or several seasoned top- and middle-level managers. It sounded as simple as that. There didn't appear to be any trick to it at all. This argument was both logical as well as intuitively pleasing. I saw no reason to question the authors' obviously expert opinions—not even to a degree.

At this point I had become a diehard and unquestioning supporter of the use of outside boards by privately owned companies. I was influenced by this view in papers and cases I prepared in graduate school. I also made a few overtures about expanding the board of our family corporation. This idea was quickly brushed off, however, due to a strong conviction in my family to "keep it in the family."

In 1982, I became involved as a board member with a new electronics manufacturing firm. One of the agenda items I repeatedly brought to the table was a plan to expand the board from four to seven members by bringing in three additional outsiders. I had a complete game plan, including a rationale, procedure, expectations, and criteria for choosing new directors, and even the names of the nominees. With hindsight, I can now see that *I was pushing a serious policy recommendation onto a dynamic, but struggling, firm based on my own theoretical perspective, rather than based on the particular circumstances and needs of that firm.* Although there was nothing particularly wrong with the theoretical perspective, my application of it was naive.

The president of the firm went along with my ideas, and the board was expanded. We met quarterly, and followed many of the standard procedures recommended in the literature. Although a few useful outcomes derived from the board (especially in the area of raising capital), my personal assessment is that it was a failure. The expanded board survived a little over two years, at which time the president decided to go back to five members, which involved dropping the three outsiders added at the time of the expansion and replacing them with a major shareholder and another new outsider chosen for other reasons. (An insider had also left the firm around this time, which left the board with a total of five members.) Since that time, the board has met only once or twice a year for the purpose of performing a superficial review of activities, engaging in a little brainstorming, and exchanging pleasantries. Yet, in spite of a lack of assistance from the board, the company competes in a tough global market, is growing at an incredible rate, and is very profitable.

While this particular board case was occurring, I had withdrawn from most of my business activity in order to enter a doctoral program in business administration, with an emphasis in management policy and marketing innovation. This gave me a extraordinary opportunity to empirically explore the board issue as a dissertation topic. The only serious obstacle I had to overcome was convincing the faculty on my research committee as to why such a question was worthy of a year or more of my time. They had no problem with the importance of small firms to the economy, or with the need to explore tools and methods to assist them. Their concern was along the line of "why do you want to study the obvious? Of course, outside boards will benefit small and entrepreneurial firms!" My counterargument was twofold: First, I pointed out that regardless of how intuitive and logical the notion that boards could be a big asset to private firms, the fact remained that the question had never been put to a scientific test to *prove* that boards benefit these firms. My second argument was that a scientific study on the subject would not only add to the academic literature, but could serve to convince firm owners of the wisdom of board utilization.

I will not go into the details of the dissertation here (an executive summary of the study is contained in Chapter 9). Rather, I will just point out that the results of the study did not produce across-the-board proof that boards benefit entrepreneurial firms. Although I did come across many examples of boards that were making numerous positive contributions to the firm and its owners—indeed, almost "model" boards—the striking observation was the number of examples of chief executive officers that were not impressed with their boards and outsiders. In fact, there were many examples of situations in which the board could have been (and often was) considered counterproductive.

At this point I must clarify that I do not mean to imply that all boards are worthless; if that were the case, there would be no point for this book. Rather, the issue is far more complicated than simply making a decision to have a board—based on theory, appointing a couple of outside directors—possibly with unrealistic expectations, and living happily ever after. There are many possible reasons why many of the firms I studied were dissatisfied with their boards, only one of which is that the firm may be better off without the outside group. Other possibilities include poor recruiting and training, ineffective organization and control, and other management-related reasons. All of this will be discussed later.

Since my study was completed, however, I am afraid that I have gotten a reputation as somewhat of a "board basher." This has been partly self-induced, and partly has been the result of the way the business press has reported the study. Let me briefly try to summarize my view on the use of boards in a very general sense, and then demonstrate why, in my opinion, my view has sometimes been misunderstood. I began exploring the use of boards by private concerns

Figure 1.1
Continuum of Board of Directors' Perspectives for Privately Owned Companies

```
POSITIVE              OBJECTIVE              NEGATIVE

<--------------------------------------------------------->


BOARDS ALWAYS         BOARDS HELPFUL IN      BOARDS NEVER
A POSITIVE            MANY BUT NOT ALL       A USEFUL TOOL
TOOL FOR PRIVATE      PRIVATE COMPANY        FOR PRIVATE
COMPANIES            SITUATIONS             COMPANIES
```

with the opinion that there was only one correct perspective, and that was that virtually all firms (at least those over some arbitrary size threshold) should have and would benefit from the use of a board complete with outside directors. This was the perspective largely hailed in the recent popular and academic literature. As a result of my study, however, I realized that there was another perspective, and that was that not all firms with boards found them useful, and perhaps boards were not necessary or helpful in all cases. I believe this is in fact a balanced view; however, some writers and their followers assume I hold an extreme antiboard view simply because I challenged the conventional wisdom.

This can be further understood by observing Figure 1.1. My personal view is expressed in the center. The views on the extreme left and right represent, respectively, the extreme "proboard" and extreme "antiboard" positions. The proboard position largely reflects the popular literature, and the conventional wisdom on the subject. I know of no one subscribing to the extreme antiboard position. Because my perspective is further away from the conventional perspective than anything else available, I am perceived as the extremist.

I also mentioned that I was in part to blame for this misinterpretation. I have done a much more effective job publishing the negative aspects of my study than the positive. It is a simple fact of publishing life that the controversial sells much better than the ordinary. Publishers of academic as well as popular journals have shown much more interest in my observations on ineffective boards and directors than effective ones. Therefore, the bulk of what has been written about my work, both by me and by professional writers and reporters, has focused on the negative. Titles such as "Who Needs Outside Directors," "The Value of Outside Directors: Myth or Reality," "Latest Board Advice Is to Keep It in the Family," and " . . . Outside Directors Are a Hindrance Because They Don't Know the Business" (see References and Bibliography) certainly have not implied an open mind on my part. I will confess that I personally suggested some of these titles, and I did not complain when they were provided by others, simply because I was interested in getting my perspective noticed. I have also written and have been quoted in a number of more positive articles, but these have received little attention in comparison to the more critical ones.

To reiterate, I consider my position free from either an extreme antiboard or an extreme proboard bias. Although I do see the many potential benefits a board can bring to a company, I also see the problems it can create, and the huge investment required to create a successful board. Although my position has been somewhat misunderstood, I am certainly not complaining as I recognize the benefits I have received from all the publicity on my research, regardless of the slant. If nothing else, I believe this publicity has served a useful purpose by raising the level of interest and discussion on the board issue.

This is a book about boards and how they can serve the privately owned company. I will attempt to cover the benefits and also include a realistic discussion on the down side as well. My goal is for the reader to go through this book and then be able to objectively and intelligently decide whether a board is an appropriate tool for his or her firm, and, if so, how to go about getting started and organized. My personal bias is that boards can be an incredible tool for the privately held company; but they are not going to work in all situations, and the investment time and cost to build an effective working board is far more than most company owners realize.

OVERVIEW

This is a book for people who own, manage, or advise privately held businesses. It deals with a subject that, in spite of much recent media attention, is largely misunderstood. Although dozens of articles (and a few books) have been written recently about boards of directors, none have presented a thorough and objective discussion concerning the use of boards by privately owned businesses.

Most of what has been previously written on the subject of boards of directors, unfortunately, pertains to larger, publicly owned businesses; that is, those companies with broad ownership that changes hands frequently through stock market transactions. The boards of directors of these publicly traded companies are very different from the boards of private firms. The lessons we learn from observing the boards of huge, multifaceted corporations are of little use to owners of small- or medium-size businesses who are thinking about developing or reorganizing their boards to help them with their enterprises. The major differences between boards of public and private firms will be addressed later in this chapter.

Over the last few years, however, a number of consultants, theorists, and academics have begun to write on the subject of boards of directors as a tool to assist entrepreneurs and small business owners. Most of this literature contains a strong proboard and pro-outside director bias. These writers typically advocate the creation and use of outside advisory or governing boards by all sorts of small, family, and entrepreneurial businesses.

A good example of the one-sided nature of the emerging board literature occurred in the Fall 1988 issue of the *Family Business Review*, a respected academic journal devoted to small and family business issues. In his introduction to this special issue, guest editor John Ward admitted that the entire issue was devoted to promoting active boards with outside directors for family firms. Although the journal's promoters should be commended for their enthusiasm, they deserve a failing mark for the one-sided way in which they treated this important issue. The reader of this publication could have easily concluded that a board of directors was a necessary and vital component of any successful small company *without exception*, because no cautionary or opposing perspectives were presented. In fact, the editor justified this editorial position by stating that they had "found no articles or advocates that opposed active boards, not even conditionally" (Ward, 1988, p. 228). In all fairness, however, I must point out that two issues later the journal published a rebuttal I submitted on the subject, along with other commentary on their continuing board of directors debate.

The emergence of this literature corresponded with the incredible surge in entrepreneurial and small-business activity that began in the early 1980s. As this entrepreneurial activity itself expanded, so did the interest level in the subject, and society's desire to find ways to make the small business "machine" more powerful and effective.

I believe that the desire to assist small businesses is highly appropriate, especially considering their tremendous impact on our economy. Further, I believe that boards of directors *can* be a valuable tool to assist these businesses. Caution should be used, however, when suggesting that a board of directors (or any other management "tool") is just what the doctor ordered to help a firm through a crisis, double its capital, make the *Inc.* 500, or some other goal.

I have observed several company owners as they invested large amounts of time and money to develop a board with unrealistic goals or expectations, or, perhaps, when they would have been better off without the board. Some of these company owners have told me that they were motivated to develop their board by some article they, or their bankers or other advisors, had read that gave them the impression that a board was some sort of magic pill that would get them out of trouble or help them reach some goal. Later, when their ill-conceived, improperly developed, and poorly managed boards failed to fulfill the owners' expectations, they were left confused and turned off to the board concept forever.

This book differs from much of the literature on boards in that the proboard-of-directors or prooutside-director bias is avoided, and a more objective approach is followed, where the benefits and the negatives of boards and directors are both considered. As previously stated, I do believe that *a well-developed board can be a very valuable tool for many firms.* However, based on my research and board and consulting experiences, *I do not believe that a working board of directors is necessary for all firms, and in some cases, they may, in fact, be counterproductive.* For those firms that are well-suited for an active board, owners, officers, and directors should be well advised that a great deal of resources, effort, and time will need to be invested before any significant benefits will accrue from these boards.

Before we embark upon the investigation of what boards are and what they can and cannot do, we should pause for a brief review of the state of small business and how it has changed over the last decade, for this is the environment that has spawned the growth of boards of directors as a tool for small business. This will be followed with a brief discussion on the differences between the boards of publicly and privately owned firms. Finally, the chapter concludes with an overview of what is in this book and how to use it.

IMPORTANCE OF PRIVATE COMPANIES
TO THE ECONOMY

At this juncture, a skeptic might ask, "Why a whole book about boards of directors, and who really cares about small business anyway?" As we shall soon see, this would not be the reaction of someone who understands the growing impact of small and entrepreneurial firms on our economy. In fact, the small-business sector has really been a bright spot in what has been, in many respects, a dull economy during the last decade. Small businesses have become so critical to our economic health that it is vital that we explore and learn about tools that can increase their effectiveness and efficiency—such as boards of directors.

The historical bias in our society has favored big business. The reasons for the existence of this bias are fairly obvious. The industrial revolution was built by entrepreneurs like Rockefeller, Carnegie, and Mellon, whose companies came to dominate our economy for most of the twentieth century. Today, business schools continue to reflect a big business bias in the examples and cases found in most text books (a fact often necessitated by the lack of publicly available data from privately held businesses) and a desire to prepare young people for professional and managerial positions in corporate America. Even the U.S. Government reflects this bias in the minute budget (proportionately speaking) given to the Small Business Administration (SBA). But the reality today is that while the influence and importance of big business are stagnant or even diminishing, the importance of small and entrepreneurial business is growing rapidly.

Based on nonfarm business tax returns, there were slightly over 19 million businesses in the United States in 1988. Bruce Phillips of the SBA estimates that 99.9% of these were small businesses (Phillips, 1989). Table 1.1 breaks down federal tax returns by corporations, partnerships, and sole proprietorships for 1980–1988. The growth rate was slightly over 46% in just eight years, and virtually all of this growth in the total number of businesses has been small business. (The SBA defines a small business as one with fewer than 500 employees.) In fact, regarding job creation, David Birch has stated that since 1970, the *Fortune* 500 (the largest industrial firms in the United States) has laid off 2.8 million workers (Birch, 1987).

Table 1.2 shows the number of new incorporations filed for each year from 1981–1988. Although not indicating as dramatic a growth rate as Table 1.1, the

Table 1.1
Nonfarm Business Tax Returns (in $ thousands)

Year	Corporations	Partnerships	Proprietorships	Total
1988e	3,978	1,831	13,328	19,047
1987	3,829	1,824	12,633	18,286
1986	3,577	1,807	12,115	17,499
1985	3,437	1,755	11,767	16,959
1984	3,167	1,676	11,327	16,170
1983	3,078	1,613	10,507	15,198
1982	2,913	1,553	9,877	14,343
1981	2,813	1,458	9,345	13,616
1980	2,676	1,402	8,944	13,022

e = Estimated

Source: The State of Small Business, 1989. Data originally supplied by the U.S. Department of the Treasury, Internal Revenue Service.

Table 1.2
New Business Incorporations

Date	Incorporations
1988	684,109
1987	685,572
1986	702,101
1985	668,904
1984	634,991
1983	600,400
1982	566,942
1981	581,661

Source: The State of Small Business, 1989. Data for 1987 and 1988 were revised from that originally published based on information supplied by Bruce D. Phillips of the Small Business Administration.

table documents the creation of over 6 million new small businesses in just eight years.

The importance of small business can be demonstrated in other ways as well. For example, small business is estimated to account for 40% of our gross national product (GNP) (Phillips, 1989). This is achieved, in part, by the vast number of small businesses relative to large businesses; what small business lacks in individual firm size, it makes up for simply by the sheer number of firms in our economy.

There is also another reason why small business is vital to our economy; and this reason also helps to explain how small business is able to contribute such a large percentage to the U.S. GNP. This other reason is the phenomenal ability of entrepreneurs and small business to innovate.

ROLE OF SMALL BUSINESS IN THE
INNOVATION PROCESS

Academics and practitioners alike have recently praised the ability of smaller and entrepreneurial businesses to innovate. Innovation can be considered from a research-and-development perspective—leading to new scientific or technical discoveries, or from the perspective of simply finding new or more efficient ways to do nontechnical things better, such as producing and selling clothing and hamburgers. Frequently, invention and innovation are lumped together in discussions as if they were a single process or concept. There is an important distinction between them, however, that should be clarified.

Invention is typically thought of as the creation or conception of a thing or an idea (Bird, 1989). Edison with his light bulb and phonograph was an inventor. Steve Jobs and Steve Wozniak also engaged in the invention process with their personal computer. Innovation, however, is not restricted only to inventors. Innovation is the process of getting an idea or invention into practical use in the economy (Twiss, 1980). This usually involves commercialization of a product, service, or process into the marketplace. The late Ray Kroc did not invent McDonalds or the fast-food concept (he in fact purchased the first McDonalds from the original owners). Yet he improved on the delivery of the idea in such an incredible fashion that his empire is one of the best known establishments in the United States, if not the world.

Fred Smith, founder of Federal Express, is another good example of an innovator. Smith did not invent the airplane, nor did he create the ideas of transporting documents by air, or of offering next-day service. Emery Air Express had been doing both for years. The symptom remained, however, that the packages were often late. Smith's innovative solution was for Federal Express to own its own planes. This removed the problem, which was dependence upon the commercial airlines to move the freight forwarders' packages. Smith was determined not to have his freight sitting idle just because American or some other carrier canceled a flight (Ford and Takas, 1988). The innovation worked, and the rest is history.

Viewing, then, the primary role of small business as bringing innovation to the market, we should ask just how small business compares to large business in this process. A study by Gellman Research Associates cited by the SBA reports that firms with fewer than 500 employees require an average of 2.22 years to bring an innovation to market, whereas large businesses require 3.05 years (*The State of Small Business*, 1983, p. 123). The magnitude of this difference can only be fully appreciated when we also compare the funding spent on innovation by the two types of firms.

Steven Solomon has stated that 95% of all corporate-financed research and development is conducted by the nations biggest 1,000 firms (Solomon, 1986). This means that, relative to its big business counterpart, the research-and-development spending by small business amounts to nearly nothing. Yet, according again to the Gellman Research Associates study, 40% of the product innovations that they followed in their research were made by small companies or independent inventors. A later study claims that small firms were responsible for 48% of innovations from 1945 to 1980, and 56% from 1980 to 1985 (Khan and Manopichetwattana, 1989). This is a simply remarkable fact considering that this group is spending only 5% of the national corporate research budget.

For any reader who previously had doubts, it should now be obvious that privately owned businesses are of enormous significance to our economy. They are in the forefront of our society in terms of job creation, GNP, and innovation. And this influence is growing. It should be clear that any tools that can aid these businesses should be explored and developed.

With this brief justification of the importance of private firms as background, we can now begin discussing some of the specifics about boards and directors, and their roles in supporting and assisting the small-business segment of the economy. Our first task is to clarify the distinction between publicly owned and privately owned firms, and how the boards of each type of firm differ.

PUBLIC VERSUS PRIVATE FIRMS AND THEIR BOARDS

A meaningful understanding of the role of boards of directors is complicated because the distinction is rarely made between boards of publicly owned firms and boards of closely held firms. It is critical that we make this distinction, because the difference between the two types of firms and their boards is enormous. This difference is essentially one of power.

In publicly owned firms, directors have the legitimate power to control the major decisions of the firm. In closely held firms, ownership of the stock is held by a single individual or a small group; therefore, directors serve completely at the pleasure of the owners. Although this is theoretically true also for larger firms, the decentralized nature of stock ownership in publicly traded companies typically results in coalitions of power rather than autocratic centralized control. This results in directors having a significant degree of stability and independence that results in real power.

In the middle are thousands of corporations with moderately decentralized stock ownership, from a few shareholders to as many as several hundred, where the question of "who has the power to control?" is a moving target. The picture is fairly clear, however, when the corporation is in the hands of a family or a very small number of individuals (which is the case for the vast majority of companies in the United States). Because these company owners can hire and fire the board at will (where the legal niceties such as notice of special meeting of shareholders are largely a matter of inconvenience), they will only have and utilize a board if they believe some benefit to the company will result, and only as long as they are pleased with the results.

For example, Fletcher (1990, p. 516) summarizes the basic functions of directors as including the selection of the chief executive officer, setting executive compensation, pension and retirement policies, and determining dividend payments. The Model Business Corporation Act specifically states that "All corporate powers shall be exercised by or under authority of, and the business and affairs of a corporation shall be managed under the direction of a board of directors" (section 35). The majority of the individual states' corporation acts also provide that the affairs of a corporation shall be managed by the board of directors. It is hard to imagine, however, a closely held corporation in which the board would really have the power required to impartially select the chief executive and set vital policies independently of the owner's wishes.

To summarize, the basic distinction between boards of closely held firms and publicly owned firms is one of power. In the closely held firm, power rests with one or a small group of owners, and the role of the board is often little more than ceremonial or window dressing. In publicly held companies, the board represents the real seat of power, where the directors are selected by a widely decentralized body of shareholders to represent their interests. The board not only is charged by law to manage the affairs of the business, but also has the authority and power to carry out the decisions of the directors. (Whether or not these big-company directors actually exercise this authority is another matter.)

In effect, this means that the board of directors of a small company can be thought of as one having more of an advisory function than a governing one. Although a firm owner can certainly assign governing powers to his or her board, the real power of the firm is concentrated in the hands of the owners. Although this is also true in a theoretical sense for the shareholders of large firms, several thousand owners of fractional percentages of a multinational company are not in a practical position to question the actions of the board members.

*   *   *

With this general introduction behind us, we are now ready to move into more of the specific issues concerning the use of boards by smaller companies. The next chapter presents the historical debate regarding the benefits and contributions of boards to their firms. Following Chapter 2 are several chapters dealing with the specifics of board development, management, and control. Chapter 8 deals with the board subject from the director's perspective. Later chapters contain a summary of the *Inc*. 500 study and three case studies. The cases deal with actual board situations in a variety of settings. Finally, the book concludes with appendices containing important information and sources presented to assist the reader to continue exploring the issues addressed in this book.

2

Pros and Cons of Outside Boards: Highlights of the Literature Debate

TRADITIONAL VIEWS AND CHALLENGES CONCERNING BOARD USE

For years, the predominant belief in management theory concerning boards of directors was that outside directors were superior to inside directors. In fact, the American Institute of Management published the following in their *Manual of Excellent Managements*:

One of the fundamental tenets of the institute is that the majority of the members of any board should be drawn from outside the company. This is, the institute is convinced, the only means whereby objectivity in approach and clear-cut decisions on corporate problems can be assured. Companies which are rated excellent in this category, but who do not fulfill this requirement, are excellent despite the condition (1955, p. 23).

Some of the advantages of outside directors typically cited in the literature are that they provide independent assessments, have broader backgrounds, are more representative of stockholders and society, and provide checks and balances (Vance, 1983).

This belief has been challenged, however, in studies on large publicly owned firms. Studies by Stanley Vance on hundreds of successful publicly owned firms concluded that companies with a majority of inside directors had superior track records as compared with those with a majority of outside directors (Vance, 1955, 1964).

The pioneering study by Vance in 1955 (1955, 1983) examined 200 major industrial corporations between 1925 and 1950. The independent variable used was the percentage of outside directors, and the dependent variable was financial performance over the twenty-five-year period. By Vance's own admission, the methodology of his first study was simplistic, yet he concluded that firms with a majority of inside directors had superior track records as compared with those with a majority of outside directors (1983, p. 254).

In 1964, he continued the investigation into the director question with a study on 103 firms during the years 1925 to 1963. In this second study, the firms were grouped into twelve industry groups, and a separate regression model was predicted for each. Again, the percentage of outside directors was used as the independent variable, and financial performance measures were used for the dependent variable. Vance concluded from this study that in eleven of the twelve industry groups, there was at least a moderate degree of positive correlation (inside boards correlated with superior financial performance measures), ranging from R values of 0.364 to 0.864 (1964, pp. 45–46). It should be noted that the cell sizes for these regression tests ranged from only five firms to a high of only fourteen firms (p. 46). From this study, Vance again concluded that inside-director-run firms invariably were better performers than their outside director counterparts (1983).

He cited the main advantages of inside directors as having superior pertinent technical backgrounds, demonstrated leadership ability through years of service with the firm, immediate availability for both regular and emergency meetings, dedication to the firm, and a keen comprehension of the wants and attitudes of the company's various constituency groups (1983, p. 46). Vance further suggests that some negative relationships might come about from having outsiders, who may frequently skip meetings due to more pressing demands. He concludes from his studies that, at least as far as large publicly owned firms are concerned, "There is no substitute for competent and dynamic internal management" (p. 256).

Pfeffer (1972) has noted that there has been very little research on corporate boards of directors, and that most of the existing literature is nonquantitative. He contributed a study on eighty, large, publicly owned corporations selected from the Dun and Bradstreet *Reference Book of Corporate Managements, 1969*. For the purposes of his study, Pfeffer defined inside directors as current, retired, and former managers in the organization. One of the hypotheses the study supported was that the number of directors was directly related to the size of the organization. He also found that the percentage of inside directors was inversely related to both the need for external capital and to the existence of government regulation over the organization. He concludes that board size and composition are not random, but rather rational organizational responses to the conditions of the external environment. Pfeffer suggests that the intention of the organizations is to coopt those external organizations with which they are interdependent. The strategy of cooptation involves exchanging some degree of control, through a position on the board of directors, for continued support from the external organization (Pfeffer, 1972).

Pfeffer also attempted to relate insider or outsider dominance to differences in net income to sales and net income to stockholder's equity ratios. The results of these tests were not statistically significant.

In a recent empirical study Cochran et al. (1985) attempted to correlate "golden parachute'' contracts with high percentages of inside directors. Golden parachutes have been cited by critics as evidence that senior managers can be more interested in their own incomes than in shareholder returns. This study was designed to test the belief that corporate boards should have a majority of outside directors in order to carry out properly their responsibilities and maintain independence of management (Cochran et al., 1985). Bacon and Brown (1977) have reported that there is general agreement among board members of major U.S. corporations that boards should have a majority of outside members in order to maintain independence of management.

The hypothesis of interest tested was that the probability that firms will give their management golden parachute contracts is positively related to the percentage of directors who are insiders (Cochran et al., 1985, p. 665). Contrary to the researchers' expectations, they found the incidence of golden parachutes negatively correlated with the percentage of the board who were insiders for the *Fortune* 500 firms studied.

The principal result from this study was that firms with comparatively higher percentages of inside directors are less likely to give management golden parachute contracts. They conclude that this finding raises doubts about the belief that insider-dominated boards allow managers to consume higher levels of perquisites and compensations, because ultimately the board must approve such arrangements.

In another recent study, a team of researchers was unable to associate higher proportions of outside board members with lower numbers of illegal acts committed by the firm (Kesner, Victor, and Lamont, 1986). Citing various "boardroom critics" who advocate that a higher proportion of outside directors strengthens a board's independence and broadens its base of power, this study set out to demonstrate that the proportion of outsiders is inversely related to the number of illegal acts committed by the firm. Relying on published data about corporate litigation, Kesner et al. looked specifically at such activities as price discrimination, exclusive dealing, price fixing, conspiracy, and several other illegal acts.

For classification purposes, they considered current or retired managers to be inside directors, and used information in *Standard & Poor's Register of Corporations* in order to decide which directors were in each class for the firms they investigated (Kesner et al., 1986, p. 794). The results of the study failed to support the contention that outsiders will lessen a firm's involvement in illegal activities, but also failed to find evidence that firms dominated by outsiders would be more likely to engage in illegal acts.

Several other studies have been done over the years to explore the debate on inside versus outside directors with publicly owned firms. The conclusion that outside directors are not superior to inside directors has been supported by Lanser (1969) and Schmidt (1975). Lanser, for example, treated board composition (inside versus outside members) as an independent measure in his study of new companies in California. This variable was related to his measure of success, which was whether or not the organization was still in existence five years later.

He found that the presence of outside directors was inversely proportional to the survival of the firm.

Studies such as those by Vance and Lanser have provided quantitative insight into an area that otherwise has been flooded with nonquantitative and normative theorizing. Their studies, however, are not beyond criticism. Valid criticisms can be made about the methodology used. The studies basically used a ratio of inside to outside directors as an independent variable, and attempted to predict the firm's financial performance (or some other specific outcome such as golden parachutes or illegal acts). Little effort was made to account for the various other factors that contribute to the overall effectiveness of the firm. It should be clear, however, that these studies seriously question the contributions of outside directors, at least with respect to larger, publicly owned firms. Empirically speaking, there is little support for the American Institute of Management's tenet that the majority of the members of any board should by drawn from outside the company (*Manual of Excellent Managements*, 1955).

Before moving on to another aspect of the literature, it is important to clarify what all these "scientific" studies really mean. A couple of important observations should be stressed to reduce the chance of misunderstandings occurring. First, these studies do not prove anything definitively beyond the limited context of the small sample of firms in each of the investigations. What the studies do suggest is that the value of outsiders, in certain situations, may be overrated. That is, these studies attempted, in most cases, to show how helpful outsiders were by comparing firms with outsiders (or with large proportions of outsiders) to firms with boards composed primarily of insiders. They found, however, that firms with primarily inside boards performed as well, or perhaps better, for the functions they examined. Note, however, that for the most part, these were very limited studies, and the results should not be generalized to all other situations.

Second, these studies are not about the question "boards or no boards?" rather, they concern board composition. These are not studies of firms without boards versus firms with boards—they all had boards of some sort or other. Perhaps a more important observation from these empirical investigations (and one seemingly overlooked) is the value of insiders as board members. From the information presented by the various researchers, it is not clear whether these studies are really reporting the inferiority of outsider-dominated boards or rather the superiority of insider-dominated boards. I believe that, as is so often the case, the truth really lies somewhere in the middle, and the real challenge is developing the right mix of inside and outside board members and then following up with extensive board development.

What Some Top Theorists Are Saying

Beyond the empirical studies being reported in the academic journals, the board debate is also raging in many distinguished publications aimed directly at practitioners. Although most of the antagonists in this debate are also concerned with the realm of big, publicly owned business, it is useful for entrepreneurs and small-business owners to review their basic arguments.

Although popular articles hailing the rise (or resurgence) of the board and outside directors abound, the opinions of serious theorists suggest that a crisis exists in the boardrooms of America's larger companies. In examining sources ranging from the *Harvard Business Review* and *The Wall Street Journal* to the *Academy of Management Executive*, one cannot fail to notice a disturbing increase of cautionary, if not hostile, board concerns. These concerns are a reflection of changes in both legal issues and societal expectations, and can certainly be a big turn-off for both management and directors when contemplating board membership and function. Some of these changes reflect very visible issues, such as the increase of lawsuits and corresponding rise in directors and officers (D&O) insurance premiums. Other aspects of this "crisis" are less obvious, and concern what could be considered an outright breakdown of the board process.

A plethora of recent articles has discussed the increase of lawsuits brought against corporate America, and these typically target the firm's directors. A *BusinessWeek* report, for example, has suggested that there is a one-in-five chance that a director will be involved in some type of shareholder suit ("The Job Nobody Wants," 1986). This phenomenon has naturally been accompanied by a dramatic increase in the cost of D&O insurance. In fact, a *Fortune* magazine report claimed that some D&O premiums has jumped 9,000% in a single year (Sherman, 1988). Critics are, of course, pointing out that there is little, if any, economic justification for such outrageous increases, and some states are passing legislation to protect directors from personal liability in the wake of this recent insurance crisis. Unfortunately, whether justified or not, the difficulty in securing D&O insurance is forcing many companies to go without coverage and, hence, many qualified, would-be directors are refusing to serve.

Another serious charge concerning the boards of big firms comes from noted business theorist Peter Drucker. In a recent article he suggests "[that in order] to find a truly effective board you are much better advised to look in the nonprofit sector than in our public corporations" (1989, p. 90). Drucker in fact suggests that much of the energy that could be directed into our for-profit businesses is being channeled into nonprofit and charitable organizations because top executives do not feel challenged on the job. He converts this negative observation into a recommendation on how to develop an effective board by suggesting that the CEO has the responsibility to design work plans for the board and review the board's performance. This board performance review, along with new board member training is routine in many nonprofits, but, according to Drucker, almost non-existent in the for-profit sector.

A similar theme was recently discussed by former GM executive and board member Elmer Johnson. In his recent *Harvard Business Review* article he called the boards of large public corporations: " . . . fat, dumb, and comfortable on a diet of postwar stability and prosperity" (1990, p. 46). He suggests a number of board reforms needed to help large corporations deal with the growing competition from global and domestic entrepreneurial firms. Among his recommendations are removing retired CEOs from the board, limiting board size to seven or nine, and having an issues-oriented agenda and true deliberation instead of the usual slide-show-type meetings. He also advocated requiring directors to own a significant number of shares in the company, which sounded like an appeal to a more inside-director orientation.

LITERATURE ON BOARDS OF PRIVATELY OWNED FIRMS

In addition to the surge of articles concerning boards of large businesses, there has also been a great deal of interest in boards of smaller firms. These firms and their boards differ significantly from their big-firm counterparts, as has already been discussed in the first chapter. The literature on board of directors and smaller privately owned firms, although lacking substantial empirical validation, overwhelmingly supports the advantages of having outside directors on the board. This literature consists of a few scientific studies; however, the bulk of the articles and books on the subject primarily consists of anecdotes and case histories from the various authors' personal board or consulting experiences. Some of the better articles will be reviewed next.

Mace (1971), one of the earlier advocates of working boards for small business, suggests that directors in these firms serve as a source of advice and counsel, exercise outside objective judgments, and serve as a source of discipline for management. He also suggests that outside directors can arbitrate differences among family members, assist with management succession planning, and act as decision makers during crisis situations such as by designating a replacement for the president in case of his death or incapacity.

It should be noted, however, that the data for Mace's research only partially applies to small businesses. His research design consisted of approximately seventy-five in-depth interviews, as well as many other short discussions, with executives and board members. Although some cases were with owners and directors of privately owned companies, the study's main concern was with large- and medium-sized, publicly owned firms.

Castaldi and Wortman (1984) have suggested that a board of directors, with sufficient outsider representation, can help the small corporation in many ways. They suggest that the most pressing and dangerous problem facing small business is managerial deficiencies (p. 9). The outside board, if properly structured, should provide expertise in technical, managerial, legal, financial, and economic fields (p. 5). (These authors propose an outline of the functions such a board can perform, which is discussed in Chapter 4.)

For maximum effectiveness, Castaldi and Wortman further suggest that the board may be broken down into committees, such as audit, finance, and executive. This board, the authors claim, will provide strength in areas where small companies have been historically weak (p. 5). While proposing their model as a conceptual scheme, Castaldi and Wortman claim that boards of directors are a largely untapped resource by small corporations. They offer no empirical support, however, for either their model, or their claim that boards are underutilized.

Heidrick (1984a), in addition to supporting outsiders for their objectivity, suggests that they bring broader experience to the firm and often serve as a bridge to new customers, new suppliers, and new sources of financing. Mueller (1984), in his collection of personal boardroom experiences, agrees that outsiders are valuable for their ability to think independently. He states: "There is no way to soar into independent governance decision making with the outside-director eagles when you are an inside turkey daily reporting to your boss who is CEO and and of course is also on the same board" (1984, p. 9).

Heidrick also points out that many firms get the same benefits with an advisory board, rather than a board of directors. The advisory board concept has recently been advocated by Mueller (1990). This concept may be more appealing to some entrepreneurs who may feel that the term "advisory board" is less threatening than "board of directors." As long as the firm is closely controlled, however, this may be mainly a semantic distinction, because the owner can hire or dismiss directors and advisory board members at his own discretion. Heidrick claims advisory boards, with outside members, bring the same type of advantages to the firm, including expertise, professionalism, and resolution of disagreements among insiders. The advisory board is also a vehicle for bringing outside talent to the small firm that is not organized as a corporation, but desires to take advantage of a professional board forum.

Danco is perhaps the strongest and certainly the best known advocate of outside boards in privately owned firms. His Center for Family Business works regularly with business owners who wish to establish or improve their boards of directors. According to Danco, an effective board in a privately owned firm assists the owner in planning, acts as a "safety fuse" (such as controlling the boss's overaggressiveness), and helps support the firm in a variety of other ways (Danco and Jonovic, 1981). Furthermore, he insists that outside directors are essential for a truly effective board. Danco suggests that in choosing the best directors:

The business owner should choose outsiders—people outside of both his family and his business, people whose views he can't buy at any price. . . . The outside director's job is to stimulate the efforts of all involved by demonstrating that the problems are not only soluble, but worth solving (1981, pp. 80–81).

The prescriptive literature in this area is plentiful, and most is similar to the references cited. Recent articles and reports on this subject have appeared in *The Wall Street Journal*, *Inc.*, the *Small Business Report*, and *Family Business Review*, among others (Posner, 1983; "Succession Planning In Closely Held Firms," 1984; Jacobs, 1985; Ward, 1988).

The *Family Business Review* citation deserves special attention. This journal, dedicated to the dissemination of new research and theory on family firms, devoted the entire Fall 1988 issue to the subject of establishing and managing boards of directors. I have already mentioned my criticism of the issue's one-sided treatment of the topic in Chapter 1. Editor John Ward later reasserted the editorial intent of the special issue by stating that

[it] was to help business owners and consultants see how an outside board may improve operations of family firms and how to establish an effective one. (We were not bashful in expressing that purpose up front in the issue.) Surely, the interest in the subject warrants that help (1989, p. 147).

A number of the articles in that special issue made strong cases for the need for, and benefits possible from, working boards, particularly those with active outside directors. These articles were written by experienced consultants, academics, company owners, and other professionals, who all endorsed the use of outside directors by family firms.

For example, firm owner Clayton Mathile (1988) calls his board "one of the company's most valuable resources" (p. 237). He attests that his board has helped the company make strategic decisions that has saved millions of potential capital. He also offers some useful insights in selecting and training directors.

Former Arthur Little chairman and prolific author Robert Mueller contributed a useful article directed toward outside directors themselves (1988). He succinctly reviews several key issues such as director roles and compensation. Drawing on his forty years of director experience, Mueller also provides three minicases to illustrate the contributions outsiders can make to family firms.

Certainly the most useful article in the issue was by John Ward and coauthor James Handy (1988). They report the results of a survey of 147 privately controlled companies. Among their more interesting findings were that nearly half of the firms had at least two outsiders (which is more than commonly believed about small firm boards in general), and that firms with what the authors called outside boards had a different expectation for the boards than did firms with inside boards. Specifically, they reported that owners with boards having at least two outsiders most often described the purpose of the board as advice and counsel, whereas owners with inside boards most often reported the board's purpose as fulfilling legal requirements. Although very interesting, these data are far from conclusive due to small sample size and other statistical limitations.

This special issue of *Family Business Review* contained several other articles that discussed topics such as legal and organizational issues for boards (Alderfer, 1988; Heidrick, 1988; Schipani and Siedel, 1988; Tillman, 1988; Whisler, 1988). My concern with this issue was not the material that was included, but rather with what was omitted. The stated purpose of the issue was to champion the use of outside boards by family businesses. The blatant one-sided treatment of the issue, however, made it appear as though there was no downside to boards and outsiders, and this left the impression that boards were a panacea waiting to solve all the problems facing small businesses.

The extensive literature challenging the supposed superiority of outside directors was ignored by the editors. As stated previously, the editors claimed that no such literature existed by stating that

While we have attempted to assemble a balanced, thorough, and objective collection of papers on boards for family firms, it may appear that we are promoting active boards with outside directors. There are two reasons for this: First, we found no articles or advocates that opposed active boards, not even conditionally (Ward, 1988, p. 228).

As if it wasn't enough to ignore an extensive body of literature and claim it did not exist, the journal carried its bias even further in a book review on one of Professor Vance's books contained at the end of the special issue. In the review of Vance (1983), the reviewers pushed his research findings under the rug by stating

Vance's own findings may confuse some readers. The research seems to conclude that firms operate best when the directors are close to the company and when they are knowledgeable about the corporation's affairs and technology. The chapter purports to be about board evaluation, but its treatment of that topic is superficial (Drexler and Nielson, 1988, p. 332).

This review is highly misleading, but it certainly helped to support the editor's claim that no opposing opinion existed regarding the value of outside versus inside directors.

On a positive note, this special issue created a needed surge in the debate on the board topic, and a subsequent issue of *FBR* contained rebuttals and additional commentary, including an article of mine (Ford, 1989c). The research I conducted on the boards of *Inc.* 500 firms raised a serious challenge to the perceived superiority of outside directors. In fact, it led me to agree with Vance's claim that the best directors may be those chosen from the internal management ranks. (For details of this study, refer to Chapter 9.)

Other writers have recently written on the importance for small firms to engage outsiders (but not necessarily as board members) to participate in their strategic planning process. It has been suggested that since small firms cannot afford full-time planning staffs, outsiders can improve the quality of decision making and help ensure systematic planning. The argument further suggests that planning interaction with outsiders will cause small business managers to take planning seriously and become motivated to allocate the necessary time (Robinson, 1982). Sexton (1976) and Dahle (1976) argue that outsiders may supplement the limited skills and imperfect information often associated with small firms. Timmons, Smollen, and Dingee (1985) also suggest that outsiders can supplement inadequate skills in the planning process of small firms.

Robinson (1982) studied a group of small firms receiving strategic planning assistance from government-supported Small Business Development Center (SBDC) programs. The study consisted of 101 small firms that had received consulting help from SBDC centers, and two matched control groups. He found that small firms that used the outsiders in the planning process had a higher increase in profitability than did matched samples of firms not using the service.

This study supports the notion that outsiders be included in the planning efforts of small firms. It must be recognized, however, that Robinson's study was not of outside boards, but rather of outsider-based planning using planning specialists. The actual contribution of outside boards to small-firm planning efforts has still not been measured.

REVIEW AND CASE EXAMPLES

This chapter has highlighted the various arguments on both sides of the boards and outside directors debate. It should be clear that the situation is anything *but* clear. The majority of the empirical or scientific literature raises serious doubts as to the supposed superiority of outside directors. This may be due to the possibility that outsiders really are not that useful, or rather that insiders may often make better directors than commonly believed. Another possibility is that many firms may simply operate more effectively without the advisory and/or governance overhead of a board of any kind.

Yet, the fact remains that the prevailing beliefs about boards are that they are very helpful and that they require a large proportion of outsiders in order to be truly effective. The persistence of these views must certainly be based on more than wishful thinking, and it is. Although not a major phenomenon within smaller firms, many firms are reporting that outsiders are making major contributions to their firms. This clearly is not occurring in a majority of firms, and many owners are dissatisfied with their board experiences. A lot of factors have to fall in place in order for a board to work effectively. Typically, this may require more work and investment than most firm owners are willing to contribute.

Table 2.1 summarizes the various strengths and weaknesses of outside directors as presented in the literature review. Similarly, Table 2.2 summarizes the strengths and weaknesses of inside directors. These tables are useful both as a summary of the literature and to assist owners and managers in formulating a plan to design (or redesign) their board, developing director classifications, and in choosing and recruiting board members.

Much of this chapter thus far has been technical and highly theoretical. In order to help put some life into the various arguments for or against outside and/ or inside directors, or for and against boards in general, we now consider a number of case examples. These are all factual situations derived from my research or board experiences. A variety of views will be discussed to demonstrate both sides of the board perspective.

Table 2.1
Outside Board Members' Characteristics

ADVANTAGES:

*Objectivity
*Provide independent assessments
*Greater stockholder/stakeholder and society representation
*Provide checks and balances
*Independence from management
*Arbitrate differences among family members
*Assist with management succession planning/recruiting
*Bring broad experience to the firm
*Serve as a bridge to new customers, suppliers, and
financing
*Strengthen the board's independence
*Supplement the skills and information of management team

DISADVANTAGES:

*May frequently skip meetings due to more pressing demands
*Limited availabity beyond regular board meetings
*Limited knowledge about firm's internal affairs
*Limited knowledge about the industry and technology
*Possible conflict-of-interest problems
*May have a lower degree of dedication to the success of the
firm
*Expensive
*Some studies suggest that the number of outside directors
is inversely proportional to the success of the firm

Some Case Examples of Highly Effective Outsiders

While conducting research on the *Inc.* 500 companies, I discovered two specific areas where outside directors appear to have a distinct advantage over insiders. These areas (which are discussed further in Chapter 9) are assisting in succession planning and raising capital. A number of CEOs mentioned that outsiders played a key role in both of these areas. A couple of examples will help highlight these issues.

The advantage outsiders may have with respect to succession and raising money is in large part due to their personal networks, that is, their extensive contacts outside the firm. These contacts can be extremely useful in seeking top-level personnel (or a replacement for a incapacitated chief executive) and obtaining debt or equity capital. Although replacing a CEO is a fairly rare event, obtaining capital is a continuous struggle for most startup and growing firms.

An interesting example of the use of an outside director to help secure capital took place in a small, high-tech manufacturing firm. The company was in the process of obtaining a second commercial bank loan (for approximately

Table 2.2
Inside Board Members' Characteristics

ADVANTAGES:

*Superior, pertinent technical backgrounds
*Demonstrated leadership ability
*Immediate availability
*Dedication to the firm's success
*Comprehension of needs and attitudes of company's
stakeholders
*Meets legal requirements
*Knowledgable of firm's affairs, technology, & industry

DISADVANTAGES:

*Must report to CEO - may be intimidated to question him
*May not be able to be objective on some matters
*More narrow backgrounds (generally)
*Weakens the board's independence
*Lesser degree of stakeholder and society representation
*Does not provide checks and balances

$250,000) using the Small Business Administration's loan guarantee program. Without this guarantee, the loan would not go through, however, the SBA indicated that it would be a routine process. Ninety days later, the paperwork was stuck in an SBA official's office, and the firm's payables were extended a similar length of time.

At a point where vendors were beginning to cut supplies and raw materials vital to the business's survival, an outside director made a number of calls to business leaders and government officials, ultimately resulting in a congressman pressuring the SBA to resolve the snag and release the needed paperwork. This transaction literally kept the firm from certain liquidation and is a striking example of how a director's connections can benefit the firm. In this case, the outside director performed a function that the entrepreneur/owner could not have performed alone.

Another example is more bizarre in that the outside contributor was not appreciated for his efforts. This firm had recently removed its outside directors after a frustrating period in which the CEO had concluded that the board would be more efficient without the outsiders. Apparently, the board meets very frequently, and the outside members could not keep up with the schedule or with the firm's activities to be of much help to the firm. One outsider was specifically criticized as not being of use for many of the "operational" issues raised by the surveys, and his frequent absences had caused some specific problems for the firm. Although the "net" contribution of this particular outsider was felt to be negative by the CEO and most inside board members, they were quick to point out the he had been instrumental in helping to identify and attract new sources of much-needed working capital during a crisis period the firm had gone through. Apparently, the board member had personal contacts and sources in his own network that were not available to the management and inside board members themselves. In spite of his overall "failure" as a board member, he made an important contribution by helping to raise capital during a time of crisis.

I know of numerous other examples where outsiders were found to be very important due to their external networks and contacts. For example, several other CEOs have reported to me concerning their outsiders' contributions in raising capital, and others have mentioned their usefulness in making contacts with new customers and just to "open other doors."

Another case example concerns a Houston firm, whose CEO emphatically hails the value of his board, which he describes as "similar to a mentor relationship." A forum that started as occasional evening dinner meetings frequently lasting until four in the morning was so helpful that the CEO later added some inside members and made the group into a real board. The real success of the board, according to the CEO, belongs to the two outsiders, who are both remarkably successful entrepreneur/businessmen in their own right. The board is a partner in all major decisions along with the management team. Management brings in proposals with lists of options, and the board often makes the final decisions. During the course of my interviews with this firm, I was informed of several key issues (both strategic and operational) in which the board had made the difference between success and failure.

Several other firm owners have reported to me that they are very pleased with their boards for "sounding-board" purposes. Typically, this includes such functions as reviewing policies, programs, and, in general, simply discussing ideas with the owner. One CEO referred to his board as a "board of critics." Another CEO said that the board "forced discipline" on him and made him "think about the planning process as [he] prepares the board agenda and background materials."

It should be pointed out that in nearly all of the cases I have encountered of successful boards, the group includes a mix of outsiders and insiders, or strictly (or at least predominantly) insiders. While singing praises of their outsiders, many CEOs were quick to point out that the vast majority of issues concerned matters that the outsiders simply could not help with much because they lacked the specific knowledge required to be useful. Therefore, the perspective that the inside directors add to the board forum is often critical to the overall success of the board.

Some Case Examples of Ineffective Outsiders

While working on board research over the past several years, I have summarized two primary reasons why outside directors seem to be of less value than their inside-director counterparts: lack of knowledge about the firm and its environment, and lack of availability to the firm. These points will be clearly evident in the next few examples of some board situations where outsiders have been ineffective, to put it mildly.

When I asked the owners of a certain manufacturing firm if they could give me an example of how an outside director had influenced them, not a single example could be found. Early in the firm's development, an outsider with a Ph.D. in a technical field related to the firm's industry was recruited to serve on the board. It was hoped that he could make valuable contributions to R&D and other product-related aspects of the firm. In fact, it soon became apparent that the opposite was true. The CEO recalled that for years this outsider's contributions were negligible because "he just didn't know enough about us and what we were doing to be of any real help. It took years of four meetings a year for him to start being helpful." The CEO's wife, the firm's treasurer and a management professor, explained that it was not just the years of meetings that finally made him useful, but rather a decision to make him an insider by giving him a salaried position (part-time) as Director of Research. She remarked, "[He] started out as an outsider, but didn't become really useful until he became, or evolved into, an insider."

An example that demonstrates the availability point comes from a consumer goods company. Although the firm's current board consists entirely of insiders (seven in all), the company had attempted to utilize outsider directors in the past. As part of a reorganization in 1980, an industry expert was added to the board as an outside director. According to one insider, "the outsider created an obstacle, since notification procedures required that he be given a 30-day notice of any meetings. This forced a lot of backdating of the minute book." When asked how, in general, the outsider influenced the firm, the CEO replied that he had been influential, but in a negative way. "He forced us to use informal methods to run the business when the board couldn't meet soon enough."

Another CEO interviewed had recently disbanded his board, which had included several outside directors. The CEO had concluded that the board was ineffective and just not worth the effort. He said that it was slow and sluggish, like a congress, as compared to a monarchy, which is able to respond faster. He commented, "I'm the one who had the vision, the outsiders were not in the day-to-day battles. [I] had to spend far too much time explaining things to them to justify the support they were able to give me."

One example should also be mentioned from a firm that currently uses outsiders on its board (both at the time of the interviews and today). The CEO began the interview by telling me how important the research was because he felt the outsiders were important and influenced him. I then asked for two significant examples that would explain how this influence worked. He then proceeded to give two examples of how the board influenced his thinking, which actually demonstrated the opposite of what he intended. The first example concerned a personnel policy issue on which he wanted the board's consensus. When the board did not support his decision, he stated that he expected their unanimous approval or their resignations. They then supported his view.

The second example concerned how to resolve a serious contract dispute with a client. An outside director with particular expertise in the area was asked to help resolve the issue. He made a series of recommendations that, according to the CEO, were only partially followed. According to the outsider himself, however, the CEO ignored most of his recommendations, and he was not sure that he had made a contribution to resolving the issue. The outsider commented that the CEO "did what he wanted to do."

SUMMARY

From the preceding pages, it should be clear why so much disagreement exists concerning the value of outside boards and directors. Theorists persist in claiming that boards are valuable and underutilized resources, whereas researchers continue to produce data that challenge these claims. We have reviewed the traditional views on boards and outside directors, as well as many of the studies on the subject. Also reviewed was the recent literature, which suggests that outside board members can make a variety of contributions to smaller, privately and family owned firms.

What does all this mean to entrepreneurs and business owners? Should they invest their limited resources on developing a board when so many criticisms have been made about them? The answer is "it depends." It should be clear that building a board is not a quick-fix solution to a variety of small-business problems. Much of my concern with the topic is that boards continue to be built up in the media as a panacea just waiting to solve any business ailment. The reality is that a carefully chosen, patiently developed, and well-managed board can definitely provide a number of real benefits for privately held firms. It is not cheap, quick, or easy; but the benefits are there if you are capable and willing to make the investment. The next chapter will help you decide if, or when, developing a board is right for you and your business.

3

Do You Really Need a Board?

OVERVIEW

This chapter is designed to help company owners decide whether they really need a board. Actually, the question may be better phrased: "Do you really want a board?" The question of need is much more difficult to deal with for a number of reasons. First, it ignores the reality that even if a firm in a certain situation needed the benefits of a board, this would accomplish nothing if the owner did not want one. The personal wants or desires of the owners are usually paramount in private company situations. Second, who can really define the needs of a business? Take, for example, a company needing an infusion of capital. A board may be able to help locate new sources of funds, but the board itself is not the capital. A board should be viewed as a tool for solving various needs of a business, not the actual solution. The answer to the question "do you need a board?" therefore becomes a personal decision of the owner/managers after carefully weighing all of the information available.

The first section of the chapter clarifies what is actually meant by the terms "inside" and "outside" directors. Without a common set of definitions, discussion of board development issues can become very confusing. Next, we cover minimum board requirements. This section addresses the fact that every corporation, by law, has some sort of board of directors, and this minimum board is the starting point to whatever more advanced board may be developed. Next, we go beyond the basics and discuss the benefits of a "working board" for firms at various stages of development, and how one decides to establish such a board.

DEFINITIONS

The terms "inside director" and "outside director" are utilized so casually by writers that an occasional reader of business literature could easily assume that the terms have precise definitions. This is not the case. Because no single set of definitions exist for outside and inside directors, it is helpful to synthesize the various definitions to give the reader a common understanding with which to proceed. This exercise also helps clarify the various perspectives potential directors from diverse backgrounds may bring to the board forum.

As stated previously, there is no agreement among theorists and writers as to the definition of inside and outside board members. On one extreme, Pfeffer (1972) has defined insiders as present, former, or retired managers of the firm only. Vance (1964) has added stockholders to the definition. Danco and Jonovic (1981) have gone to the other extreme and included any family member, friends of management, and paid advisors, such as the company attorney. There are other approaches to the definition problem as well.

Cochran et al. (1985) suggest that insiders can be classified by degree. For example, they refer to board members who are current employees of the firm as Insider One. Adding former employees to this group yields Insider Two. Finally, adding employees of customers or suppliers, employees of the firm's investment bank or corporate counsel, and employees of the firm's parent firm or subsidiary to this group yields Insider Three. Insider Three is, therefore, supposed to represent all affiliated directors.

Occasionally, various governments have attempted to deal with this definitional ambiguity. The New York State Insurance Law, for example, requires that a minimum of one-third of the directors of domestic stock life insurance companies be "independent" directors. Section 1202 defines independent directors as

persons who are not officers or employees of such company or of any entity controlling, controlled by, or under common control with such company and who are not beneficial owners of a controlling interest in the voting stock of such company or any such entity (*New York Insurance Laws*, 1985, p. 86).

The law further sets the minimum number of directors at thirteen. This requirement effectively guarantees that each corporation governed by the statute will have at least five independent, or outside, directors.

In order to conduct my *Inc*. 500 research, I needed a set of definitions that gave a clear distinction between inside and outside board members, without the added complexity of varying degrees of each definition. To reduce confusion for the participants of my study, as well as readers, I felt that these definitions needed to be as dichotomous as possible. That is, for research as well as conversational purposes, I wanted a set of definitions in which any director could easily be classified as an inside director or an outside director, with no, or as little as possible, overlap. (As a researcher, I was also interested in the greater statistical power that was achieved from a simple two-category classification system.)

By synthesizing the definitions of other theorists, there appears to be two basic criteria for classifying inside members. First, they need to have a strong understanding and knowledge of the firm. This could result from personal access to reports and other data and involvement in the general management of the firm, or from a close fraternal relationship with a top officer or manager, such as a spouse or children might gain through years of "dinner table" conversations.

A second criterion is that insiders are viewed as being dependent upon, or having strong loyalties to, the CEO or firm. This is in sharp contrast to outsiders, who are seen as being more independent, or having an "outside" perspective. This dependence could be the result of employment by the firm, causing actual financial dependence, or a close family relationship, where the dependence or loyalty could be either financial or emotional. The notion of dependence as a criterion for classification as an insider is clearly supported by Danco and Jonovic (1981) who suggest that outsiders are "people whose views [the CEO] can not buy" (pp. 80–1).

This leads to a definition of inside directors as follows: Inside directors are present, former, or retired officers or managers of the firm, and their spouses and children. The present officers and managers easily meet both criteria, having direct access to data and other information, as well as a financial dependence on the firm. Spouses and children are included due to the perception that they will have information and knowledge through the eyes of the officer/manager spouse or parent. This relationship also makes it most likely that a financial or emotional dependence, or both, exists. Former and retired officers and managers and their spouses and children are included in the insider definition due to the belief that their position on the board, even though no longer working in the firm, indicates that both the knowledge and dependence/loyalty criteria are probably met.

Arguments can probably be made on a case-by-case basis as to why others who fall outside of this definition should be classified as insiders. This has been demonstrated over the years by the proliferation of definitions on the subject. This definition, however, appears to capture the vast majority of inside members, while simultaneously satisfying the desire for a dichotomy. All other board members will be classified as outside members under this definition system.

Some typical types of outsiders can be examined to demonstrate how the definitions function. A board member might be appointed from a bank or other financial institution with which a firm does business. This person would not meet either criteria for classification as an insider. He or she would not have day-to-day access to data or information and would not be financially or emotionally dependent upon the firm. This member would also clearly bring an outside perspective to the board.

A representative of a venture capitalist group or individual investor would also be classified as an outsider. Although having an equity position, this board member also would probably not have access to information on a day-to-day or even week-to-week basis. Furthermore, this person's primary loyalty would be to his or her employer, or self, rather than to the firm's management. This representative would be expected to speak out if the investment in the firm seemed threatened. Others, including Vance (1964), have suggested that stock ownership is a sufficient criterion for classification as an insider. In the case of privately owned firms, however, the opposite may be true. Rather than being a "rubber stamp" to the CEO, this board member might be the first to challenge management if it appeared that the member's minority equity position was in danger. Not having any particular dependence upon the firm, and lacking first-hand information, the minority equity owner, if not part of the family or management team, might act more like a banker or venture capitalist than like an insider.

Other types of board members are relatively easy to classify under the outsider definition. Lawyers, owners of other small firms, and professors are not dependent upon the firm or CEO, and have the outside perspective of their various fields. Also, these members are unlikely to have in-depth knowledge of the business or regular access to data and other internal information concerning the firm.

To summarize, then, this leads to the following definitions, which are assumed throughout the book:

Inside directors are present, former, or retired officers or managers of the firm, and their spouses and children.

Outside directors are all other members of the board. This group frequently includes, but is not limited to, representatives of financial institutions or investor groups, various professionals and academics, and officers of other privately owned business.

It is not expected that these definitions will satisfy all readers and all situations, however, it is believed that they are general enough to serve for most purposes. The simplicity of these definitions also provides us with a much needed common vocabulary.

MINIMUM BOARD REQUIREMENTS AND DIRECTOR QUALIFICATIONS

From a legal perspective, the question "does my corporation really need a board?" is, as lawyers say, moot. That is, corporations are required to have a board of directors by law. The correct question is not, therefore, "board or no board?" but rather "legal minimum board or working board?" The actual composition of this legal minimum board is very thin. It is important that we examine the minimum board requirements, however, because these become the foundation from which to build an expanded working board, should you decide to do so.

The U.S. Model Business Corporation Act (Model Act) establishes in Section 35.1 that corporations shall have and be managed by boards of directors stating that

The business and affairs of a corporation shall be managed by a board of directors except as may be otherwise provided in the articles of incorporation. . . . Directors need not be residents of this State or shareholders of the corporation unless the articles of incorporation or by-laws so require. . . .

Section 36.1 of the same act adds clarification concerning directors with the language:

The board of directors of a corporation shall consist of one or more members. . . . The names and addresses of the members of the first board of directors shall be stated in the articles of incorporation. Such persons shall hold office until the first annual meeting of shareholders, and until their successors shall have been elected and qualified. . . . Each director shall hold office for the term for which he is elected and until his successor shall have been elected and qualified.

Unfortunately, the rules and regulations governing corporations do not stop with the Model Act. Each state also has its own corporate laws that can create additional restrictions and requirements to complicate corporate life. Although the Model Act has served to create some consistency in corporation law across the United States, a good deal of variation remains among the individual state corporation acts concerning board and director regulations and qualifications. Issues such as the minimum number of directors, director qualifications and eligibility, and board powers are all dealt with under the Model Act.

Historically, the various states typically required a minimum of three or more directors. The Model Act, however, states that a board may have as few as one director (see Section 36 of the Act) and many state laws have increasingly moved toward this easing of restriction. Several states, including, for example, Colorado, Oklahoma, and the District of Columbia, still require a minimum of three directors. This fact is complicated by the large number of variations in the state laws created either by the actual statutes or caused by developments in case law (where the results of a specific law suit has an effect on other corporations or on corporation law in general). For example, although Oklahoma's Business Corporation Act requires that a corporation have a minimum of three directors, a professional corporation may organize with only two directors under Oklahoma's Professional Corporation Act.

Many other traditional rules governing boards have also been eased due, in part at least, to the widespread acceptance of the Model Act by the individual states. For example, the various state corporation acts used to require directors to be shareholders, be citizens of the United States, meet a residency requirement, and be of some minimum age. These conditions have been widely lessened or eliminated today. Some theorists would claim that the rationale for reducing restrictive eligibility requirements would be to allow corporations to seek top-quality directors regardless of whether or not they meet some "litmus test." Others would argue that the effect of easing restrictions (with respect to closely held firms at least), regardless of the intention, was to reduce the value or power of the board by allowing more discretion to owners and managers.

Even with the adoption of the Model Act by most jurisdictions, however, a tremendous variation still exists among the states regarding the eligibility of directors. Some states, including Hawaii, New Hampshire, South Carolina, and Vermont, still require that at least one director be a resident of the state. Others, such as Nevada and Florida, require that at least one director be a citizen of the United States. There still remains many circumstances, particularly including financial institutions, where directors must be shareholders. Vermont, for example, still requires that all directors must be shareholders. Age is still a condition for eligibility in a number of states, including Georgia, New Jersey, New York, Florida, Nevada, Pennsylvania, Oklahoma, and Tennessee. Legal age, however, is defined in a number of different ways and this requirement is, of course, subject to change as are all of the legal conditions summarized in this section. There are also wide variations among the state laws regarding such conditions as to whether an individual can hold more than one corporate office, and regarding the level of fiduciary responsibility assumed by directors. Also, there is a wide range of laws and special conditions governing whether or not a director is allowed to serve on the board of more than one corporation of a similar nature (*Bank Directors Responsibilities*, 1987, p. 10).

These subtle and frequent legal variations present a formidable maze for most business owners, and help to ensure an ample supply of work for lawyers. Because the laws of each state are complex and subject to change, you should consult with your attorney or call your state's corporation commission to verify the specific minimum board requirements and director qualifications in your jurisdiction if you are uncertain on any point. A current directory of state corporation commissions addresses and phone numbers is contained in Appendix 1.

DO YOU NEED A WORKING BOARD?

Once the corporation is established and the initial board of directors named, the question becomes: "What are you going to do with it?" It is widely believed that the vast majority of closely held corporation boards exist in name only, often with only one or two directors, those typically being the husband and wife (Ford, 1986; Ward and Handy, 1988). Many other firms may list an additional director or two, such as another relative or the family attorney, but in reality many of these boards serve primarily as window dressing.

In his recent survey of over 300 readers of *The BusinessWeek Newsletter for Family-Owned Business*, Harvard College senior Marc Schwartz found that only 31% of the sample had outsiders on their boards (Moskowitz, 1990, p. 1). (This corresponds almost exactly to the 32.6% of firms with at least one outsider that I discovered in my *Inc.* 500 study.) More interesting was Schwartz's discovery regarding the CEO's perception of the usefulness of his board. When asked to rank the board somewhere between "waste of time" (1) and "extremely valuable" (5), the average response was markedly higher for boards with one or more outsiders than for all family or family and management only boards.

The minimal board established when the corporation was chartered could serve as a foundation from which to build a functioning, working board or it could remain a paper tiger content to meet only those requirements dictated by law. The decision to create a working board needs to be made from the dual context of (1) your objectives for the board and (2) the current stage of development of your company. Danco and Jonovic (1981) have suggested that a family company is not ready for a board unless it meets several performance criteria, including being successful and having stable management that was competent and well-chosen. Unfortunately, these criteria may be unreachable for a large percentage of businesses and should not be taken too seriously. Rather, firm owners should look at their circumstances as a unique situation and avoid trying to follow any cookie-cutter decision rule as to when they should develop their boards. Boards can be implemented for almost any objective and at almost any stage in the life of a company, but as the circumstances vary, so will the difficulty of the task and the probability of successfully meeting your objectives.

Setting Board Objectives

There are countless potential objectives one could have when contemplating board development or expansion. These vary from simple legal requirements for incorporating a new firm to establishing a sophisticated committee system to help direct a rapidly changing firm. Some of the most frequently mentioned board goals include assisting with company strategy and policies, providing an independent audit and/or review, and helping to maintain management continuity. Other objectives could include providing specialized expertise, helping to arbitrate feuding family members, or simply serving as "window dressing" to impress bankers or other capital providers. These and other more common board objectives are summarized in Table 3.1. In an ideal situation, a board may be able to provide assistance in all of the areas listed. In the real world, however, it may take years just to master a modest number of objectives. An overly ambitious agenda may quickly lead to burnout and disillusionment by both owners and directors.

It is important that board objectives be realistic. A owner/manager could perceive that his or her board is a failure when, in fact, it was never given a fair chance. This lack of a fair chance could be due to a variety of conditions, including no real objectives (the board was established for legal or window-dressing purposes only), unrealistic objectives (the board was brought in at the eleventh hour before the creditors pushed the company into bankruptcy), or the board was unqualified to handle the objectives (a primarily inside board expected to deal with a complex international undertaking, with no board member experience in international situations).

When setting the board objectives, consider the nature of each goal and whether

Table 3.1
Common Objectives for the Board of Directors

*   Legal requirements (organization)

*   Window dressing (public relations)

*   Stockholder/stakeholder involvement

*   Networking (access to capital/markets/agencies/people)

*   Strategy/policy formulation

*   Independent assessment/review/audit

*   Management continuity and succession

*   Specialized expertise (financial/international/technical)

*   Innovation (new venture/product development and expansion)

*   Arbitration (family members/multiple owners)

*   Crisis management

*   Committee assignments

it is realistic to expect the board to be successful. For example, it is unlikely that a newly formed or expanded board will be able to contribute much to day-to-day operational activities, simply because it won't know what is going on. No number of occasional board meetings will be likely to prepare your directors to handle recruiting and training of hourly personnel, preparation of weekly newspaper advertising, or purchasing raw materials. Also, it would be unrealistic to expect that a hastily recruited board would be able to help the firm attract a significant amount of investment capital at a time when the firm is showing nothing but red ink on the income statements. There certainly are a number of spectacular board success stories along this line, but they are very rare and probably not as simple in actuality as the magazine writer would have you believe.

As a general rule, you need to set objectives that match the needs of the company with the abilities (and time availability) of your (potential) directors. No qualified director will long tolerate boring, do-nothing meetings nor will he remain committed to activities that may be insufferably complex, tedious, or otherwise inappropriate. I cannot provide a simple list of objectives dos and don'ts. Let a dose of common sense, along with a preliminary discussion with directors and potential directors before commitments are made, be your guide. The theme of board objectives will continue into the next section when we discuss what the board may be able to contribute at the various stages of firm development.

Stages of Firm Development

The value of a working board can vary greatly from firm to firm based on an endless number of variables. Some of these variables include industry type, size of firm, geographic location, number of employees, number of products and/or strategic business units, and the size and sophistication of the management team. Accounting for all of these here (or perhaps anywhere) would be an impossible task. One variable that is probably more significant than any other when considering a new board, and must be discussed here, is the stage of firm development. The location of the firm on its life cycle is an important context for the questions of "do I need a board?" and "what could the board do to help me?"

The major needs or issues facing businesses vary greatly, and somewhat predictably, according to their stage of development. By considering each stage separately, we can view some of the particular advantages, as well as disadvantages, a board can bring to the firm at each stage of growth. A number of entrepreneurship theorists have developed frameworks for discussing firm life cycles (Timmons, Smollen, and Dingee, 1985; Kuratko and Hodgetts, 1989). Figure 3.1 represents my interpretation of the business life cycle, along with descriptions of the various stages. This framework is now discussed, with particular emphasis on the role of the board for each stage.

Embryonic/Seed Stage. The earliest stage of a business's development is the embryonic or seed stage. Perhaps 100 or even 200 potential new firms will wither away and die at this juncture for every business that will actually make it to the next stage of development. The seed stage attracts far more dreamers than doers. Only the doers usually go beyond this point. The dreamers are typically glued to armchairs, boasting about how great their businesses "could have been" like so many of their Sunday quarterback counterparts.

The major task during the first phase of the life cycle is to determine the feasibility of the proposed venture. This involves proving the viability of the concept for all of the major aspects of business creation. The most important aspects of the feasibility study include business definition and description, product/service development, market and competition assessment, production and operational concerns, management and personnel requirements, and financing. Perhaps the most difficult task of this stage is to objectively analyze the major risks and potential problems inherent in the venture in order to predict its overall risk. This is extremely difficult for most entrepreneurial types, who tend to get overly emotional and zealous about their ideas.

A major advantage to involving a board during the first stage is that the outsiders will not suffer from the emotional attachment to the idea that may cloud the entrepreneur's judgment. This objectivity could serve as a critical counterbalance to the entrepreneur's "love affair" with the concept. Outsiders can also greatly facilitate the gathering of information and resources needed to arrive at the "go" or "no-go" decision. Of course, a team of outsiders involved

Figure 3.1
Stages of Firm Life Cycle

STAGE 1 EMBRYONIC/SEED STAGE

> This stage is the conceptual phase of the business's development. Emphasis is on the idea generation, learning, research, interest and support building. The major task during this phase is proving the feasibility or viability of a proposed new venture.

STAGE 2 STARTUP

> At this stage, the business begins to move from concept to reality. Management is concerned with gathering together all the resources necessary to begin operations. A strong and dynamic entrepreneur (or entrepreneurial team) is essential to survival at this phase in the cycle.

STAGE 3 EARLY GROWTH

> Once the doors are open, the major emphasis turns toward increasing sales and improving operational systems to support growth. Capital requirements beyond that raised for startup becomes an issue.

STAGE 4 RAPID GROWTH

> This stage is not achieved by all firms. Millions of small, family run businesses start small and never achieve sales growth beyond that needed to support one or a few families. Rapid growth firms are typified by the Inc. 500 rated companies, with annual sales growth rates often exceeding 100-200%. Capital infusion is critical to maintain sales growth.

STAGE 5 MATURITY

> Once a firm reached maturity, sales growth slows and eventually stagnates. Markets are usually saturated and highly competitive. It is critical that firms innovate in order to reverse a nearly inevitable decline.

STAGE 6 INSTABILITY

> A firm in this stage may be undergoing a leadership transition, or could be facing other serious problems. Typical concerns would be an entrepreneurial manager attempting to bring on a more professional management structure, or a solo entrepreneur (or his estate) trying to find a successor to the throne.

---

in the business early on will be more likely to really feel a part of the venture than would outsiders brought in at later stages.

A major disadvantage in involving an outside board during the seed stage is that it can stifle the entrepreneur's creativity and flamboyance. Entrepreneurs are unique in that they frequently go against the grain of conventional wisdom and thought. Directors, on the other hand, tend to provide advice and counsel based on more traditional experiences and ways of doing things. Strong directors may try to stop the entrepreneur from swimming upstream. Granted, sometimes this may be necessary, but often it will result in yet another mediocre, marginal business, whereas the flamboyant entrepreneur, left to his own counsel, could have created a truly innovative business concept.

At a recent chamber of commerce dinner in my city, Jim Wheatly, a highly successful automobile dealer was honored as the Entrepreneur of the Year. In his acceptance remarks, he mentioned that had he known twenty years ago what he knows now about the automobile business, he never would have tried to create his auto auction, at least in our city. According to conventional wisdom, it was impossible. Yet, the creative, tenacious efforts of hard-working entrepreneurs can often succeed in spite of the conventional wisdom. The outsiders can be helpful at this stage, but only if the lead entrepreneur can utilize their wisdom without dampening his or her own enthusiasm and creativity.

Another argument against bringing in a board at this stage is the uncertainty inherent in this stage of a venture. Like the boy who cried wolf, you must avoid inviting busy, successful, potential director types to join you unless you are certain that you are really serious about the venture. Inviting someone to sit on a board of a business that never gets started wastes everyone's time and destroys your credibility.

Startup. At this phase, the business moves from concept to reality. The feasibility study was completed and the concept was found to be viable. A business plan has been developed, and the entrepreneurial team goes to work to implement it. This is an extremely exciting time, and the energy level of all concerned is typically off the scale and highly contagious.

There is much that a board of directors can do at this stage. The major task involved is gathering all the appropriate resources in order for the business to function. Underscoring this, of course, is the need for startup and working capital. Whether equity capital, debt, or both is desired, the odds are that raising it will take far more effort than expected. I tell my students and consulting clients that they should come up with their best guesstimate of their total capital needs and then multiply by 2. This usually proves to be a good rule of thumb.

It was shown in Chapter 2 that outside directors can be very helpful in external functions such as raising capital. They are also very helpful in general networking activities, which can be most useful in gathering other needed resources, such as key personnel, government agency or foreign contacts, and a variety of other "people" resources. A board can often substitute, at least on an occasional or temporary basis, for the internal management functions that have not yet been filled by a full-time staff.

Some directors may appear at your doorstep at this juncture, whether you are ready for them or not. Your banker, accountant, or investors may insist that they or their agent be given a seat on your board so that they can watch over their investments. In some cases, this is fine and you will get a good director to work with. In other cases, the person appointed will take on an adversarial role as if his or her only concern is protecting the family jewels.

You can take steps to avoid getting stuck with a potential problem director by setting standards and policies for board membership early, and by insisting that any stakeholder-designated directors be persons of high quality, and that you have a say on the selection. Once appointed, do your utmost to get them educated and involved so that they will become part of your team, and not just an investor watchdog.

A negative side to involving outsiders at this stage can be summed up in the old and tired cliche "too many chiefs, not enough indians." During the startup stage, hundreds of key decisions need to be made quickly, and by a unified (if not a single) voice. Involving a board early can seriously slow down what needs to be a fast process. Directors can easily assume that they need to be consulted on everything from which bank to use to what color chairs for the reception area. This can create confusion and replication of effort that can cripple the venture before it is really moving.

Boards rarely create businesses. In fact, from the research that has been done, it is clear that only a small percentage of private corporations use boards at all. A competent board, however, when combined with a strong lead entrepreneur can be a powerful combination during startup.

In recent years, I have been involved as an organizing director for a new commercial bank. Due to legal and other considerations unique to the banking industry, a group of directors is almost essential to successfully chartering and opening a new bank. Directors were carefully screened and chosen to represent a careful geographic, industrial, and social balance for the community involved. Each director played an important role in a variety of organizational activities, including such areas as stock sales, public relations, recruiting and staffing, site selection, building design, policy formulation, and budgeting. Yet, all of this significant board effort and contribution would not have made the bank a reality without the presence of a lead entrepreneur. In this case, the bank president, who came up with the decision to leave his old position and create a new institution, played the role of lead entrepreneur. Although he does not own 100% or even 50% of the stock as do most entrepreneurs, he still embodies the drive, vision, talent, and other abilities found in other successful entrepreneurs. Without his leadership, the bank would not have happened. Yet, without the directors' contributions, he would not have been able to start the business on his own.

Early Growth. Once the doors are open for business, the major emphasis turns toward increasing sales and improving internal operations in order to meet the demands of business. Struggles with cash flows, suppliers, and staff needs become a nearly daily occurrence. At this stage, the owner is often so overwhelmed with operational concerns, that a board of directors becomes a back-burner concern, at best, and a nuisance, at worst. Efforts to "keep up with the flow" eliminate any well-intended plans to sit down from time to time with advisors to recapture the big picture.

The very difficulty of using a board forum at this stage may be the best reason for making the effort. As Marc Schwartz reported in his recent board study, outside directors' greatest contribution is bringing an objective viewpoint to the table. "Outsiders help us to see the forest and not the trees" (Moskowitz, 1990, p. 10). The trade-off, of course, is the time required to prepare for the meetings, prepare the directors, and the actual meetings themselves. A half-hearted effort will accomplish little other than to create frustration for directors and owners alike.

Rapid Growth. The rapid growth stage is not reached by most firms. Millions of smaller, family owned firms will start out small and remain small for a variety of reasons. The rapid growth firm is characterized by the *Inc.* 500 list of rapidly growing, privately owned firms. Whereas only 500 firms a year are named to this prestigious list, *Inc.* magazine estimates that the number of potential candidates for its ranking exceeds 500,000 firms (*Inc.*, 1984, p. 136).

Rapid growth is a time of whirlwind activity. Sales growth may be increasing by as much as several hundred percent per year. Managing this growth is a formidable task and requires a herculean effort from all involved. Capital requirements will grow seemingly one step ahead of sales growth. There is much that a board of directors can do at this stage. Unfortunately, there probably is not a more difficult time for the owner to make the time necessary to develop a board. On the other hand, this is an excellent time to attempt to recruit top-level directors who will find the challenges of serving a dynamic firm attractive.

The advance preparation of a working board during an earlier stage will almost certainly pay off here, because the groundwork and process for board utilization are already in place. If a firm does not already have a working board at this stage, circumstances may force one into being as various suppliers of expansion capital attempt to place tentacles onto the business. Unfortunately, as discussed previously, this sort of board may serve the stakeholder's interest, but provide little assistance for the business itself.

Much of the benefit that a board can provide is similar to that discussed in the earlier sections. You may wish to refer back to the case examples of effective and ineffective use of boards that were discussed at the end of Chapter 2. These examples were based on interviews with rapid-growth firms, therefore, they will not be repeated here.

Maturity. Maturity is marked by a slowing, ceasing, or even decreasing of sales growth. For smaller firms, this may be at a level of $100,000 or even less. For the larger private companies, this could occur at a level of several hundred million dollars per year. Firms reaching maturity usually find their markets saturated and highly competitive. Strategies usually involve capturing market share away from competition or innovating. Innovation is the best way to reverse sales decline.

Nolan Bushnell is an excellent example of an innovator. His entrepreneurial success began in 1972 when he invented the Pong video game. After quickly saturating the market with this relatively unsophisticated technology, he introduced several other games under his Atari name. The later games offered an important innovation in that they used cartridges that, unlike Pong, allowed several games to be played on the same machine. Shortly after Atari came Pizza Time Theater, an arcade where young people brought their parents to eat pizza and play Bushnell's video games. In spite of his strong innovative skill, however, Bushnell's Pizza Time Theater went bankrupt in 1984 (Gilbert, 1984; Garrett, 1989). Innovation alone will not make or save a business.

As with the other stages, there are pros and cons to boards for mature firms. On the positive side, the company should be in an excellent position to devote the time and resources needed to establish the board. A strong internal management team should be in place, and some of these insiders would make excellent board candidates. The firm and its founder most likely has a strong reputation that would make recruiting outside candidates relatively easy. The board members may provide an important catalyst to inspire needed innovation and change. On the other hand, boards often seem better qualified to urge caution and maintain the status quo than to innovate. A lot will depend on the qualities of the directors, the objectives set for the board, and the implementation of the owners and managers.

Instability. This final stage does not necessarily follow the others sequentially; rather, it could occur at any time that the firm faces a crisis. For the purposes concerned here, the discussion will be focused on a leadership transition, but instability could result from a variety of internal and external forces, such as government actions, liability resulting from product failure, fluctuations in the economy, and changing consumer trends. The question of whether a board can be of value in times of crisis is a particularly difficult one. On one hand, the CEO may benefit from having several good minds to engage in a brainstorming session. On the other hand, some crises arise from circumstances outside anyone's control, and the board may provide little more than a commiseration session. In my study, inside directors were ranked as having much greater value than outsiders for crisis management.

Related to leadership, however, instability can come about by the temporary incapacitation of the owner, a feud between the partners, or the death of an owner. Each of these situations can spell imminent disaster for a privately owned firm, and a board may be of great value. My study found outside boards to rank high in this area, and this finding was confirmed in several follow-up verbal discussions. Schwartz, however, found evidence to suggest that outsiders are of little help in choosing a successor or mediating family conflicts (Moskowitz, 1990, p. 10). A possible explanation to the contradiction in these studies may be the uniqueness of each sample. My study was of *Inc.* 500 ranked firms, whereas Schwartz surveyed readers of *The BusinessWeek Newsletter for Family-Owned Business*. The Schwartz sample could easily have been heavily weighed with family firms whose successor issue was preresolved by birth and other relationship variables, and not an issue open for board discussion.

The time to face the succession question is, of course, when the founder is living and active. Unfortunately, this is not always the case, and a board or estate executors may be forced to find a leader overnight or have a fire sale in the morning. Certainly, the likelihood of finding a qualified successor is improved by having a competent board with broad experience and networks in place. The board can also play a vital role in the orientation and adjustment phase of the leadership transition. In a time of crisis, such as a death, it is unlikely that family members not actively involved with the affairs of the business would be able to execute an effective succession.

SUMMARY

This chapter has addressed the question "do you need a board?" We have defined the two major types of board members (inside and outside) and have established the minimum board requirements as prescribed by law. Also, board objectives and the stages of firm life cycle were discussed. In considering the general question of whether or not to utilize a working board, we covered some of the basic advantages and disadvantages for boards for each of the major stages of firm development.

In closing, it should be pointed out that it is easier to establish a board in the early stages of development than in the later ones. This provides the opportunity to take advantage of the board longer, while also allowing the board members to go through the learning curve with the firm. This can reduce the common problem of board members being of little value because they do not know what is going on in the company. On the other hand, the more established the firm, the easier it is to attract good board members, and, furthermore, more established firms will have greater resources with which to establish the board. The final decision, of course, rests with each firm's owners and officers.

4

Getting Started: Strategies for Developing a Working Board

INTRODUCTION

This chapter is designed to help the owner/manager develop a personal framework for building a working board of directors. The first section contains a brief discussion on the need for personal commitment to the concept on the part of top management in order for the process to succeed. Next is a discussion of the basic board types in terms of the expected function of the board. The remainder of the chapter contains discussions on a number of special considerations one must face when making decisions during the early organizational stage of the board-building process.

IMPORTANCE OF OWNER'S COMMITMENT

The first and most important step in building a working board was introduced in the preceding chapter, namely, the desire of the owner/manager. Unless the chief executive is willing to make a serious personal commitment to the board process, all effort toward developing a board is wasted energy. This is not a task where an underling can take the initiative and succeed. An uncooperative owner/manager will quite naturally thwart any attempt to, as he perceives it, make him subordinate to a board.

Countless family firms have been subject to power plays in which disgruntled shareholders (family or otherwise) have attempted to exert control over the company management. These power plays often involve the creation of a board in an effort to "share" power. At best, these situations accomplish their objectives after some degree of emotional bloodletting. At worst, these efforts only exacerbate existing tensions until legal measures are taken. Although there certainly may be situations that justify a hostile board creation, for the purpose of the following discussion, we will assume that the owners are in support of and leading the board creation process.

Table 4.1
Generic Board Types

---

* WINDOW DRESSING	Exists primarily to enhance image and prestige of the firm. Duties are largely ceremonial.
* STRATEGIC	Deals with a variety of long-term and policy-related functions of the firm. Role may be either advisory or decision-making.
* OPERATIONAL	These boards are involved in a wide variety of routine and day-to-day activities of the firm. Typically composed of mostly inside directors.
* NETWORKING	Established to create and enhance the firm's external linkages to the outside world through the personal contacts of the outside directors.
* ALL PURPOSE	A hybrid of all the other types. Involved in all levels of the firm's activities. Difficult to create from scratch; requires much time and commitment to achieve.

The decision to build a board is one of serious long-term cost and consequence, and, as such, should not be taken lightly. Top management must come to the decision only after weighing the pros and cons, as well as considering the experiences of others who have been in a similar situation.

In addition to making the personal commitment, management must set goals and objectives for the board. This involves a number of subdecisions, but begins with deciding upon the general purpose of the proposed board. In reality, there are probably as many board types as there are firms. Further, the type of board a firm should develop ought to reflect the current needs of the company, considering its situation and environment.

GENERIC BOARD TYPES

In order to simplify the discussion, I have developed the following generic board typology that classifies boards according to the primary purpose for which they are formed. This typology, outlined in Table 4.1, is certainly not exhaustive, nor does in account for boards which may evolve from one type into another. I believe it is useful, however, as a starting point for developing your board strategy.

These categories were selected to reflect common "triggers" that often initiate the board creation process. That is, as the title of each board type suggests, the decision to create a board is often triggered by the recognition of a specific area of need or opportunity, where the entrepreneur believes some sort of formal board forum would be of benefit. Hence, the trigger also represents a major objective area for the board.

Window Dressing

The reality of many supposedly working boards is that they were created and exist primarily for "window dressing." The typical scenario goes something like this. A firm is growing rapidly, and, as such, is experiencing capitalization problems. Knowing that the company's history is short and shaky, the owner (possibly at the advice of a consultant) decides to "dress up" the company's image by creating an outside board. This usually can be helpful in getting a little free publicity on the newspaper business page, and the presence of a few high-profile directors may give the firm's image a quick (but short-lived) burst of professionalism. In some cases, this may help the firm, as long as short-term image building is all that is expected.

The downside of this type of board should be fairly obvious. Good people typically do not associate with do-nothing causes and organizations. The directors recruited to a window-dressing board will quickly become disillusioned with their role. This is not to say that a window-dressing board should be avoided. In fact, probably many private firms would benefit by simply realizing that window dressing is all that is desired of the board. This would eliminate much frustration on the part of outsiders who keep waiting for something to happen, only to eventually realize that it was all a public relations game.

Another negative to this sort of motivation for creating a board is that most professionals will quickly see through the facade. The most that should be expected from this strategy is that it will "dress you up" sufficiently to help in a few marginal situations. Bankers, venture capitalists, and other investors will not long be fooled by a board that exists in name only. On the other hand, in this information age, it is amazing what can be accomplished with good public relations. One CEO put it very succinctly when he told me: "The membership of the board lends credibility to the private corporation." I once served on an outside advisory panel for a corporation whose CEO told me directly that one of the main reasons the panel was formed was to give an "appearance" of objectivity to the employees who would be affected by the panel's assignment.

If window dressing is all that you want from a board (at least in terms of your initial goals and objectives), be warned that you still have to pay for it. Most potential directors will turn down the invitation to serve on a do-nothing board. They value their time and reputation too much to affiliate with such an organization. You cannot buy their association cheaply. On the other hand, if you offer a reasonable retainer or meeting fee, and throw in enough other perks, such as nice dinners and occasional parties, you will find some suitable nominees. You also should consider retirees for such positions. Retired professionals and business owners often have a good deal of free time on their hands, and they enjoy having an audience to share "war stories." It is precisely for this reason that I do not usually recommend retired people for positions on more active boards, however, they may serve very well if window dressing is all you are looking for.

Strategic

Probably the most common trigger in the decision to create a working board is the need for help in strategy and long-range planning. This is the area of the business concerned with major goals and objectives, and the policies established to achieve them. The popular literature abounds with anecdotes concerning the use of boards to help in strategic matters, such as succession planning, and to simply serve as an objective sounding board for management.

Typically, a new firm begins with a particular vision of an entrepreneur. This vision, whether in the form of a business plan or simply a mental picture, serves as the long-range plan while the business is young. At some point in the future, however, the original vision becomes inadequate to guide the firm's future direction. This may occur due to changes in the industry or competitive situation, technical breakthroughs, or simply because the founder is thinking more about retirement or other matters than driving the business into the future (and, perhaps, driving himself into the ground). For whatever the reason, once the original vision fails to fill the need for a long-range plan, a replacement is needed, and a board is often viewed as a tool to help fill that need.

Strategic issues typically are considered those that concern the long-term consequences of a firm. These might include decisions such as buying out a competitor, entering a foreign market, closing a plant, and developing a succession plan. Most of the boards I am personally familiar with engage primarily in strategic issues. In some cases, the board is used as a sounding device for the owner/manager to bounce ideas; however, the final decision is made by the CEO, not the board. As one outside director told me: " . . . we really don't make any decisions. This board is more than anything else a 'sounding board.' "

In other cases, the board is actually given a decision-making role regarding the strategic issues facing the firm. In these situations, the owner/manager chooses to share power with the board for key decisions. Examples of power sharing can be found when the board is composed of primarily insiders or primarily outsiders. One example from a decision-making inside board follows. According to one inside director,

[the] board of directors are all insiders as well as managers of different functions in the company. However, we leave all parochial interests outside the door when we have board meetings. The board makes major decisions and truly is not a rubber stamp for the CEO.

An example from an outsider-dominated board comes from a CEO who told me that "the advisory board consisting of five board members worked to develop criteria for succession, and we just employed [someone] as a result." Kenneth Andrews has stated that

[an] effective board should require of its management a unique and durable corporate strategy, review it periodically for its validity, use it as the reference point for all other board decisions, and share with management the risks associated with its adoption (Andrews, 1986, p. 58).

Whether or not this actually happens (or if it is even desired) is completely in the hands of the business owners, who ultimately control the privately held firm.

Operational

Quite different from a board developed for strategic purposes (and also less common) is a board designed to guide operational functions. Operational concerns are those decisions and activities made on a routine and day-to-day basis. In larger firms, these are dealt with exclusively by management and staff assigned to the various tasks and functions of the firm. Boards are rarely advocated as a boon to operational decision making. Outsider-dominated boards are of little use for the day-to-day issues due to the outsiders' lack of information and availability. However, I am aware of boards that review and often make decisions concerning day-to-day functions. These boards are usually dominated by, if not completely composed of, insiders. One such firm holds weekly board meetings, and insists that this process is largely responsible for their continued growth and success. I spent nearly an entire Saturday observing this board work. They dealt with a broad range of issues, mostly routine, and were striving for consensus on nearly every point. If consensus was not reached, the issue remained on the table. Conventional wisdom would suggest that this firm would die from analysis paralysis; yet the extraordinary success of the firm demonstrates otherwise.

Regardless of the occasional example of a board regularly making routine decisions, I will not recommend it. The situations I am familiar with typically arose out of necessity, where a limited size staff had to rely on a few outside directors and some insiders wearing two hats to deal with situations where no permanent staff was available, and financial circumstances made additional hiring unfeasible. There are countless outside directors who have helped with public relations, advertising, shareholder/stakeholder communications, personnel decisions, and many other tasks that typically are considered to be operational, not strategic. Fortunately, this is usually only a temporary situation, and the board will eventually get the tasks reassigned to the staff where they belong.

Networking

I first proposed the creation of a board of directors or advisors for the primary purpose of networking at a national conference for women entrepreneurs held at Baldwin-Wallace College in 1988 (Ford, 1989b, 1990). At that time, I was addressing the concern that young and new entrepreneurs often begin a business activity with a serious deficiency in the area of general business experience and contacts. The typical female entrepreneur, for example, has been described as married with children, has a liberal arts degree, and work experience as a teacher, secretary, or administrator (Hisrich and Brush, 1984). This can result in major problems for the embryonic firm in both startup and growth stages unless the owner is able to compensate for this deficiency, especially the lack of contacts.

Although this problem is more common for female entrepreneurs, men may also lack this key information source, especially if they are young or if it is their first entrepreneurial endeavor. In a study of about 50 members of a women's entrepreneurs association, networking was found to have the highest ranking among a list of useful information sources (Nelson, 1987). A board of directors or advisors can be an important tool to increase the network power of a business owner.

Viewing the entrepreneur from Say's perspective as one who "unites all means of production" (1816, p. 28), we see that the entrepreneur needs to have linkages between the various factors of production or the components of the entrepreneurial process. The sum total of these linkages becomes a network giving the entrepreneur access to information and other resources needed to manage the entrepreneurial process.

Networking involves three important dimensions: density, reachability, and centrality (Aldrich and Zimmer, 1986). Density refers to the extent of the ties, in both absolute numbers and their strength. Reachability considers the path between two persons and may include one or more intermediaries (such as a board member). Centrality examines the total distance between a focal person and all other persons in the network.

An experienced, seasoned company owner may have an extensive personal network in place. A newer business owner may need to obtain a surrogate network, and a board may well serve this purpose. Board members can often assist in the network process by serving as a broker, or connecting link, between the entrepreneur and the outside environment. A number of the examples concerning contributions of outsiders mentioned in earlier chapters deal with situations where the board member brought resources or solutions to the firm as a result of personal connections outside of the firm. Chapter 2, for example, highlighted examples of directors' connections with government officials and venture capitalists that solved survival-level problems for their firms.

The value of establishing a board with networking as a primary objective will vary inversely with the quality of the entrepreneur's (and management team's) personal network. As previously stated, the typical female entrepreneur may not have the same quality and quantity of network as her male counterpart. This is particularly true if the female was out of the work force during childbearing years, or if she was employed in a nonmanagement capacity, such as teaching. For any entrepreneur whose network may be inadequate to access the information and resources needed by the firm, a board established to assist with the network function may be a useful strategic tool. As one CEO put it, " . . . the board's role as an interface to the community is most important."

Such a board may not be easy to establish, however. Outside board members will be of little use for any matter unless they are fairly knowledgeable about the firm. This means that an extensive education and training program will be necessary. Also, you must be careful about inviting someone to join a board under such restrictive terms. A prospective board member may well balk at serving a firm under such a limited charge. A balance must be struck between the limited needs of the entrepreneur (if networking is what you are after) and the ego needs of prospective directors, who may wish to do more than simply open doors for company management.

All Purpose

The previous generic board types dealt with a specific focus, namely, appearances (window-dressing board), long-term planning (strategic board), short-term issues (operational board), or connections (network board). These are the major, broad purposes for which boards are typically formed or expanded beyond that minimal board required by law. The final generic board type is a hybrid of all four, and, depending on implementation, could represent the best, or the worst, of each of the other board types.

An all-purpose board is much more difficult to establish than the other types simply because it is set up with multiple expectations. This form of board can easily fail (or be perceived to fail) like anything or anyone that tries to be "all things to all people." On the positive side, such a board can be created as long as sufficient time and other resources are committed to the process, and the rewards can be significant.

The reality one must face if an all-purpose board is desired is how much time and other resources it will take simply to get a board up and running to deal with a limited agenda. The entire process of board development, from concept to recruiting and organization to functioning, will take an enormous amount of energy. Each level of expectation that is added to the board will only delay the return on investment. This, more than any other reason, may be why numerous CEOs and board members have made negative board comments to me such as "Common tendencies appear to be survival or defense of the position rather than attack the new ground," or "Board members—in this and prior ventures—have generally voted with management because they cannot spare time to really comprehend the business decision," and even "[the] board is viewed as an obstacle to be overcome rather than a partner in planning and running the business."

If an all-purpose board is desired, try to achieve it gradually, rather than all at once. Recognize the enormous amount of information you will be expecting your outside directors to absorb and master, and do not expect them to be able to give you wise counsel on every aspect of your business overnight. A few hours of meetings a few times per year will not make someone an expert in someone else's firm. Even inside directors will need time to learn to how to function in their new role as a director of the whole, rather than as a manager of the part.

The composition of the board may change several times as it evolves from a limited-purpose forum into a broad, multipurpose tool. Be prepared to invest patience in addition to time and other company resources as the board process unfolds. If you expect the board to be an instant solution to all your problems, you will most certainly be disappointed. Over time, however, the board may evolve into an all-purpose tool that can help the firm in all sorts of areas. As stated by a director who feels that his firm's board has successfully gone through such an evolution, "The board of directors has contributed significantly to our success. Without this resource initially, we would certainly [have] made major errors . . . their value is ever present."

OTHER CONSIDERATIONS

The preceding sections addressed the generic purpose, or broad goals, that will typically serve as the foundation for the board development process. This section covers a number of important variables that the owner/manager should deal with prior to or during the initial board formulation. Most, if not all, of the following issues have at least some relevance to any of the generic board types.

Board Size

The optimum board size is a widely debated topic, and there is little scientific evidence to help settle the issue. Most studies on board size suggest that the boards of public corporations average from 12 to 14 members (Vance, 1983). The typical size for boards of privately held companies is much smaller. In my *Inc.* 500 study, board size ranged from 1 to 22 members, with most falling into a smaller range of between 3 and 6 total members. Of those firms with outside members (roughly 50%), the most common number of outsiders was 1, 2, or 3. (See Chapter 9, Table 9.1, for details.) In the Ward and Handy study of 147 smaller firms, the median number of board members was 5, with 37% of those being "nonshareholder outsiders." Of the roughly half of those firms that had what the researchers defined as outside boards, the mean number of directors rose to 8, with 56% being outsiders (Ward and Handy, 1988, pp. 294–297). A recent study sponsored by the National Association of Corporate Directors suggests that the average size of private corporation boards is 8 directors, with financial services firms having 14 members, and all other types of firms averaging 7 members (Giardina and Tilghman, 1988, p. 13).

One should take caution not to assume that these studies prove that smaller firms ought to have small boards and large firms ought to have large boards.

The studies simply reveal the size of typical boards. You cannot conclude that a larger board will help you become a larger firm or make any other success or performance conclusions from data of this type.

The number of directors a board should have depends largely on how many directors the board needs. The choice is relative; there is no magic number. As Danco and Jonovic put it, "Five is much better than three, but more than six or seven is usually too cumbersome to be effective. The size, complexity, and needs of the company are the determining factors" (1981, p. 106). The logical starting point is to determine what the board will be expected to do, and then determine how many members it will take to get the job done. Care must be taken not to make the board too large, because it can easily become clumsy and unmanageable. You can always add a member, but it is hard to get rid of one.

In general, boards developed for more of a window-dressing or networking purpose can be larger, because names and contacts are desired. Boards that will engage regularly in either strategic or operational decision making should be smaller, because the members need to be kept up to date and brought together more frequently. On the other hand, if an extensive committee structure is anticipated, then more members may be needed to avoid overextending any individual member.

As a general rule, you probably should start with just a few members, and add additional ones on an as-needed basis. This will help avoid creating an unwieldy and ineffective forum that may be regretted and abandoned later.

Director-Type Mix

Once the initial number of directors is selected, the next decision that needs to be made is the balance between inside and outside directors. The literature is mixed on this question, and the correct answer is, again, largely relative. Some of the theorists strongly advocate using strictly outsiders, and others have built strong cases for the use of at least a few, if not several, carefully chosen insiders.

The two opposing arguments are best summarized by Leon Danco, who is opposed to insiders on the board, and Stan Vance, who questions the value outsiders bring to the board. Danco has stated that insider directors will not challenge the owner's judgments since "They work for him after all. Their livelihood depends on his funds, his goodwill, and his continued blessing" (Danco and Jonovic, 1981, p. 39). Vance has taken the opposing position and has stated the following concerning the value of many outside directors: " . . . no one would hire a plumber to perform surgery or a barber to build a bridge! . . . Coming from all sectors of society, many [of the outside directors] have not even mastered the business alphabet" (1983, p. 258).

There is wisdom in both positions. Many inside people are not cut out to serve as directors, and many outside types are equally unqualified to contribute to a board. In making this decision, carefully consider the expectations for the board, along with the advantages and disadvantages of inside members and outside members as cited in Chapter 2 (refer especially to Tables 2.1 and 2.2). For example, if you plan to use the board for long-term planning, perhaps simply as a sounding board, then outsiders can offer a fresh and objective perspective. If you think you may want the board to help develop or review a marketing plan or chose a data-processing system, then your insiders may have much to offer.

Sometimes insiders are unfairly criticized when they are labeled as narrow functionaries incapable of wearing a director's hat and being objective at board meetings. Although this may be true for some inside types, it clearly is not the general rule. When dealing with many critical board issues, an insider's informed subjectivity may often be of greater value than an outsider's uninformed objectivity. The owner/manager should not overlook the potential contributions that an internal staff already in the company's inventory could make to the board.

Advisory versus Governance Board

As the general issue of boards of directors for smaller firms has grown in media attention, so has the topic of advisory boards. Gardner Heidrick (1984b) has suggested that advisory boards can bring many of the same benefits to firms as can boards of directors. Says Heidrick, "I recommend to many family run businesses that they set up a board of advisors rather than a board of directors. You get outside advice without giving up any control" (Adkins, 1989, p. 5). Robert Mueller (1990) has recently devoted an entire book to the advisory board concept, although it focuses primarily on public corporation boards.

On the surface, the distinction between a board of advisors and a board of directors is enormous: the former deals with advice, whereas the latter deals with governance. The reality is quite another matter where privately owned companies are concerned. In the case where all power is in the hands of one or a few stockholders, all directors are, in the final analysis, advisors only. The owner/manager can call a special meeting of the shareholders and elect new directors or advisors on a moment's notice. Powerwise there is no difference between the two.

The differences that are most often perceived deal with semantics and prestige. Semantically, some business owners seem to prefer the term "board of advisors" because it may sound less threatening. Having a board of advisors sounds less like having a boss than does having a board of directors. In terms of prestige, there is no doubt that directors and potential directors prefer the title "director" than "advisory board member." This is only logical because in the world of large corporations (where most business jargon originates), "board of directors" means all the way at the top, whereas "advisory boards" usually deal with more narrow or specialized matters.

Take the example of banking. During the 1980s many smaller banks were bought up by larger banks and regional bank-holding companies. When the mergers took place, the old boards of directors were usually left in place (at least temporarily) under new names such as "branch advisory boards" or "local advisory boards.'' Typically, these boards are largely ceremonial, left in place to help with public relations while bank customers get accustomed to the power shift from the local offices to the regional offices. The directors kept their titles, but it was well known that power was elsewhere, and the prestige of these positions was, accordingly, diminished.

My basic suggestion on the matter is that the board should be called a board of directors unless the owner has some compelling argument to the contrary. The owner ought to realize that the directors serve at the pleasure of management—no one else, and, therefore, should not be threatened by a title. For whatever it is worth, give the more prestigious title. There is very little else to say about the matter, other than that the term board of directors appears to be the overwhelming choice of private firms using a board. I asked the respondents of my *Inc.* 500 survey to indicate whether their board was a board of directors or board of advisors (or if they had both). Of several hundred responses, only a handful indicated that they had an advisory board.

Committees

Related to the issue of advisory board versus governance board is the notion of committees. Here I am referring to the idea of establishing a committee instead of a board, not committees within the board, which is discussed in Chapter 6. It was stated earlier that one of the very first steps in creating a board is to establish the objectives the board is to accomplish. Occasionally, the objectives developed simply do not justify the creation of a full-blown board—in this case, perhaps a committee will suffice.

Some of the common objectives that may be more appropriate for a committee than a board include employee-of-the-month selection, health benefit and compensation review, scholarship awards selection, computer and data-processing equipment selection, and productivity or suggestion box review. All of these issues are similar to those often dealt with by a board in that they require a fairly regular discussion and decision process, and they are well suited to involvement by outsiders or an expert panel.

The question is do any of these concerns (or a combination of them) justify the creation of and commitment to a high-level board? The answer is ''probably not.'' For each of these issues, a special committee, either standing, or selected and convened when needed, will probably get the job done more effectively, and with far less effort, than your regular board. If you do not have a board in place, issues of this sort are probably insufficient to trigger one into formation. Should you have a regular board in place, you may not want to involve them in decisions of this type anyway.

Special committees can quickly and easily be formed to deal with specific problems and issues. It is also much easier to recruit functional experts than qualified directors. I have served on several corporate committees that were formed for one specific purpose. Typically, after the work is completed (which may take a week, or, occasionally a year or more), the committee is disbanded.

A scholarship award panel is a good example of a useful committee. Outsiders are often desired for decisions of this type to eliminate the charge of favoritism by the employee whose child was overlooked. Active or retired educators are usually thrilled to serve on panels of this sort, and rarely expect to be paid for their services. Another example would be a productivity or suggestion box review team. Again, outsiders may be desired for this type of function for their objectivity or perhaps due to their functional expertise. A qualified outsider can be recruited from industry or academia, although a small fee may be expected.

The point is that a general-purpose board may not be necessary or appropriate for many functions that an ad hoc committee can perform. It is much easier to recruit members to a special-purpose committee than it is to recruit board members. Further, most of the people that you would recruit and appoint to a committee would not meet the criteria for a directorship. A retired teacher would make an excellent choice for the scholarship panel, and an electrical engineer may serve well on a productivity review committee. It is unlikely, however, that either would make an effective director of the whole corporation.

Special-Purpose Boards

The list of objectives and purposes for which boards and/or committees are formed is endless, and it would be impossible to try to cover them all in this chapter. Two very specific types of special-purpose boards merit a brief discussion before the chapter closes: the family council and the Employee Stock Ownership Plan (ESOP) board. These boards are becoming more widespread, and, as such, deserve a special mention here.

Family Council. The family council, or family board, is a forum used by many family businesses as a means to educate and communicate with family shareholders, siblings, children, and other interested, related parties about the business's affairs. This council is usually a separate and distinct entity with little relation to the main board (if one exists). Consultant Roy Williams, an advocate of this type of family forum, has said:

It allows the family to address some of the gut-level issues nobody wants to talk about—and to address them in an open and direct manner without the animosity that often occurs when concerns are not dealt with in a loving and caring manner (1989, p. 7).

Some of the types of issues this council may address include succession and (family member) retirement plans, allocation or abuse of perks and/or expense accounts by family members, sibling rivalries related to possible nepotistic promotions or pay raises based on favoritism. Oftentimes, what is perceived as nepotism or favoritism is, in fact, based on rationality that is not understood by all family members. Regular and good communication can reduce the tensions and potential hostility before they arise.

The family council may also be a way to identify early those family members with a genuine interest in the business, and serve as a training ground for future managers and directors. The keys to a successful family council are to treat the forum professionally (i.e., regularly scheduled meetings with an announced agenda, adequate time allocated, etc.) and be certain to have all interested and appropriate parties included. Like any other organization, it may take a few meetings, or even a few years, to really break the ice and get effective output from the forum. If the business is successful, and especially if the family is large, the use of a family council may have a big payoff in the future.

ESOP Boards. The Employee Stock Ownership Plan concept has been growing during the last decade as an equity-transfer strategy for small businesses (Wallen, 1989; Wood, 1989). The basic idea behind the ESOP is for the employees of a company to be able to invest in the shares of the firm over time. The amount of equity in the plan can vary from as little as 30% to as much as 100%, according to the owner/entrepreneur's desires and other circumstances surrounding the company. (An ESOP can legally be formed with less than 30% of the company equity, however, 30% is the minimum amount required in order to qualify for tax benefits, which is a primary incentive to create such plans.)

A common dimension of many ESOP firms is the creation of an ESOP advisory board. This is a distinct and legally separate entity from the board of directors, and has its own special role and function. Sometimes ESOP boards will be given the power to elect one or more representatives from the ESOP member employees to the firm's governing board to assure that the interests and concerns of the employees are represented. The actual impact of the ESOP board on the corporation as a whole can vary widely, especially in relation to the actual percentage of the company stock controlled by the ESOP.

The specific operation of an ESOP and its board is complex, and a firm must meet certain legal criteria to qualify. More information concerning the concept can be obtained through the ESOP Association based in Washington, D.C., which is referenced in Appendix 1.

SUMMARY

This chapter has addressed several strategic considerations concerning getting the board development process started. It was stressed that the first consideration in developing a successful board strategy is the desire and commitment of the owner/manager. Without this commitment, the process will fail before it even begins. Next, a generic board typology was presented to help guide the basic objectives and goals for the proposed board. Finally, a number of basic considerations were discussed, ranging from board size and composition to special-purpose boards. All of these concepts should be thought out well in advance of extending invitations to potential board members. With these basic board strategy concepts as a foundation, we will now move into the area of choosing and recruiting directors.

5

Choosing and Recruiting Directors

OVERVIEW

This chapter deals with staffing the board of directors. The initial section discusses the team concept, that is, a board is more than just a collection of individuals. Next, minimum qualifications are discussed, followed by sections on ideal directors (what every CEO looks for), generalists versus specialists, and setting classifications. These sections are followed by topics including choosing insiders, sources of and recruiting outsiders, and making the actual invitation. The chapter concludes with a section on how directors view their selection and role on the board.

A TEAM CONCEPT

When recruiting for key functional personnel, the most important factor may be the individuals' talents in their fields. For example, if a new director of the computer and information-processing function is needed, then the most talented computer-type individual would be desired. The person's ability to perform outside of the functional area would be of secondary importance. An effective board, however, is a team, not just a collection of talented individuals. Mavericks and prima donnas may serve well in sales, computers, manufacturing, and other specialized areas, but they may not be the best board members.

A complete board may be thought of as a pie, where each board member constitutes one slice. As individuals, no one member is complete, rather, they come together to form the whole. When filling the board, then, it is important to consider how each potential board member relates, not only to the owner/manager doing the recruiting, but also to the other board members, and to the board as a unit. Think of the total relationship as a matrix, not just a series of binary relationships between the owner and each individual board member. This means that you will try to recruit individuals with complementary talents, rather than all financial experts, for example. It also means that you should strive for individuals with a good mix of personalities. A board built upon a team strategy will be more enduring, and will offer the additional benefit of synergism, where the value of the board overall will be greater than the sum total of the value of each of the individual board members.

MINIMUM QUALIFICATIONS

Although I would like to avoid suggesting a cookie-cutter approach to board building as much as possible, there are a few common-sense generalities regarding director qualifications that are worth mentioning. These should be thought as rules of thumb as you begin the recruiting and nominating process.

Age

Chapter 3 dealt with this topic from a legal perspective, where it was pointed out that some states have a minimum age requirement for directors, whereas others do not. More important than calendar age, however, is mental age. Some 18–21-year-olds have a mental age and maturity that far surpasses many 30–40-year-olds. This may especially be the case for children of family business owners who instilled a knowledge of the business and a strong dose of work ethic at an early age. In these, and possibly other, situations, a young person may make a suitable director. Also, many startup businesses are being created by very young people these days, and the energy and enthusiasm of youthful officers and directors often compensate for a lack of business experience.

These situations are exceptions, however, and, as a general rule, individuals with several years of experience will make better directors than very young and inexperienced candidates. This usually means that anyone under 30 may not qualify, but, of course, there are always exceptions. Also, directors should usually be avoided who are retired. By this I am referring more to a retirement "state of mind" than retirement age. Many individuals are blessed with health and energy that allow them to remain mentally and physically active long after qualifying for social security. These types can make excellent directors. The "mentally retired," however, should be avoided. I have observed this type at meetings where they dominate conversation after conversation with war stories and other tales about how great things were in their day.

Generally speaking, then, directors should be sought who are actively engaged in their careers, not too young, and not too old. Ideally, this means an age range of 30 to 60, with all the usual exceptions inherent in any generalization.

Character

A reputation of good character and high integrity is absolutely essential for a prospective board member. A good company image can take years to build, but can be destroyed overnight by the association of unethical characters on the board. There are many ways to inquire into someone's character. These can include memberships (clubs, churches, political/social organizations, etc.), employers, and other peoples' opinions, among others.

Membership checking is an easy way to learn about the interests of an individual, as well as identifying others who could be used as reference checks. This is also a good preliminary indicator of community acceptance and respect. Caution should be exercised that the criteria for membership for various clubs, churches, political associations, etc., vary widely from "pay your dues" only at one extreme to adherence to a specific doctrine or statement of belief on the other. Also, social and professional climbers have been known to seek a wide range of memberships simply for the purpose of credential building and networking, therefore, memberships alone will not tell the whole story.

Employment, or occupation, also can be a good way to check character. Employment in certain fields automatically implies something about character due to restrictions that may govern who can practice or be licenced to conduct or work in a certain type of business. The medical and legal professions are obvious examples of this. Educators, insurance brokers, and bankers also are typically thought to fit a high ethical profile due to the nature of their work. In today's scandal-ridden society, however, many of these generalizations are becoming obsolete as high-profile individuals in virtually every field are being exposed for various corruptions. Still, employer checks, along with possible calls to various accreditation, certification, or licensing boards, are appropriate measures that will, at least, identify major ethical or legal character questions that would disqualify a potential nominee.

Probably the best method of character checking is the opinions of other persons who are mutually known by you and the potential nominee. These are persons who will be more likely to give a frank and candid assessment of the individual without being concerned about avoiding possible lawsuits for liable, which seems to be the primary concern of personnel directors these days. Especially useful would be the opinions of others who have worked with the candidate in some other board capacity, whether a business board, or some sort of nonprofit group such as the Chamber of Commerce or the United Way. These individuals will be able to comment about the candidate from a point of reference very similar to the forum for which they are being considered for membership.

For all of these methods, care must be used to keep the checking quiet and informal. Any potential embarrassment caused to candidates that are passed over would be unfair, and a poor reflection on the organization doing the investigation. This preliminary checking cannot be avoided, however, since the best way to deal with questionable directors is not to appoint them in the first place.

Knowledge and Skills

Obviously, the knowledge and skills of a potential director play a key part in the decision to extend an invitation to join. It is important to carefully consider the match between those skills possessed by an individual and the skills most needed by the board. For example, a financial services firm will need a board with members that are capable of reviewing and understanding sophisticated and complex financial tools and issues. Similarly, a manufacturing firm ought to have board members with manufacturing knowledge and experience.

This does not mean, however, that every board member needs to be expert in all relevant areas of the business. The important thing is that, if the firm is in the financial services business, most members know something about the industry, and at least one member ought to really be an expert in the field. Because the number of board seats will naturally be limited, individuals chosen for specific areas of functional expertise should be the very best attainable. Do not rule out someone because you may believe that he or she is too busy to bother with you. Most people are flattered to be considered, even if they turn you down for lack of time or other reasons. Further, the best person will often provide a list of other well-qualified candidates, some of which may not have been known to the nominating person or committee. Finally, do not rule out the use of insiders when seeking board members with specific areas of expertise.

Interest

Another key qualification for board membership is interest in the firm itself. This ought to be included in any litmus test used to prequalify potential board members. Most individuals will be flattered to be asked to serve on a board— especially for the board of a visible, successful, business. This flattery is not the same as a genuine interest in the industry, business, and people that the board member would be serving.

It may take more than one meeting or phone call to distinguish between flattery and real interest. Someone who is genuinely interested will tend to show real enthusiasm in one or more ways. Some will simply express themselves verbally. Others will demonstrate their interest with nonverbal cues. One good way to gauge interest is through the type of questions the candidate asks. Does he or she ask discerning questions about the nature of the business, or, rather, questions concerning director compensation, or questions that make it clear that the person is only interested in status and prestige? Some candidates will give themselves away by talking about themselves exclusively. Real interest is not an easy characteristic to measure, and may also fade over time even for the most enthusiastic board member. It is clearly in the best interest of any board, however, to filter out prospective directors who are far more concerned with self-interest than with the business.

Time

It goes without saying that a board member who never has time to attend meetings or other functions will be of little value, if any, to the firm. On the other hand, one should be suspicious of any candidates who do not have a full agenda of their own. As the old saying goes, ''busy people do busy things.'' Good directors are people who have busy schedules—busier than most—combined with the excellent time-management skill needed to get things done efficiently and effectively.

One of the first things a board candidate will want to know will be the required (or anticipated) time commitment. A CEO should not respond with a fuzzy answer like ''we are still trying to figure that out.'' A specific meeting schedule, including frequency of meetings and tentative dates and times, should be available to allow the candidate to realistically assess the time requirement. Often, persons will decline membership due to the time issue. At other times, candidates will be able to work the commitment into a crowded calendar—especially if genuine interest exists.

I know an entrepreneur with businesses scattered across the country, a president of an international company, and a busy surgeon who all serve on boards of other businesses. They are all very effective directors, and have no problem making meetings as long as they are scheduled in advance. On the other hand, these individuals will frequently have difficulty making meetings called at the last minute. The owner/manager must carefully calculate the relative trade-off of having great directors with outstanding credentials who will not always be available—especially for hastily called meetings.

No Conflict of Interest

Conflict of interest is one of those fuzzy concepts that people frequently cannot define, but say they know it when they see it. Avoiding conflicts of interest can be a painfully arduous and time-consuming task. Sometimes the search for conflicts can take on the appearance of a witch hunt, especially if the firm has recently been the subject of any sort of ethical or legal investigation. Many corporations will have a stated policy that director conflict of interest will not be tolerated, however, rather than having a detailed policy defining conflicts, each situation will be considered separately on a case-by-case basis.

There are certain obvious and legal situations where conflicts of interest are clear and must be avoided. These would include situations such as recruiting a government employee to a board where unfair or even illegal influence could be used to obtain government contracts. Or one could imagine a situation where interlocking directorships could be sought to attempt to fix the pricing in an industry—a clearly illegal activity. In cases like these, there is no question about the inappropriateness of the conflict.

However, there are thousands of more subtle situations where the presence of a conflict is not clear. One example would be to recruit a retired government worker or former official of an industry competitor. Is this a conflict or just good business? I cannot answer this question for you, but would suggest that the board discuss the matter of conflict of interest to be sure that sufficient sensitivity is given to this serious issue. The Arthur Young/NACD study offers insights that could be used to suggest some "rules of thumb" when formulating conflict policies (Giardina and Tilghman, 1988, p.10). For example, the study reported that 28% of companies require approval before a board member can serve on another board. Further, 20% of the reporting companies restrict the number of boards that a director may serve on. Although these methods still do not say just what constitutes a conflict, they will at least ensure that the question is raised. In the final analysis, if you are bothered by a situation, but are not sure if it is a conflict of interest, get legal advice before making a decision.

THE IDEAL DIRECTOR

The title of this section is intentionally misleading. Although life would be far simpler if there were a standard test for finding ideal directors, in reality, there is no such standard. One of the numerous peripheral questions that I explored in my *Inc.* 500 board study was the common characteristics that CEOs looked for in ideal directors. Although there was some similarity in the responses given, there were far more dissimilarities discovered.

Table 5.1 lists the characteristics mentioned by the chief executives in response to an open-ended survey question. A few responses, such as specialized knowledge, industry experience, financial expertise, and successful track record, received sufficient mention to consider part of the core requirements for "ideal" directors. Others, including general business knowledge, personal contacts, complementary background, compatibility, judgment, and dedication, certainly also deserve consideration.

The characteristics that received only one or a handful of votes are also worth noticing. These help to underscore the incredibly complex, and often personal, task of selecting, identifying, and recruiting directors. Characteristics such as creativity, humor, Christian value system, women or minority, and willingness to serve without insurance may not have broad appeal to director seekers in general; however, there is certainly a place for special and/or personal characteristics requirements for many firms.

The bottom line in seeking ideal directors is that there probably are no such candidates. Each nomination process should define a set of minimum, "must-have" characteristics, along with a secondary set of "would-be-nice" characteristics, and then be prepared to be very flexible. It may also be helpful to draft a set of disqualifying characteristics to speed up the nomination and selection process.

GENERALISTS VERSUS SPECIALISTS

The topic of generalist directors versus specialist directors comes up frequently, and can create some confusion. Typically, the situation will arise where a new board is being designed and the nominating committee (or individual) is trying

Table 5.1
Characteristics CEOs Seek in New Board Members

Characteristics	Frequency
Specific technical or specialized expertise, including tax, legal, medical, computers, etc.	31
Experience in same industry/ field	21
Financial Expertise	21
Successful track record (entrepreneur, CEO, mgr.)	21
General business knowledge/ experience	20
Personal contacts	16
Complementary experience background	15
Compatibility, personality, chemistry	11
Judgment, maturity, common sense	10
Dedicated interest in serving on board	10
Nepotism (must be related)	9
Successful manager, employee with "the" firm	9
Honesty, integrity	8
Intelligence, brilliance	8
Action oriented, problem solver	7
Objectivity, broad perspective	6
Outspoken, opinionated	6
Advanced degree (M.B.A., Ph.D., M.D.)	4
Prestige, reputation	3
Creative	3
Availability	2
Communication skills	2
Vested interest (own stock)	2
Willingness to serve without insurance	1
Humor	1
Christian value system	1
Gambler, risk taker	1
Women, or minority group	1

to strike a balance between recruiting good "general business" types and specialists that have a lot of expertise relevant to the business. Occasionally, this can be manifested in the extreme by recruiting one specialist, such as an electrical engineer, and one generalist, such as a retired business owner. Usually, however, the distinction is more subtle. In this case, someone is needed with a specific expertise, such as electrical engineering. However, in choosing such a candidate, someone is sought who also possesses as much general business background as possible. One could imagine recruiting a "hyperspecialist" who was outstanding in his or her own field, yet could not begin to carry on a meaningful conversation with the board on general business matters. This sort of director should be avoided at all costs. If assistance of this type is needed, it can be obtained via a consultant or, possibly, by hiring an appropriate full- or part-time staff person.

Likewise, generalists can sometimes be too general—resulting in little real contribution to the board. Someone can be a generalist by virtue of having owned his or her own business, yet have very little relevant knowledge or understanding that would be necessary to be an effective director of, say, a medical instruments company. Take the generalist out of familiar surroundings and he or she could be as ineffective as someone who is overspecialized.

As a general principle, then, one should avoid selecting directors solely based on their specialized expertise or their general business background. Instead, try to seek individuals who have some specialized training and knowledge in an area relevant to the firm *and* evidence of the broader background and experience necessary to function in the general policy and/or advisory capacity of a board member.

SETTING CLASSIFICATIONS

Before any individual offers of board membership are made, it is important to think out what the final board composition should look like. This starts, of course, with the decision of board size. Another parameter may be precommitted board seats, such as for one or two partners or key stockholders (this point reflects reality, not necessarily a recommended ideal situation), or for a top manager, or heir apparent that needs to be included. Once these preconditions are all sorted out, the remaining number of desired board seats will be ready for assignment.

A number of theorists and consultants have recommended schemes to distribute board positions. Castaldi and Wortman (1984, p. 10), for example, proposed an ideal board with one seat representing owner's equity, one for a technical expert, two with management experience, two with legal and/or financial expertise, and one representing a broad economic perspective. As a rule of thumb, this is a useful proposal in that it stresses diversity without creating a board that is large and cumbersome.

I have previously proposed a somewhat similar board structure, the main difference being that my model is a bit more flexible. This model suggests that board positions be mapped out in advance according to the specific areas of knowledge, skills, and connections desired to create an effective board (Ford, 1989b). Some of the characteristics sought may include banking and finance, labor and professional associations, export regulations and foreign markets, marketing and competition, and legislative and regulatory agencies. These characteristics should be chosen to custom fit the firm, however, and should not simply be a copy of those chosen by some other firm or those depicted in anyone's model (including my own).

Well-qualified inside directors may be available to cover some of the functions. For example, the personnel manager may fit for the area of labor markets and professional associations, and the marketing director may be well suited to fill the need for someone with a handle on marketing and competition. By the process of elimination, outside directors may then be sought to fill the gaps, while simultaneously meeting the objective of having a mixture of inside and outside directors.

Regarding the notion of specialists versus generalists, the intent is to recruit based on some area of specialization, however, in every case those individuals selected should possess abilities and credentials that are as broad as possible. Like any rule made to be broken, these guidelines are only suggestions. Board positions should be used simply to ensure that the board has a good balance and that key areas of expertise are represented. They should never be viewed as static, inflexible job descriptions.

NOMINATING DIRECTORS

The decision as to who should be selected as directors obviously rests with the owner/manager of the firm. For some, this means that the decision will be a solo one with no input from others. Most decision makers, however, will desire, if not require, the advice and input of some sort of nominating committee. This group should be charged with collecting names and reviewing credentials of both outside and inside directors.

Caution should be used about the potential for conflict when choosing the nominators. For example, unless you are certain about which insiders you are going to select, potential inside candidates would be in an awkward position serving on the nominating committee. It is better to avoid this situation and use only board definites and others who are clearly (and knowingly) not under consideration for the nomination process.

The specific charge to the nominating committee will vary from situation to situation, however, a few general duties apply. First, the committee needs to be briefed on any and all preconditions such as number of positions, position descriptions, preselected directors, etc. The committee also needs to be clear on the rationale for any conditions that may be less than obvious. Next, the committee should be given a timetable and a set of specific outcomes expected. For example, is the committee being asked simply to generate a list of names or is a detailed review and actual selection desired? The level of involvement of the committee will naturally depend on the leadership style of the owner/manager.

CHOOSING FROM AMONG YOUR INSIDERS

Referring back to the section on classifications, recall that all directors should be selected because they have certain characteristics that are desired by the board. This applies equally to outsiders and insiders. Insiders are usually considered first, simply because the pool of potential insiders is fixed, therefore, less flexible than the universe of potential outside directors.

Typically, well-qualified insiders can be found with marketing/sales/competition knowledge or financial background or R&D/manufacturing skill. Insiders may also have many other areas of expertise, depending on the nature of the firm and its workforce. Whether or not these types will also make good directors depends on a number of factors, primarily centering around the minimum qualification criteria as suggested earlier in this chapter. These would include such points as maturity, compatibility, and other personal attributes, in addition to the specific skill area.

Another potential complication in choosing insiders is protocol. Assuming the marketing person considered for a board seat is also a senior vice president, there is no problem. Fortunately, seniority, rank, and board qualifications usually coincide.

However, if the marketing person is junior in rank and seniority to a couple other persons (persons not being considered for board positions), then a situation of envy and jealousy will inevitably develop. This is the unfortunate truth of corporate politics that often undermines the rational intentions of top management. Even if there is a good reason for selecting a junior person for the board, the mere oversight of one or more senior people could cause more damage to the firm than the potential benefits to the board from the appointment.

Another potential pool of inside directors consists of those related to the owner/ manager, but not actively involved in the management of the firm (refer back to Chapter 3, where inside directors are defined). Far too many company owners automatically appoint their wives (spouses) and/or adult children to the board with no real expectation that they will perform any duties as board members. This is unfortunate in that it sets up an attitude early on that the board is a do-nothing, rubber stamp of the owner.

I will not advocate that relatives be appointed in this manner, although I will admit that I am aware of situations where spouses, dormant for years, suddenly jump into action and exert authority during times of crisis. Perhaps this would have occurred even without the title of director; we can never know. Nevertheless, I can see little benefit in appointing someone to the board expecting that they will play the role of a "comatose director." The only possible benefit I can see from this strategy is in a situation where power is shared by more than one family and there is a desire to stack the deck by having a spouse who can give an automatic proxy to her owner/manager husband.

There are often, however, situations where a spouse, child, or sibling would be a well-qualified candidate for a board seat, even though the relative is not employed by the firm. There are spouse-directors who are college professors, CPAs, and lawyers, brother-directors who are managers and officers of major corporations, and children-directors who are engineers, and entrepreneurs, and just about every other combination one can imagine. In these cases, the insiders may truly possess the specialized knowledge and expertise sought by the firm, and they bring with them the added benefit of a close, personal association with the owner/manager. Of course, one must also be sensitive to the potential pitfalls of nepotism when several family members are placed on a board. One or two well-qualified relatives can certainly add value to the firm, however, related parties that are unqualified will only create hard feelings and an unprofessional atmosphere.

CHOOSING AND RECRUITING OUTSIDERS

The key to finding good outside directors hinges on what sort of candidates you are looking for. As Table 5.1 suggests, there are numerous characteristics sought, but the more common ones contain the clues to where to locate good directors. The pool of candidates having good director qualifications will be found to include attorneys, accountants, bankers and financiers, company owners and managers, business school professors, and others (Whisler, 1988, p. 315.) A good place to start looking for these persons is the manager's own contacts, including clubs, professional and trade associations, and business contacts. According to one CEO:

I started out by approaching a very well known local entrepreneur who eventually turned me down. Fortunately, he gave me a short list of potential directors who were all influential businessmen. From there I started networking, and each person contacted either confirmed other names or added new names to the list. The entire process took about four months.

An important dimension to the procedure is the confirmation process, whereby potential directors are approved informally by consensus by several others prior to the final selection and election process. This can often allow the manager (or whoever is doing the checking) to gain important background information on each candidate before any commitments are made.

I was recently involved in a situation where a director had to be removed after only about one month on the board when it was discovered that he had falsified his credentials. In this case, he was recruited and selected without sufficient background checking, and the board had no choice but to ask him to resign in order to avoid potential embarrassment. Fortunately, this taught the entire board a valuable lesson on the importance of reference and background checking.

The bottom line in choosing outsiders is that you only get a few choices, so use them wisely. It may take time to recruit really top-level directors, but the benefit will be worth it in the long run. The board is no place to train raw, green recruits. The governance and advisory roles of directors are too important to leave in the hands of inexperienced or second-rate board members.

THE INVITATION TO SERVE

Prior to any actual meetings or interviews with potential board members, the term and compensation policy need to be established. The purpose for predetermining term and compensation policies is that it reduces the likelihood that these details will bog down the negotiations. For example, it may be decided to elect and/or reelect directors on an annual basis. Or, commitments may be made for 3-year terms of office, perhaps staggered so that some directors rotate off the board each year. Of course, exceptions can always be made to allow outstanding directors to be reappointed.

Likewise, the amount of compensation and other director benefits should also be determined (at least the basics). The interviewer should offer this information when appropriate, rather than leaving the candidate in the awkward position of wondering or having to ask. For example, a certain annual retainer, or per-meeting fee should be set, along with any other benefits such as mileage and directors' and officers' insurance.

Sometimes the purpose of the initial interview will be immediately clear, and other times the purpose may be veiled. For example, if a candidate is well known, and his or her credentials impeccable, then it is probably best to come right out and state the purpose of the meeting up front. Especially where the manager and candidate have an established relationship, a direct, to-the-point approach should be used.

If the candidate is less well known, at least personally, then a less direct approach may be desired. For example, candidates may have been recommended by others or may have been identified due to their reputation. In cases such as this, the manager may try a strategy such as asking the candidate for advice on establishing a board based on the candidate's own board experiences. Or a meeting could be requested to discuss candidates. Once the manager decides whether or not he or she is compatible with the candidate, a decision can be made whether or not to make an actual invitation. This less-direct strategy may take more than one meeting, because it could be awkward to set a meeting for one purpose and then move quickly to another.

In some cases, it may be desired to extend the invitation with tentative language, such as "would you like to be considered a candidate for board membership? Your nomination would, naturally, be subject to full board and shareholder approval, but I feel confident that you would be considered a strong candidate." This approach will give both parties a graceful out if for any reason it is decided that a good fit does not exist.

Table 5.2
Reasons Board Members Attribute Their Selection to the Board

Reason	Frequency
Vested interest (own stock)	27
Successful manager, employee with "the" firm	18
Specific technical or specialized expertise	18
Financial expertise	11
Friendship with CEO	6
Successful track record (entrepreneur, CEO, mgr.)	6
General business knowledge/ experience	3
Nepotism (related)	2
Prestige, reputation	2
Elected by workers (ESOP, union)	2
Personal contacts	1
Complementary experience background	1
Compatibility, personality, chemistry	1
Judgment, maturity, common sense	1
Outspoken, opinionated	1
Advanced degree	1
Christian value system	1

A final consideration is whether to conduct the interview alone or if an additional director or officer should also be included. This question needs to be approached on a case-by-case basis. If the two parties have a close relationship, then it is probably best to keep the meeting private. If the manager and candidate are not close, or even acquainted, then an intermediary is a good idea. Having a third party present who is well known to the other parties will help warm up the meeting and be able to add both information and credibility to the process.

HOW DIRECTORS VIEW THEIR ROLES

So far, this chapter has focused on the recruiting and selection process from the sole perspective of the company owner/manager seeking to build a board. This is as it should be, because the owner of the firm is responsible for making the key decisions. It may be helpful, however, to pause and try to view the process as well from the director candidate's perspective.

In my *Inc.* 500 board study, I included an open-ended question in the board member survey asking board members to comment on their opinion as to why they were asked to serve on the board. The results of this question, shown in Table 5.2, make an interesting comparison with Table 5.1, which was the response to the CEO question as to what characteristics they sought in new directors.

Note that the main reason cited by directors was a vested interest, or stock ownership. This compares with only two such vested interest comments from the CEO group. This may indicate that, although more knowledge and experience credentials are preferred by CEOs, the reality is that most are chosen to privately owned firm boards due to their financial stake in the business. Similarly, the next frequently mentioned reason cited by directors was their success as an employee (insider) of the firm.

Beyond the notable leaning toward insiders, there is some similarity between the two sets of responses. Specific technical or specialized expertise, and financial expertise were mentioned by a large number of board members, and these were two of the most frequent comments made by the CEOs. Therefore, we can summarize by saying that, ideally, directors are chosen due to their specific expertise and experience, but, in reality, many are selected primarily because of relationships and other connections.

SUMMARY

This chapter has addressed the process of choosing and recruiting directors. An attempt has been made to clarify each step of the process, from defining the team, setting qualifications and classifications, using both insiders and outsiders, and generalists and specialists, to extending the invitation to serve. The selection process was considered from both the owner/manager's as well as the director's perspectives. The next chapter deals with the process of board management and control.

6

Management and Organization

OVERVIEW

This chapter discusses a variety of issues related to the effective management and organization of the board. The first topic area is the term of board membership. Also covered is the termination of ineffective directors. Next follows a section on training and educating directors. Simply put, directors are only as useful as they have been prepared to be. This section is followed by a discussion on board positions and roles. Specifically, the various board offices are defined and their duties are discussed. Finally, commonly used board committees are described, along with some suggestions as to if and how they should be utilized.

TERMS AND TERMINATION OF DIRECTORS

Owner/managers need to pay heed to this particular warning: Directors, especially outsiders, can be very difficult to remove, so be careful not to give them the impression that they are being appointed for life. It can feel awkward asking someone to serve under some sort of limited, fixed policy (''I would like to put you on our board until March 30 of next year''), unless it is part of a normal board policy to rotate directors via some sort of routine schedule. If a rotation schedule is to be used, it needs to be in place before making any invitations.

One common rotation scheme is to divide the directors into two or three groups, where each group rotates off the board on different years. This will create the opportunity for new blood, while also offering a good deal of continuity. A CEO certainly has the right to ask a director that is not working out to resign or to decline standing for reelection at any time, however, this can get very embarrassing and uncomfortable for all parties involved. It is preferable to ask all directors to rotate off the board in some manner.

Of course, some directors will work out so well that it would be desirable to keep them on past a normal term. It is much better to treat these cases as the exceptions rather than the reverse. That is, it is much easier to find a way to ask someone to remain than it is to ask someone to leave. Some factors related to asking directors to stay on the board include their equity position, the need for continuity, and general usefulness of the directors. Some boards may stagnate if all "old timers" constitute the group. Others would suffer from a domination of inexperienced "young turks" unless a few senior members are kept on. Every case is a unique situation. Each director should be recruited as if he or she could contribute forever. However, reality suggests that some standard, useful life, period of time exists (perhaps 3 or 4 years); therefore, the new member should expect to leave after the term expires.

No matter how well the nominating team does its homework, an occasional director will be appointed who just does not work out. In this case, it may be necessary to terminate the individual prior to the end of the term. Some reasons for this could include poor attendance at meetings, a change in the individual's personal situation or employment that creates a possible conflict of interest, or, simply, a personality clash between the board member and the other directors and/or company officers.

Poor attendance can be the result of many factors, including a relocation to a new job and/or city, or simply a lack of interest. Conflicts of interest could develop if a director changes employment (perhaps working for a competitor of the firm whose board he serves) or if some personal event or situation creates a cloud of ethical suspicion around the individual. Personality conflicts can occur any time, and these are the hardest to deal with, because they are terribly subjective, and hard to rationalize with facts and specifics. Nevertheless, they can become very disruptive in meetings and otherwise, and occasionally require extreme action to rectify.

The best way to handle any situation where a director needs to be removed would be to counsel the director to resign. This method allows the director to save face, and reduces the amount of chatter in the rumor mill. The action can be softened by offering to continue whatever compensation or perks were due as a working director for some period of time beyond the resignation date. Unfortunately, not everyone will accept the gracious way out, and, especially in cases where personalities are involved, more direct action will occasionally need to be taken. Should a forced termination be required, it may be necessary to call a special meeting of the full board, or even a shareholders meeting. In any event, legal counsel should be sought to avoid any possibility of a lawsuit or other negative reaction from the action.

TRAINING AND EDUCATING DIRECTORS

The responsibility for training and educating directors falls squarely on the shareholders of the company's leadership, namely, the CEO or chairman who recruited and selected each director. Obviously, the directors already possess a high degree of knowledge and expertise or they would not have been selected in the first place. However, directors can improve their effectiveness, both as individuals and as a group, through an ongoing program of director education. This education should include company-specific information, as well as more general training aimed specifically at directors and corporate leaders. There are several general approaches to continuing the education of board members that are now reviewed.

Individual and In-House Training

Director training begins at the one-to-one level when each director is interviewed and recruited by the company's owner/manager. At this time, a detailed package of company information was probably presented and reviewed in order to give the director candidate a reasonable picture of the business. This type of orientation needs to continue on a regular basis, although not necessarily on a one-to-one basis.

As a part of regular board meetings, directors need to be given information for review, and an opportunity to ask questions about virtually all aspects of the business. It is a good idea to schedule such items as a plant tour, brief reports from vice presidents and/or division managers, and a review of financial statements into the regular agenda of board meetings. By including one or more review items at each regular meeting, the directors will gradually become more familiar with the firm, which will keep them interested and more effective.

Using Professional Trainers and Consultants

Another method of director education is the use of professional trainers and consultants. There are essentially three approaches to using these outside professionals for director education: enrolling the directors in regularly scheduled, continuing education seminars and workshops; hiring a consultant to conduct an in-house workshop on a general topic; and using a consultant to help address a specific or difficult issue or problem facing the firm.

There is an endless number of regularly scheduled, "off-the-shelf" seminars that directors may benefit from. For example, certain directors may be deficient in some skill areas that pertain to board functions. For example, a director who is a medical doctor may not be comfortable reviewing financial statements and spreadsheets. If this is a problem, the individual could be encouraged to take a short course at a local college or Small Business Development Center to learn the basics of financial analysis. These programs are typically very inexpensive, and usually have highly trained professionals for instructors.

In addition to such general-purpose seminars, the entire board, or representatives, could benefit from specialized workshops that specifically address board matters. For example, the National Association of Corporate Directors

(NACD), referenced in Appendix 1, offers special workshops for directors on a regular basis. These are offered in a number of cities across the country, and they also offer programs through local chapters of the organization. Some of the topics covered at their annual sessions include "CEO/Board Relationships," "Compensation Criteria," "Smaller Company Boards," and "The New Director: Criteria and Selection." These sessions can benefit both experienced and inexperienced directors as well as corporate officers.

In addition to these general-purpose seminars, there are numerous opportunities to enroll in more specific director-training workshops offered by various industry and trade groups. These programs often coincide with national or regional association meetings, and include a wide range of topics. For example, the Virginia Association of Community Banks (VACB), an independent trade association, occasionally offers a Board of Directors Seminar specifically targeted for directors of smaller Virginia banks. This seminar covers such topics as directors' liabilities, running the board efficiently, lenders' liability, strategic planning, and recruitment and turnover. Readers may find it helpful to contact the appropriate trade associations for their organizations to inquire if similar seminars are or can be offered for their industries.

Enrolling in open-to-the-public seminars may not appeal to everyone, and they are not always available when and where they are needed. In this situation, it may be desirable to bring in an appropriate trainer to conduct an in-house workshop exclusively for the board members. This may seem expensive, but when the value of time and the advantages of having everyone together for a session are considered, it is good investment.

At the general level, a trainer could be utilized to discuss general themes such as team building, director roles and liabilities, or trends in the industry. Consultants could also be used to assist with a broad orientation program for new directors. As a consultant, I have personally assisted boards with training in the areas of strategic management and long-range planning. Although most firms have the ability and talent to deal with these issues with existing staff, many choose to utilize outsiders for training and educational assistance for a variety of reasons, including the outsider's objectivity, familiarity with the material and teaching skill, and convenience.

Another case for the use of consultants and trainers is when the organization is challenged with a major issue or problem, and its leadership believes that it lacks the ability to deal with it alone. Such an issue could be as routine as dealing with foreign competition or as serious as discrimination or restraint-of-trade lawsuits. In any similar situation, an outside expert may be desired to be brought in to help educate and sensitize the board members to the challenges, issues, and potential solutions to the problem. By bringing the professional before the entire board, issues can be brought out and ideas discussed as a team, and all the board members will have the benefit of the information and insights directly from the expert.

Journals, Magazines, and Periodicals

One very easy and inexpensive method of continuing the education of directors is to invest in a number of professional journals, magazines, and periodicals and have them sent directly to each board member. A larger company may assign the responsibility to an employee to scan various publications on a regular basis and select key articles for distribution to directors. Another method is to select interesting ideas and references from various publications and summarize the key points in the in-house newsletter, if one exists. Firms without the staff to perform this function may simply choose to subscribe to a few appropriate publications and have them sent directly to the directors.

A drawback to sending entire publications is information overload. I receive at least a half dozen complimentary publications from organizations I serve or belong to and must confess that I rarely make time to read them all. One way to combat the problem of overload is for the company officers to be on the lookout for good articles and send a note to directors that they might enjoy a certain article in a particular issue. This will help get the directors in the habit of scanning the literature when it arrives.

Choosing the best periodicals can be very difficult. There are more magazines on the market now than anyone can count. As a general principle, try to keep the number of items selected to a minimum, such as three. One selection should be industry-specific such as *Progressive Grocer*, for a firm in the wholesale or retail food business, *Sight and Sound Marketing*, for electronics retailers, and *Restaurant News*, for businesses in the food service industry. There are literally hundreds of industry trade journals, and many specific industries have several within each niche of the industry.

When choosing a trade publication, one must be careful to find the right balance between trade publications written by and for academics and those aimed directly at practitioners. The academic titles may offer the latest in theory, but be difficult to read and of little practical value for people out in the field. On the other hand, many practitioner-geared magazines are nothing more than advertising and swapsheets with little useful information for those concerned with corporate advising and governance. Outside directors in particular can benefit greatly by regularly reviewing a top trade journal pertinent to the firm's industry. This will help them stay abreast of the latest trends and techniques, as well as the activities of competitors, which will enhance their boardroom performance.

Another publication selection could be board-specific, such as a subscription to *Director's Monthly*, the newsletter of the National Association of Corporate Directors. This newsletter is available as a benefit to Association members. Although it is fairly expensive, a corporate group membership is available, and the investment is probably well worth the price. The newsletter includes regular briefings for directors on subjects such as accounting, law, and regulatory actions affecting board practices. It also offers important special features on topics ranging from inside versus outside directors, corporate codes of conduct, and board considerations in overseas marketing strategies. Another possibility is a subscription to a bimonthly newsletter called *Boardroom*. This publication offers general advice to managers that directors may find useful. Still another selection is *Across the Board*, a monthly publication of The Conference Board (referenced in Appendix 1). This publication covers leading-edge issues for senior-level executives, such as global strategy, education, and business outlook.

A final category of publication that could be purchased for directors is general business periodicals such as *Fortune*, *BusinessWeek*, *The Wall Street Journal*, *Inc.*, *Entrepreneur*, and others. Each has its own particular emphasis and strength, yet offers coverage and appeal for a wide readership. More than likely, directors already have access to many of these general publications, but it may be useful to ensure that all directors are equally prepared and up to date by offering complimentary director subscriptions to whichever title is deemed most appropriate. The bottom line in purchasing any periodical for board members is to improve their effectiveness as directors by making them better educated and informed about the industry and business in general.

Junior Boards and Committees

A final suggestion for training and educating directors is the use of some sort of "junior board" or committee device to develop future members for the actual board of directors. As early as 1932, the McCormick Spice Company established a junior board of directors as a device for grooming qualified directors for the full board (Vance, 1983, p. 207). Mueller has referred to a similar concept, which he calls a "probationary farm club." This club allows the firm and individual under consideration to assess the value of a relationship without the obligations of a statutory board (Mueller, 1990, p. 82). The same objective could be accomplished by inviting a prospective board member to serve on a committee prior to an actual invitation to join the board.

The actual duties of these groups could vary widely, from reviewing and advising, to reconsideration of past company actions in a case-study format, to various tasks assigned just as with any other working committee. In some cases, especially with "official" junior boards, it may be known to the members that they are being considered for future appointment to the full board. In other situations, such as when regular committees are being used for the job, the "grooming future directors" motive may be concealed. In the case where prospective board members are simply recruited to serve on some sort of corporate committee, with a task and function independent of screening future directors, it may be perfectly appropriate to keep the director screening motive quiet. This will allow the personalities to get to know each other in a work environment without the concern of the candidate "wearing his Sunday manners" because he knows he is on trial. Should a decision be made later not to invite the person to join the board of directors, no harm has been done, because the only expectations that were established were those of the actual committee itself.

Personally, I like the concept of grooming future directors by involving them in corporate committee work, but I am not all that comfortable with "junior boards." The committee concept allows for the company to involve any number of outsiders in the affairs of the firm, at a wide variety of levels, such as personnel issues, productivity improvement, and educational leaves and scholarships. The junior board concept, however, simply strikes me as somewhat deceptive as well as demeaning to those being scrutinized. Nevertheless, it is a valid technique that has been successfully utilized by a number of organizations, so the readers should make up their own minds on the practice.

BOARD ORGANIZATION AND ROLES

This section defines and describes the function of various board officers and committees. Smaller and new boards often possess only a very loose, informal structure. As an organization expands and matures, however, greater formalization and delegation of tasks and responsibilities often become practical, if not essential. Each of the major board positions are now discussed in turn.

Chairman

The board of directors is typically headed by one who has been selected to serve as chairman. In this role, the chairman of the board is responsible for calling the meetings, preparing (or approving) the agenda, conducting the meetings, and any other duties specified by the firm's by-laws or the laws of the state. Many small business boards do not have a chairman, or the chairman's title is held by the president who runs the board.

There are a number of reasons why a separate chairman may not be necessary. One reason would be that the board is new, and, as such, the president desires to keep a tight rein on its development. Another reason could be that the board is small, and there is no real need for delegation of the responsibility. Still another reason is control.

Most business owners are rightfully sensitive about giving up, or appearing to give up, control to another. Most people would consider the role of chairman to be a powerful position, which it is, or, at least, can be. In fact, the chairman is the one person in a position that could most easily threaten the president's position in the organization. Although this may not be true for most small businesses, where the president may have majority control of the stock, the perception may still be formed that the president has lost or given up control when a chairman is appointed. This perception can, of course, be managed, but it is still a major stumbling block that keeps many entrepreneurs from desiring to be a chairman of the board.

Putting the negatives aside, there are many positive reasons for appointing an outside chairman of the board. One reason is that appointing a director to the position of chairman can serve to greatly empower that individual to greater interest and contribution to the firm. Empowerment is a buzzword that has recently become popular in the management literature. Basically, it simply refers to the attitude behavior change that can occur in people when they are given real power to make decisions in an organization (Swoboda, 1990). By asking one of the more capable and interested outsiders to serve as chairman, that person will usually rise to the challenge to become even more useful to the organization. This happens, in part, as a return for the confidence shown in that person by the appointment. That is, people generally want to succeed, and a challenge serves to drive motivated individuals to new levels of success. Also, people simply enjoy work more if they have a real say in the activities and decisions affecting their organization.

Another reason for appointing an outside chair is prestige. An organization's image and standing in a community or industry is partly contingent on the reputations of the individuals associated with it. Appointing someone of high standing to chairman, therefore, often leads to a corresponding increase of the reputation of the organization. An example will highlight both the prestige and empowerment principles.

I served on a business advisory board at a state university. This organization demonstrated an astute understanding of the prestige principle when it appointed an outsider as board chairman in 1989. The individual selected holds a high-level management position with one of America's leading high-technology, manufacturing firms. He also is an alumnus of the university, and was already a member of the advisory board. His appointment brought instant recognition to the board from the resulting publicity, and it caught the attention of the new chairman's employer as well. The appointment also empowered the chairman to new levels of commitment and contribution to the board and the organization it advises. His increased enthusiasm is obvious and visible both in person and through the various correspondence and other written material that he now generates himself or collaborates on with the organization's officers.

Another very important rationale for an outside chairman is succession planning and continuity. This issue is especially critical for family owned firms where a visible organization chart and line of succession may not exist. A chairman of the board, even if largely ceremonial, can play a vital role in helping to identify likely successors both in a planned succession process as well as during a succession forced by a sudden death. This is very important when the founder of a business is trying to decide who should take over at retirement time. Sometimes, it may even take an outsider to get the founder to face this issue.

A chairman can also play a key role in times of emergency. As an officer of the corporation, the chairman of the board would have the legal authority to step in and make key decisions, such as those related to finances and personnel, during such crises as when the president may become temporarily or permanently disabled. I served as a director of a business during such a crisis where the chairman of the board was a stabilizing force when the president left the firm suddenly. There were other officers and managers in place, but the reputation of the chairman was a key factor in soothing the nerves of the financial community and shareholders during the leadership transition. He provided the assurance of continuity as well as legitimate and stable authority to those concerned both inside and outside of the organization.

Vice Chairman

The position of vice chairman is fairly uncommon in the boards of privately held businesses. It is a position that is largely ceremonial and has no routine function. The primary purpose for appointing a vice chair would be to have someone to officiate at board meetings in the chairman's absence. Usually when this happens, however, the president runs the meeting. Another reason to appoint a vice chair is to enhance the prestige of the person appointed. Technically, the vice chair falls between the chairman and the president on the organizational chart, hence, the associated prestige factor. Much like the Vice President of the United States, however, the vice chairman of a business may, in reality, be "out of the loop" in terms of the real day-to-day operations and power of the organization. The decision to appoint a vice chair is largely one of ceremony. It is a nice way to give a deserving director a title, but the appointment will typically contribute little to the operation of the firm, unless the person is an actual full-time line officer of the business.

President and Chief Executive Officer (CEO)

The president and chief executive officer is the person in the organization charged with the actual responsibilities of running the business. The president is appointed by and reports to the board, although, as discussed earlier, the real power in closely held firms rests with the owner(s), who often is the president. The president is the pivotal figure in the organization and, as such, is the primary decision maker regarding the strategic, long-term issues and much of the day-to-day affairs of the firm.

Secretary and Treasurer

The positions of secretary and treasurer may be assigned to a single person in a small firm or may be treated as separate positions held by two separate persons (which is often the case in larger organizations). The position of Secretary has numerous official duties in the corporation, including preparing (or at least approving) corporate minutes and records, and signing various official documents, such as banking-related corporate resolutions, official paperwork pertaining to the state corporation commission, some tax and other government-related forms, and other similar documents.

The position of treasurer is often responsible for various financial matters of the organization, including opening and handling of bank accounts. In practice, however, the CEO of smaller firms may not relinquish these duties, preferring to handle them alone, or by an appointed staff member without the title of treasurer. In these situations, the titles are often held by relatives of the firm's owner.

Although I have no data to support this claim, it seems to me that the position of secretary/treasurer is held more often by the owner/president's spouse than by an outsider in small firms. As long as the spouse is somewhat active with the firm, this is probably a reasonable situation. If the spouse holds the titles purely as an honorific appointment, then the company would be wise to consider appointing someone who would be able to legitimately carry out the positions' responsibilities, if for no other reason than to be prepared to function during a crisis.

Assistant Secretary/Treasurer

As stated in the section just concluded, the secretary and treasurer are often called upon to perform certain legal functions, specifically related to preparing, approving, and signing various documents. If the titles of secretary and treasurer are held by board member(s) who are not a full-time employee of the firm, this can cause a problem because the individual may not always be available when needed to approve and sign important documents. This situation could create a bottleneck that could seriously affect the routine operations of the firm.

A solution frequently used to alleviate this situation is to appoint an assistant secretary and an assistant treasurer, or a combined assistant secretary-treasurer. The assistant secretary and treasurer will carry out the duties of the secretary and treasurer in their absence (with the approval of the president, of course). The person(s) given the ''assistant'' title will almost always be a full-time employee of the firm so that availability will not be a problem. I personally hold secretary or treasurer titles for three corporations whose boards I serve. In no case am I available to sign all the documents that the companies need prepared on a day-to-day basis, and the assistant secretary-treasurers normally perform this function for me. To the best of my knowledge, this has never created a problem for any of the three firms.

BOARD COMMITTEES

This section defines and discusses some of the more common board committees used to handle specific functions by many corporate boards of directors. The purpose of including them all here is not to advocate their use, but rather to give a sort of encyclopedic directory to enable the reader to choose what is useful in his or her situation.

The boards of some companies will function quite well with no additional structure. Others, especially boards attempting to keep up with the increasing complexity of growing firms, will find the use of committees to be an effective method to delegate and distribute the work load, especially for routine board duties. In their study of large, public corporations, Giardina and Tilghman (1988) found that the use of the committee format was an increasing trend throughout the 1980s by corporate America.

Executive Committee

The purpose of an executive committee is to carry out roughly the same duties as the full board, with the exception of major functions and other matters that may be reserved for the full board's action. Typically, such a committee will not exist in smaller board situations or where the full board is able to meet on a frequent basis. The usual role of an executive committee is to meet in between full board meetings or, as called, to deal with matters that arise between regular meetings of the board. An executive committee is usually composed of mostly inside directors because availability is very important. The committee is usually chaired by the chairman of the board, vice chairman, or president. The Giardina and Tilghman study found that 71% of the large companies polled had an executive committee (1988, p. 11).

Audit Committee

Every corporation listed on the New York, American, or NASDAQ stock exchange is required to have an audit committee (Dooley, 1990, p. 4). It should be no surprise, therefore, that audit, with 97%, was the most prevalent committee in use discovered by Giardina and Tilghman (1988, p. 11).

According to an NACD monograph on audit committees, they " . . . should be informed, vigilant, and effective overseers of the company's financial reporting process and its internal control system" (Verschoor, 1989, p. 5). This monograph reviews the Securities and Exchange Commission literature, and finds the basic functions of the audit committee to be: recommending engagement of discharge of the independent auditors; directing and supervising investigations into matters within the scope of its duties; reviewing results of the audit with the independent auditors; reviewing the scope and results of internal auditing activities; approving each professional service provided by the independent auditors prior to its performance; reviewing the independence of the independent auditors; considering the range of audit and nonaudit fees; and, finally, reviewing the adequacy of the system of internal controls (Verschoor, 1989, p. 9).

Simply put, the auditing committee is the direct conduit between the board and the independent auditors, which helps to guarantee that the board has sufficient, high-quality financial information needed to advise and govern the firm. Important as this committee's role sounds, however, it cannot be completely effective unless company management (and/or owners) supports the audit process—which is not always the case with closely held firms where a single owner likes to keep all financial matters private. As stated in a *Harvard Business Review* article, '' . . . the corporate audit committee can make a substantial contribution to corporate governance, but it will do so only when it is properly constituted and competently staffed, and when it exists within a corporate environment that encourages, rather than discourages, its activities'' (Mautz and Neumann, 1970, p. 91).

Nominating Committee

The functions of the nominating committee were briefly discussed earlier under the section on choosing and recruiting directors in Chapter 5. This committee serves to help perpetuate the board by developing and screening a pool of potential directors to fill vacancies whenever and however they occur. The committee may be a standing one or may be appointed when the need arises. The full board may provide appropriate methods for the nominating and selection process or may ask the committee members to develop their own. The Giardina and Tilghman study reported that 51% of the companies surveyed utilized a nominating committee (1988, p. 11).

Compensation Committee

Compensation is another popular committee that, according to the Giardina and Tilghman report, is used by 87% of the boards surveyed (1988, p. 11). The main function of a compensation committee is to review and make recommendations concerning the compensation packages of the CEO and other top-management employees. By using such a committee, the CEO and other top executives are relieved of the inherent conflict of interest they would encounter if they acted alone in setting their own compensation (Dooley, 1990, p. 5).

Compensation expert J. E. Richard points out that executives of closely held firms can burn out from too much, too little, or the wrong kinds of compensation. This problem can be managed with a properly developed compensation committee. Richard advises that membership should include board members who are not too personally close to the CEO, and will have the time necessary to study the latest ideas and trends in compensation theory (1990, pp. 1–5).

Finance

Another committee found to be quite popular in the Giardina and Tilghman study is the finance committee. The researchers found that 29% of the firms they surveyed used such a committee (1988, p. 11). A finance committee might be useful for a privately owned company that had a complicated capital structure or some other characteristic that would make it unfeasible to review and deal with financial matters during regular full board or executive committee meetings.

From my personal experience, however, I do not know of very many smaller firms with an active finance committee. Any issue or function of the board that tends to dominate and eat up a large portion of the board's regular meeting time, however, would certainly merit consideration for a board committee.

Strategy/Long-Range Planning

One of the most critical functions of the board and top management is to develop the firm's long-range plans and strategies. This is a function that is difficult to delegate because the responsibility ultimately comes back to the CEO and the board. However, the actual process of data collection and review is often assigned to others who assist the top management in the preparation of the plan. Some firms use a board committee in the long-range planning process in order to have director involvement in the activity, while avoiding spending countless hours on this process with the full board.

The Vice Chairman of the Board of Mead Corporation once said: "The board of directors' most important function is to approve or send back for amendment management's recommendations about the future direction of the corporation" (Wommack, 1979 p. 98). This committee typically would include the CEO (as chairman), one or two other insiders or staff members, and one or two outside directors. It is a committee whose work is never finished, because shortly after a plan is completed for one time frame, it is time to begin the review-and-update process again.

Public Policy

Although not mentioned in the Giardina and Tilghman study, the public policy committee (also referred to as the public responsibility, public interest, social responsibility, or corporate responsibility committee) is growing in its use by American corporate boards. According to Vance, such firms as General Motors, Mobil, American Telephone & Telegraph, Bank of America, Chrysler, Dow Chemical, General Electric, Gulf Oil, and Metropolitan Life are included in the group of around 150 major corporate boards using such a committee (1983, p. 86). The purpose of these committees is to meet a few times per year to review trends in the political and social environment that may affect the firm in some way. This committee may also set and/or recommend policy regarding charitable contributions (Vance, 1983).

One might rightfully ask if there is any need for such a committee for the board of a smaller firm or if public responsibility is the sole purview of the *Fortune* 500 crowd. I believe the answer is definitely "yes" regarding the need for smaller firm boards to be concerned with public responsibility, but only "maybe" regarding whether a separate committee is necessary to carry out the function. Lovdal, Bauer, and Treverton offer a strong justification for these committees by pointing out the widespread (and growing) publicity about the relationship of business to social issues. One only need consider the increasing prevalence of consumer boycotts, affirmative action lawsuits, and other legal charges levied against business concerns to realize the seriousness of this issue. By giving attention to trends early, organizations may be able to be responsive before problems occur (Lovdal, Bauer, and Treverton, 1977). Whether or not a special committee is needed to perform this function is largely a matter for individual preference, based on the nature of each business's industry and environment, and, of course, the size and complexity of each firm.

Et Al.

The preceding list of board committees is by no means exhaustive. It is, I believe, a list of the most common and useful of the standing (or permanent) committees in wide use. There are, of course, countless special-purpose and temporary committees used by boards, and no limit to the committees one could think up to deal with any number of contingencies. For example, financial institutions have loan committees, medical groups often have ethics committees, diversified firms have investment committees, businesses looking to expand have building committees, and firms with large labor pools have pension review committees.

Whether to use (or create) a committee depends largely on the nature of the task, and the availability (or lack) of other means and resources to deal with the task. A corporate manager is advised to avoid creating structure simply for the sake of structure. We teach in business policy class that *structure needs to follow strategy, not the other way around*. A board with too many committees can be even less effective than one with too few. The decision to use any board committee should be made only after a thorough discussion as to other possible means to deal with the task, and when convinced that the full board can no longer deal effectively with the issue in a timely manner. The positive benefits can include cutting down on marathon board meetings and creating a special-purpose forum that can really develop an expertise in an area. Of course, this requires a comfort with decentralization, which may take time to develop.

7

Control, Cost, and Assessment

OVERVIEW

This chapter deals with a variety of topics related to the actual running of the board meetings and assessment of the results. The chapter begins with control issues, including the running of meetings, record keeping, and corporate communication. Next are sections dealing with estimating the cost of having a board, including compensating directors, D&O insurance, indirect costs and overhead, and management's time. The final section discusses overall board assessment. That is, how can you tell if the net contribution of the board is positive, and, if so, is it worth the cost?

RUNNING THE MEETINGS

Frequency and Timing of Board Meetings

When it comes to the calendar and the clock, there are numerous methods of selecting days and times for board meetings. One of the first issues to address is the frequency of meetings. On one extreme would be holding a single perfunctory meeting once a year in conjunction with the annual shareholders meeting. There are many firms that operate their board this way, but, as should be clear by now, these are not really working boards. On the other extreme are boards that meet every week. I know of at least one *Inc.* ranked firm that does this, and I have had the privilege of observing one of its meetings. The idea of a board meeting this frequently is very unusual, and certainly not for everyone. On the other hand, who can argue with success, at least for this one firm?

But what about the average board? How frequently do they meet? The Giardina and Tilghman study reported that the average number of board meetings overall was five per year for the firms in their study. They also discovered some variation depending on industry type with financial services firms meeting eight times and durable goods manufacturers meeting only four times, as the extremes (Giardina and Tilghman, 1988, p. 14).

There are three basic variables that help determine the optimum meeting frequency for a board: (1) the level of activity the board is engaged in, (2) the presence (or absence) of a committee structure, and (3) the number-of-meetings versus attendance issue. The level of board activity is largely in the hands of the owner-management team that leads the board. If only a few concerns are going to be put before the group, then few meetings will be necessary. A board should not be called unless there is something of substance for the board members to do. Meetings called for routine reviews of the same old stuff will only lead to boredom, frustration, and the eventual turning off of interest by the directors.

The presence of a committee structure will also affect the optimum meeting frequency of the board. If no committees exist, then the board may need to meet more frequently because there is no other forum through which to deal with various board-related issues. The existence of various committees, such as audit, executive, and/or personnel advisory committee, would alleviate the need for more frequent meetings of the full board as long as an appropriate committee had the authority to act or advise on relevant issues.

The last major variable that should be considered when establishing meeting frequency is the relationship of frequency to attendance. When only a few meetings are planned for a year, a couple of things happen. First, there is a greater likelihood that sufficient news and events will have occurred since the last meeting to ensure that a robust, busy meeting agenda can be planned that will keep the directors interested and involved. Second, busy outside directors (and inside members as well) will find it relatively easy to commit the time to attend the meetings.

When meetings are held more frequently, however, there is a danger of the opposite effects taking place. Instead of more new information to deal with, the board is likely to rehash much of the ''same old stuff'' at frequent meetings. To some extent, more frequent meetings can lead to board involvement in operational issues, which may be all right in certain cases, but frequently could make management and staff feel ''micromanaged'' by the board. Management should carefully consider whether or not there is sufficient agenda to justify calling a meeting because few people enjoy meetings simply for the sake of meeting.

The other opposite effect concerns the board members' willingness and ability to attend more frequent meetings. When meetings are called too frequently, attending them can be difficult and your directors may simply burn out. Although I do not have empirical statistics to prove that attendance decreases with meeting frequency, Table 7.1 sheds some light on this issue. This table represents an actual attendance log for a twelve-member board of directors. Due to certain extenuating circumstances, this board called nine meetings during a 5-month period. This was approximately twice as many meetings as normally held by the company.

Table 7.1
Example of Board Attendance When Meetings Are Frequent From an Actual Twelve-Member Board

	4/26	5/24	6/07	6/21	7/12	7/23	8/02	8/30	9/27	Att
A.	X	X	X	X			X	X		67%
B.	X	X	X	X	X	X	X		X	89%
C.	X	X	X	X	X	X	X	X	X	100%
D.	X	X		X	X	X	X	X	X	89%
E.	X	X		X	X	X	X	X	X	89%
F.	X		X	X		X	X			56%
G.	X	X	X	X	X	X	X	X	X	100%
H.	X	X		X		X	X			56%
I.		X			X		X	X		44%
J.	X	X	X	X	X	X	X		X	89%
K.		X			X	X			X	44%
L.	X	X	X		X		X	X		67%
AVERAGE ATTENDANCE										74%

At the end of the period, the president decided to check the attendance records, because he realized that meeting attendance had been below normal. He and his directors were all concerned when they realized that average attendance had slipped to below 75%, and that a third of the members had attended less than 60% of the meetings. Had certain directors lost interest in the firm? In this situation, it was believed that the real culprit was the increased frequency of the meetings. Otherwise active and highly motivated board members (mostly outsiders) simply could not juggle every other week meetings with their busy schedules. As soon as the meeting frequency returned to once a month, the board's attendance rate went back up to normal high levels.

Meeting Time and Duration

There is no best time to call a meeting, nor is there a magic number of hours in which to conduct a standard meeting. Obviously, extremes (20 minutes or 10 hours without a break) should be avoided. Many boards meet first thing in the morning (beginning at 6:00 or 7:00 a.m.) for one to a few hours, and others meet late in the afternoon. If the directors' schedules permit, some meetings are simply scheduled during regular business hours. Still another approach is to meet Friday afternoon, with a social event in the evening (sometimes including spouses), and a follow-up meeting Saturday morning.

Finding the right timing mix involves experimentation in consultation with the board members. Once a workable time is found, however, it is a good idea to fix a long-term meeting schedule and stick to it. No calendar will suit everyone, so the best way to minimize complications is to announce a schedule one or even several years in advance. This will allow the directors to schedule their other activities around the meetings as much as possible.

Agenda and Supporting Materials

Meetings are rarely effective when everyone comes to a meeting without advance preparation. The directors cannot prepare in advance on their own, therefore, the burden of advance preparation falls squarely on the chairman or CEO who runs the board. One complaint I have heard over and over is that directors are not kept up with the company's activities in between or prior to board meetings. This situation seriously reduces the potential contribution of the board members because they must react instantly from a cold start to the various issues presented at the meeting. I have served on different boards where the extent of advance material ranged from zero to two full days of reading matter. Although neither extreme is appreciated by directors, too little material is worse than too much.

A good advance package should be received by directors about two weeks before each meeting. (If meetings are frequent, the package may be sent with less lead time.) This package should contain a tentative agenda (which will be followed as close as possible), current financial statements, and whatever background material may be needed (and/or available) for each of the agenda items. For example, if the board will discuss land acquisition, a plat and appraisal sheet for each of the possible sites would be helpful. Or if a presentation will be heard by an expert on some particular topic, a summary of his task and a brief biographical sketch will bring the directors up to speed quickly and help them to evaluate what they will hear.

Other information useful to send to directors would be all sorts of public relations and marketing-related material, including newsletters, brochures, media coverage, press releases, and promotional material. Don't assume that directors (especially outsiders) will automatically learn about new products, employee accomplishments, and new hires through the grapevine or general media. Directors should be included automatically on databases to ensure that they will receive important communication even when the board leader forgets to have it done. This will all help to educate and keep the board better informed about the company, and will save valuable board meeting time for more important things that cannot be sent through the mail.

Obviously, the advance package will never be perfect, and the agenda will not always stick to the plan. One must also resist the trap of going overboard with advance preparation to the point that the cost of preparation exceeds the importance of the task. This is a situation where the old 80–20 rule applies well. That rule suggests that 80% of the value of a thing can be obtained with 20% of the effort that it would take to accomplish the entire 100% of the task. Simply interpreted, be sure to send advance material, but don't get carried away trying to make it perfect.

Cleaning Up After Meetings

From the typical director's perspective, the meeting is over when everyone packs up their briefcases and leaves. This is not the real end of the meeting, however, at least not for the CEO or chairman who will have to deal with all of the loose ends. Although it is true that board meetings are called to deal with issues, and, in one sense, tie up loose ends, they also produce an agenda of their own that creates new work and new loose ends to be tied.

Much of this clean up can be anticipated. For example, if an agenda item dealt with a land acquisition decision, then it can be expected that as a result of a board decision, someone will have to do the actual work of carrying out the real estate purchase. Although the board will help with the decision itself, the actual work will need to be handled or assigned to the company management or staff.

But much of the meeting clean up deals with unexpected matters. Simply as a result of a meeting occurring, many new ideas, suggestions, and recommendations will arise. For example, directors may suggest new sales leads, a unique corporate novelty that they would like to see developed (i.e., they want a coffee mug), a specific report on some facet of productivity could be requested, and so on. Each of these "ideas" represents real work for someone (usually the leader him or herself). Although innocently and helpfully submitted, collectively these "leads" can result in several hours or even days of work for someone. One board chairman told me that he can expect a full half day of new work just cleaning up loose ends after every single board meeting.

I am not suggesting that all this make-work by the directors should be avoided. In fact, the opposite is true. Many of the leads and ideas of the directors will be innovative and useful—that's one of the reasons boards are created. But many of the calls made and reports generated will be done simply as a courtesy to please the director who suggested it. Not all the board's input will be useful, but the good will hopefully outweigh the bad.

Managing Your Directors

As the previous section suggested, not all the behaviors of directors will turn out as planned, nor will they be positive. In extreme cases, this may lead to the termination of a director (discussed earlier in the book). In those cases where the good clearly outweighs the bad and the director's usefulness is appreciated more than his or her occasional shortcomings, it is possible to "manage" individual directors to increase effectiveness and downplay weaknesses.

On a positive note, some directors' performance can be improved with a little extra coaching or preparation. An example of this is the case of an outsider serving as board chairman. This person would be expected to "manage" the board meetings, although the president would be the one who really develops the agenda and has the insight and knowledge necessary to move the meeting along. In this case, the president could meet with the chairman in advance of the meeting to go over the agenda and any special details that would allow the chairman to run the meeting more efficiently.

I know of one very effective situation where the chairman is provided at the board meetings with a special copy of the agenda that contains marginal notes and other amplifications to allow him to keep control of the meeting without the awkwardness of having to defer to the managing officers on every single point. These notes may say "Joe has prepared an update on this issue" or "counsel has advised us to delay executing plan B," etc. Although this may seem like unnecessary fluff (or even ego stroking), these little details can greatly improve the efficiency and professionalism of the meetings, and can improve the performance of the chairman or other directors who are being coached.

Another board situation that sometimes must be managed is the case of the busybody director. This is the director who attempts to micromanage every move the company makes, or perhaps simply likes to gossip and know everybody else's business. The best way to deal with these types is to keep them off the board in the first place. If this is not possible, however, then good management of the person can help to reduce the problem.

The first step in managing the board busybody is not to give in to his or her moves to interfere with business. An occasional bit of input from directors on nonboard-related operational issues is tolerable, and maybe even desirable. But when Mr. Busybody starts telling you who should be fired, who should get a raise, and why the advertisements with so and so should be dropped, then you have a potential problem.

I discussed this issue at length with an executive who had had numerous board experiences with various firms for over 20 years. He stated that every board he had ever served on or worked with had a micromanager type. The danger, he added, was much more than simply annoyance or antagonism. He explained that subjective issues are tough to deal with anyway, and that boards will typically go along with anyone that happens to have a strong opinion on a subject, even if that opinion is not held by management. Hence, in extreme cases, this type of director can dominate particular issues, even though his opinion is in the minority, simply by being persistent and not letting go of the issue until he gets his way. He gave the following example:

We had a director that for some reason did not like our advertising agency or its work. He simply did not understand our industry and the need for our advertising program. At every opportunity he suggested that we get rid of the agency and replace its ad campaign with newspaper advertisements that simply stated who we were and included pictures of all of the directors. As silly as this seemed, he kept pushing for it until the rest of the directors went along with it. Eventually (once the manager telling the story left the firm) the company fired the ad agency and ran the advertisements with the directors' pictures!

Although the example is extreme, it points out the danger of not managing the busybody director before he or she gets out of control.

A final point on managing directors deals with controlling the timing of certain potentially time-consuming issues. Although the previous section described the busybody as a particular individual (or individuals) that may serve on a board, sometimes many or perhaps all directors can engage in this type of nonproductive behavior. This is particularly true for certain issues for which nearly everyone has an opinion, but in the final analysis is quite subjective; therefore, endless board discussion is of little value. The simple fact is that sometimes subjective decisions cannot be made (or at least efficiently made) by a committee.

An example of this is planning a new building. Nearly everyone has opinions concerning matters of taste and style, yet the relative value of one opinion over another may be slight. Usually, experts are hired to help make these decisions, in part, because of the subjective nature of the task, and, of course, the complexity of the project. Because the board's input is desirable on major issues, however, building plans will inevitably wind up on the agenda. The danger is that long-winded discussions on matters of style and other subjective issues will tend to dominate the meeting and keep the board from dealing with other matters.

One way to manage these situations is to have a special meeting, or perhaps a committee, to address the topic. This allows the directors to have their say, but not in a way that eats up valuable meeting time. Another possibility is to simply make unilateral decisions about such an issue and bring it before the board only as an informational matter. The board leader needs to carefully consider whether each potential agenda item is one that is for information, discussion, or actually merits a board decision.

Of course, every group is different, and not all will be oriented toward long-winded and wasteful discussions. I have, however, observed groups burn up meetings for years discussing matters of style and other minutiae while getting absolutely nowhere until someone took control and made the decisions that the committee was unable to reach.

Another way to deal with such issues is to selectively develop the agenda to place potentially time-wasting issues at the end of the meeting. For example, if a board tends to micromanage advertising copy, yet it is felt important to keep the group informed about such information, plan on handing out the samples or copy as a final agenda item. This allows everyone the opportunity to comment, but catches the group when its energy is low and thoughts are on adjournment. Although some might view this technique as manipulative, it can be quite effective, and, after all, some agenda items need to be last.

CORPORATE MINUTES AND RECORD KEEPING

In many entrepreneurial-run companies, the recording of corporate discussions and decisions for inclusion in the minute book is viewed with disdain. This activity is considered a needless and time-wasting process that interferes with the important action of running the business. A thorough and complete record of board activities is more than busy work, however—it is required by corporate law in an overwhelming majority of the states. Also, as suggested by attorney Charles R. McCarthy, detailed corporate minutes are essential in cases where the board may be called upon to defend its actions in court (McCarthy, 1989).

Board minutes are also an essential part of the preparatory and supporting materials that should be sent to directors prior to meetings. Each meeting should begin with a reading of the minutes of the last meeting, for purposes of review and approval of the official written record. These are important functions that justify more than cursory care in preparing the minutes.

McCarthy (1989, p. 3), in a monograph prepared for the National Association of Corporate Directors, offers seven suggestions for what should be included in good minutes:

1. Time, place, and date of the meeting.
2. Notice procedures or waivers thereof.
3. Attendees—both as to members and invitees, including departures and reentries into the meeting.
4. Type of meeting.
5. Quorum requirements satisfaction.
6. Actions taken, including dissents and abstentions.
7. Reports presented—either in summary fashion, or, if possible, as an appendix to the minutes.

Of course, once the minutes are amended (if necessary) and approved, the appropriate signature should be obtained from the secretary or designated officer, and the document should be stored in the record book or some other storage place for safekeeping. A good set of corporate minutes serves as a useful management tool that can help to chronicle the history of the firm's direction, as well as to focus the decisions of leadership into a coherent plan of action.

CORPORATE COMMUNICATION

One concern that may arise when a board is created, or its function is expanded, is that misunderstanding, envy, or even fear could develop within the corporate organization. When a company has been managed almost totally by a single manager or a few key insiders, the remainder of the company staff probably know where they stand. Once a board of directors or advisors comes on the scene, however, employees may become confused about how they may be affected by this new power group. This can be avoided by giving careful attention to appropriate internal communication.

A board of directors will be thought of as a powerful and mysterious group at a minimum. Depending on what the board does (or is perceived to do), it could be viewed by company insiders with suspicion or even contempt. I have heard comments many times from hourly workers as well as managers that "the board" (often stated with a ring of dislike or distrust) "is up to something," always with the implication that something heavy was underfoot that would interfere with business life as the employees knew it. Often this concern is valid, because the board may have been used to help make a hard decision by management. Sometimes, the business owner will make the board out to be the fall guy when taking a hard position that may affect peoples' jobs, pay raises (or cuts), benefits, etc.

If the board does play a role in making hard decisions, then a little distrust by the workforce may be inevitable. However, the rumor mill may greatly exaggerate the "evil" tendencies of the group. Good employee communications about the composition, purpose, and activities can help the other units of the firm to understand what the board is about, and how (if at all) the board's role may affect the company.

If the business has a newsletter, make sure that board activities are covered. Include brief biographies of the chairman and other outsiders. If insiders are included, mention how they were selected. Also, be sure to mention the scope of activity and authority that the board will have. If a newsletter does not exist, then use some other means, such as a presentation and discussion at a company meeting or through the use of a memorandum or brochure that may be produced simply to explain the board's role.

Basically, the board is a tool to make the business and its leadership more effective. Let everyone else in the firm know this, so that the board is not misunderstood and feared as a black box that is somehow going to make life more difficult for the employees.

COST

At this juncture, all pragmatic, bottom-line managers are asking "what will it cost?" This section attempts to answer this question, not with a specific number, but by suggesting a formula that a board organizer can use to calculate the cost for his or her situation. The total cost of a board includes those costs incurred during the planning, recruiting, and development process, as well as the cost of maintaining and running the board.

There are essentially four major components of overall board cost: director compensation, directors and officers insurance, indirect costs and overhead, and management time. These vary from circumstance to circumstance, and not all costs apply in every situation. Let us now consider each of these component costs in turn.

Director Compensation

The first cost usually anticipated is how much the directors will be paid. Director compensation typically falls into one of three categories: cash, stock and options, and perquisites. The total cost to the company for director compensation is, naturally, the sum total of cash, stock, and all other perks. The amount of each a company may decide to pay is based primarily on two factors: the market rate for directors and what the company is willing to pay.

There is no fixed "market rate" for directors, especially for boards of smaller companies. The market for directors of large corporations, however, is another matter. Survey data indicate that directors of major corporations typically receive both retainers and per-meeting fees, which can total as much as $15,000 to $21,500 per director, depending on the type of industry and other factors (Giardina and Tilghman, 1988, pp. 11–12). The same study found that 25% of the responding companies also provided some sort of stock compensation, such as stock options, stock grants, or phantom stock (p. 12). Some of these firms also offer other forms of compensation, including expense reimbursement, liability insurance, travel insurance, retirement plans, medical insurance, and life insurance (p. 12).

But smaller firms do not begin to compare with their big-firm counterparts when it comes to director compensation. Danco suggests that directors should be paid $2,000 to $10,000 per year, depending on the size of the firm (Danco and Jonovic, 1981, p. 109). Ward and Handy found in their survey of smaller firms that the average compensation was about $1,000 per director per meeting, and this also varied with the size of the firm. For example, they found that the average annual director compensation in firms with less than 100 employees was $2,465, 100–499 employees was $2,872, and 500 or more employees was $8,400 (Ward and Handy, 1988, pp. 292–294).

It should be pointed out, however, that some smaller firms do not offer any compensation to directors—even outside directors—at least during the startup phase of the board's development. Many CEOs and directors have told me that they have no problem finding qualified director candidates who are willing to serve on their boards simply for the experience, enjoyment, and prestige of membership. I know of *Fortune* 500 company vice presidents, bankers, professors, farmers, successful entrepreneurs, medical doctors, and others from virtually all walks of life that have served on private company boards for no compensation—at least for a time.

In the middle of the no-fee to large-fee continuum is a board compensation scale that I believe is appropriate for most small-firm boards. This scale, which I know encompasses the compensation plans used by many boards, ranges from $50 to $300 per director, per meeting, with perhaps a modest retainer and/or a stock option plan. This middle ground recognizes the value of the director's time, without attempting to emulate the lavish, and unnecessary, policies of the *Fortune* 500 crowd. Following a middle-of-the-road compensation policy, each director will cost anywhere from $500 to $3,000 per year in total compensation. This amount compares, appropriately, with the legal and tax advice services of many small businesses.

As a final note on this point, it should be clarified that most compensation plans distinguish between inside directors and outside directors. Insiders are already paid by the firm, and a board position could simply be considered part of the job description, therefore, additional compensation may not be necessary. Each company needs to develop its own policy concerning whether insiders should receive additional compensation for board service.

Directors and Officers (D&O) Insurance

I have frequently heard CEOs state that they refuse to establish a board because they cannot afford D&O insurance. Similarly, I have heard director candidates say that they would not consider a board position unless the board had D&O insurance. This concern has been verified in research studies (Mueller, 1990, p. 28). This section attempts to clarify some of the key facts about as well as the approximate cost of this insurance.

Laws bring corporations into existence. The very nature of these laws carries with it the liability of directors and officers who are responsible for actions they take while carrying out their duties. For example, the Model Act states in Section 8 that " . . . all corporate powers shall be exercised by or under the authority of . . . its board of directors." And these directors are expected to act " . . . with the care an ordinarily prudent person in a like position would exercise under similar circumstances." Similarly, state corporation laws often expand upon these principles and hold directors personally responsible for many activities of their corporations (Schipani and Siedel, 1988, pp. 279–281).

The purpose of D&O insurance is to minimize or protect directors and officers from liability that may result from the carrying out of their duties. For example, much of the small business world became aware of D&O insurance during the mid–1980s, when the cost of this coverage, as well as its availability, skyrocketed. According to one report, between 1984 and 1987, the cost of this insurance increased 1,000%, whereas the coverage limit and scope decreased (Wollner, 1991, p. 10). This resulted in a minicrisis for many boards who debated the relative merit of paying the increases versus going without the insurance.

A logical question arises: "Does every business need D&O insurance?" One report claimed that lawsuits against directors and officers in general are increasing at a compound annual rate of 10% (Wollner, 1991, p. 10). This same report points out, however, that the growth of these suits are primarily affecting banks and other highly regulated companies, whereas claims against directors and officers of small and private corporations are leveling off. I doubt if anyone would argue that D&O insurance is unimportant. The real question is can the firm afford it or does the risk justify the cost? Ward and Handy's study discovered that only 49% of the firms with outside boards they surveyed had this insurance. As could be expected, the smallest of the reporting firms (36%) were the least likely to have D&O insurance and the larger firms (63%) more likely to have it (Ward and Handy, 1988, p. 295). When they added firms whose boards they referred to as inside boards to their sample, the total percentage with D&O insurance dropped to just 35%. This suggests that firms using primarily insiders on their boards are very likely to go without this insurance.

There are other means, both structural and contractual, to limit the liability of officers and directors. This is a very technical legal issue, however, and one that is far beyond the scope of this book. Legal counsel should be sought to address this point if it is deemed necessary. Should D&O insurance be desired, however, the cost may be considerable, and obtaining it can sometimes be difficult. For example, I inquired about rates from two insurance companies and found that the minimum premium for D&O insurance ranged from $5,000 to $15,000 per year. Factors affecting actual rates for any specific company include scope and extent of coverage, number of directors and officers to be covered, company total assets and annual sales, industry type, location, profit or nonprofit status, and company legal track record. Therefore, if D&O insurance is going to be obtained, this item quickly raises the total cost of developing a board.

Indirect Costs and Overhead

The third category of board development and operation expense is indirect costs and overhead. Like the other costs, these will vary widely from situation to situation, but must be approximated in order to ensure a reasonable estimate of total board cost.

During the initial board formation steps, expenses that could occur in this category would be related to organizing and recruiting. Specifically, this may include travel expenses, meals and entertainment, legal advice and organization expenses, extensive telephone and mail expenses, including numerous overnight delivery packages, and so on. Also, one-time expenses may include a variety of supplies and benefits for directors such as notebooks, orientation kits, business cards, insurance enrollment, credit card issuance (possibly issued for business travel), coffee mugs, and anything else that is deemed appropriate to get the group started.

Once the board is operational, the routine overhead and indirect costs remain, such as meeting rooms (which go up greatly when off-premise locations are used, such as hotels or resorts), supplies, photocopying, postage, travel and telephone reimbursement, and insurance premiums. Don't forget to include the down time of however many of the staff that will be assigned board-related work, whether clerical or professional. Again, these costs will vary widely from excessive to nearly non-existent, depending on the needs and style of the firm.

In general, however, it is a common tendency to overlook or at least underestimate many of these "hidden" costs. By trying to come up with a reasonable estimate of the costs in this category, the chances of frustration and disappointment later are significantly reduced.

Management's Time

Perhaps the greatest cost of all in putting together a board of directors is the time of the leader and other managers involved in the process. It is very hard to put a real dollar value on this. How much is a top manager's time worth? Is a day worth 1/365 of his annual salary or perhaps 1/365 of the firm's annual profits (assuming the manager is the owner)? Possibly the manager's time is his billing rate (such as used by attorneys, doctors, accountants, and engineers). Another way to calculate what a manager's time is worth is the opportunity cost. This is the value of the other opportunities passed by or given up in order to spend time on the board issue. Perhaps a major contract or acquisition could have been completed if so much time was not absorbed by the board "thing."

A real danger is to discount management time as unimportant. Often managers will jump into some new idea without asking the question "where will the time come from?" Most managers I know are very busy, if not downright overextended. They cannot take on new time commitments lightly or without first considering what they will have to give up for the new project. This danger is magnified greatly when the number of hours needed is underestimated.

I have personally found (as a director) that the amount of time I spend with a firm is always about twice what I originally expected. Also, one CEO recently told me that he figures that he spends about 2 hours for every 1 hour given to him by each of his board members. Depending on the number of board members and frequency of meetings, this can really add up. Of course, even the best estimate of management time will probably overlook the occasional unplanned or emergency meetings that may occur.

I do not really expect that many readers will actually take the time to come up with an exact dollar amount that the board will cost. However, a reasonable estimate can be calculated in order to help the manager enter into the process with a realistic understanding of what he or she is getting into. Otherwise the quickly rising cost of the board process will soon create a dissonance within the manager, who then may become frustrated, disappointed, and discouraged with the board experience long before any benefits from the board could accrue to mitigate the expense.

ASSESSMENT AND SUMMARY

Assessment is a before-and-after proposition. On one hand, it involves trying to estimate the total cost of developing the board before the fact so that a go or no-go decision can be made. On the other hand, it involves measuring the actual costs against the actually benefits—if the board was actually built. Both the pre- and postassessment processes are very difficult to reduce to numbers, because assessment involves many intangibles.

Simplistically speaking, one adds up all the benefits, subtracts all the costs, and if the balance is positive, then you build (or keep) the board. Trying to explain this vicariously, however, is a little like the judge who was attempting to define pornography—he couldn't really define it but, "he knew it when he saw it." When you listen to dozens of company owners describe the difficult and costly process of managing their boards, one quickly wonders if it is actually worth it. The managers using the boards, however, know. Some have told me that they decided to abandon their boards because they were not worth it. Others, such as Warren Braun, author of one of the cases at the end of the book, state unequivocally that they have found that "both our outside and inside directors' opinions and observations to be particularly helpful in developing the successful corporation we have today" (see case by W. Braun for quotation).

A major complication in the assessment process is trying to sort out the short-term effects from the long-term effects. For example, the costs involved are rather easy to measure, because they occur in the short term. Director compensation, overhead, and management time are all felt immediately as they accrue. Benefits, however, may not really be noticed in the same time frame. The real contribution of a working board may take months or years to be realized. This fact dictates that management must have patience and be willing to take the long view in order to fairly assess the value of the board.

Another difficulty in assessment is accounting for the intangibles. These are the various factors that affect or are affected by the board process, but are not always seen or easy to quantify. An excellent perspective on the intangible factors of board effectiveness was expressed by Tom Harris in a *Family Business Review* article. Harris, who has board experience with both a family business and a number of other firms, is concerned that a board may undermine the potential contributions that family members might make to their firm (Harris, 1989, p. 151). That is, he recognizes that most of the businesses in this country are owned by families. These families may, in fact, benefit from the counsel of a board of directors, however, the presence of the board may also reduce the possibility that similar advisory and management support would flow out of the family group. Because the board is doing the job, the various family members may take for granted that their help is not needed and, therefore, never have the opportunity to develop.

There are numerous other intangibles, ranging from the personality differences that might develop between any combination of insiders and outsiders to the possible charges of conflict of interest or favoritism. The problem with these factors is that they are hard to predict, difficult to manage, and impossible to prepare for.

If the decision is made to go for it, much of the potential problems of the board can be minimized by careful planning and development. By taking care early, the chances of a negative overall assessment later will be greatly reduced. *Careful planning begins by setting clear, but realistic goals—recognizing that a board of directors is a tool, not a panacea.* Next, build the board carefully, being sure that you select the best mix of directors available, because regardless of the quality you buy, you may be stuck with your directors for a long time. Finally, be sure to invest the necessary time and energy to nurture the board into an effective group. This will not happen overnight, nor does good raw material guarantee that the final product will be one of quality.

With careful attention to both the big-picture goals and the details of implementation, most organizations will wind up with a board that is a useful and effective management tool—one that will challenge and complement the leadership team. The board will not be the answer for all problems, however, and it is probably not appropriate at all for some firms. Time and a careful process of assessment should allow each leader to make the right decision. In some cases, this leads to a negative decision, which may result in no board being created, or possibly an existing board being downsized or eliminated. If this is the conclusion a manager reaches after careful consideration, then the appropriate action should be taken. Perhaps at another time when circumstances have changed, the possibility of creating a working board will look different to management.

8

The Director's Perspective: Things Every Director Should Know

Plans fail for lack of counsel, but with many advisors they succeed.
—Proverbs, 15:22, NIV

OVERVIEW

This chapter is written especially for directors and potential directors. Everything written previous to this chapter (as well as the material following this chapter) was focused primarily toward the interests of the owners and managers who do the actual creating and running of boards. This special chapter considers the perspective of those asked to serve on boards. The major sections address clarifying expectations, legal liability, the director's vantage point, inside versus outside directors, dealing with crises, benefits of directorship, and a wrapup section on how to be an effective director.

CLARIFYING THE EXPECTATIONS

When someone is asked to join a board of directors, the typical reactions are flattery and bewilderment. The flattery is a normal response to being paid a compliment, and an invitation to board membership could be considered a compliment in most cases. The bewilderment is the result of not knowing exactly why the invitation is being offered. The flattery passes quickly; then it is time to satisfy the bewilderment.

A (potential) director needs to be very clear as to what is expected. As covered in Chapter 4, there are different types of boards, ranging from window dressing to networking to strategic and/or operational. The expectations of directors vary widely with each general board type. Also, as discussed in Chapter 3, businesses go through distinct growth stages, ranging from startup to early growth, maturity, and instability. The demands of directors can also vary widely, depending on what stage the business is in. Far more important than the expectations created by these structural conditions are the expectations of the person or group making the invitation.

Regarding these personal expectations, nothing should be assumed or left to chance—the director nominee needs to ask questions, sometimes from more than one person. A good first question is "why me, what do you think I can contribute to your board?" Listen carefully to the answer. It should be a reasonable reflection of the nominee's talents and capabilities. If not, perhaps the nominator does not really know the candidate. Other questions to ask concern the time requirements, liability, board structure and composition (who are the other members?), term, and, of course, compensation and other benefits. Of course, don't forget to ask for a thorough set of financial and annual reports so that you can verify the overall health of the company.

These questions should be asked of the nominating committee (or person), the chairman and/or CEO, and the other directors. You may also wish to seek input from others in a position to know about the company and its people, especially if you are not particularly knowledgeable about the situation. You may be surprised at the wide variation of answers that you may get from the chairman vis-à-vis the other directors. This is not to suggest that one or the other would intentionally mislead you (which may certainly be true in some cases), but, rather, that directors and chairmen often have very different perceptions of situations. This is why I strongly recommend that the expectations be checked out via more than one party.

As an example of the danger in only using a single source for background checking, consider the following situation. A new board was being formed a few years ago. Much of the work of nominating and director recruitment was performed by an existing outside director who was a friend of the CEO. At least two new outside directors accepted the nomination based on the assurances of the outside director nominator. Shortly after the expanded board began operating, the original outside director (who brought in the new outsiders) left the board due to his (employment-related) move out of state. The two new outsiders then compared notes and discovered that both felt uncomfortable because they had relied solely on the departed outsider for background and insights into the firm. They had not performed independent checks on the business or its leadership, and now were suspicious that things might not be as they seemed. Although in this situation everything turned out fine, and the new directors quickly got over their "minicrisis," the example helps clarify the need to use more than one source to clarify the situation before accepting a board position.

Another set of expectations that should be examined would be the director's personal ones. Anyone nominated for board duty more than likely would already have a busy and successful personal agenda. Busy people will not typically add things to their schedule simply for the résumé line. They like to do things that interest and challenge them. A good question to ask, therefore, is "can I make a difference in this firm?" If not, why do it? If you are interested in being a director just for the connections and prestige, then I suspect you would make a poor one. If you are not prepared to make the personal commitment of time, energy, and emotion to serving the company, then you should decline the nomination.

DIRECTOR'S LEGAL LIABILITY

As suggested in Chapter 7, directors assume legal liability for their decisions and actions. The Model Act states that directors are expected to act with the care of a prudent person. Further, state corporation laws often expand upon the principles of the Model Act and hold directors personally responsible for many corporation activities (Schipani and Siedel, 1988). This, of course, is the primary reason why directors and officers (D&O) insurance is such a major issue for many prospective directors.

D&O insurance is not, however, the only answer to the liability issue. In fact, recall that the Ward and Handy (1988) study found that only 35% of the small businesses in their study carried D&O insurance (49% when those boards classified as outside boards were considered separately). Obviously, there are countless numbers of directors serving thousands of boards without D&O insurance. As stated earlier, the growth of the use of D&O insurance is a relatively recent phenomenon, one that seems to mirror the growth of the litigious attitude in our country.

So what is the legal risk to directors without insurance? First, it needs to be clarified that insurance will not always protect directors. Certainly, the underwriters could balk at paying out claims in situations where the directors were clearly engaging in illegal acts, or were particularly negligent. Directors with or without insurance may be protected from loss through indemnification. To indemnify means to secure hurt, loss, or damage. Directors may be able to obtain indemnification from the company by asking for it in some sort of contract. This cannot protect you in all situations, but it is a good start.

Another question that should be asked concerning liability is "what is the company's track record?" If the business seeking your services has a history of antitrust violations, or is involved in a major environmental cleanup battle, or has a general habit of running in and out of court, then the exposure of their directors is probably quite high. On the other hand, if the company has a long history with little or no litigation experience, then the risk to their directors is much lower.

Each director candidate needs to use good judgment to evaluate the liability issue, consulting appropriate legal counsel, if necessary. Although I believe that this matter is somewhat overrated, especially in the popular press, it is nevertheless a serious issue and should never be taken lightly. Directors can be held responsible for the actions of the firm even if they missed a relevant meeting. They can also be held responsible in cases where they did not understand a particularly complex situation. So ignorance and being green and inexperienced are not particularly strong defenses.

Because such a large percentage of directors serve without insurance, they must feel that liability is not a particularly big issue. On the other hand, about half of all directors are covered by expensive D&O insurance, so this group apparently is concerned about liability. The bottom line is this: If, after carefully evaluating all the data available concerning the directorship, you are still troubled by the possible risk of serving, perhaps you should turn down the invitation, regardless of the presence (or lack) of insurance. If you cannot proceed optimistically into a situation, looking forward to the challenges ahead, then that particular opportunity is probably not right for you.

DIRECTOR'S VANTAGE POINT

In order to fully understand the director's role, it is necessary to understand where power is located in the company. When studying corporate law and large companies, one gets the clear impression that the board of directors is the ultimate seat of power in the company. In larger, publicly held businesses, this is usually true. If a new director joins a closely held board with this preconception, however, that person is grossly ill-informed. Because in smaller businesses the majority of stock ownership is typically held by one person (the top manager) or a small group, the board serves purely at the owners' pleasure, and real power rests with them.

Well, then, what does this suggest about the director's role in this situation? Are directors expected to be company yes men, serving only to please the owners? Sometimes this may be the case, and goes back directly to what was said in the previous section about clarifying expectations. But even if the owners really do want thinking, contributing, challenging directors, the classic model of the directors wielding ultimate authority over the officers still does not apply. If the majority owners have their minds set on something, the directors are powerless to stop them. Whether this is a problem depends on the situation.

When owners are arbitrary simply because of taste and preference (arbitrary regarding routine business decisions such as where to build a plant or what target market to go after), that is really their prerogative. The director needs to distinguish between arbitrary behavior that is relatively harmless and arbitrary behavior that is potentially dangerous to the firm. For example, the decision to build a new plant close to the owner's home versus building in a bigger town a few miles away may be totally arbitrary, but not really a harmful business decision. If, however, this building location does not have access to a needed utility or other resource vital to the business, then this may be a harmful business decision.

Challenging the owners on small issues will not serve either the director or the business well in the long run. Challenging the owners judgment on serious issues, however, sometimes may be necessary, and the directors need to be ready for this possibility—even if it results in the owners finding new directors. There is an old saying about it being hard to manage from a subordinate position. Regardless of what the theories may say about the power of the board, it just isn't that way in privately owned firms. Therefore, if directors are going to be effective, they need to understand where power is, and learn to manage from a subordinate position.

INSIDE VERSUS OUTSIDE DIRECTORS

The discussion thus far has tended to favor the perspective of the outside director. In fact, the majority of the board of directors literature is oriented toward the independent, outside director. Much of this section, therefore, focuses on the perspective of inside directors. Insiders are often taken for granted because they are just there. That is, no special effort is usually made to recruit insiders because they are already present through their involvement as family, investors, or managers. Insiders can be great directors, however, and, with a little care, the quality of the inside component of the board can be increased to the benefit of the board as a whole and company at large.

Qualifications and Recruiting of Insiders

Recall from Chapter 3 that inside directors were defined as "present, former, or retired officers or managers of the firm, and their spouses and children." This establishes the minimum qualifications for an inside director. From this starting point, it can be seen that the pool of potential inside board members may be quite large. I believe that for an effective board of five members, two or three should be insiders. For a board of seven, three to four should be insiders. This gives the board that critical balance between outside objectivity and intimate knowledge of the firm's activities, processes, and people.

Insiders that could easily be given an opportunity for board membership could be divisional or departmental managers, spouses or adult children of the owner(s) or manager(s), or retired managers from the firm. Each of these could bring a unique vantage point to the board. All of the various management types bring their superior technical knowledge to the group. They also are available, which can be crucial to getting the board together for an emergency meeting.

Spouses can also be effective board members. Granted, some spouse-directors do not know the difference between a balance sheet and a bed sheet, but most bring their own accomplished careers and life experiences know-how to the forum, in addition to their intimate knowledge of their spouses. Adult children can also bring their academic and work experiences to the board, in addition to the unique family business perspective they have from growing up with the business dominating dinner table conversation.

Managers, spouses, and children also can serve the board well in terms of preparing for planned as well as unplanned succession, which is one of the most ignored problem areas of many small firms. Family members and other insiders should look at board membership as a unique opportunity to serve and learn at the same time.

Wearing Two Hats

One of the main concepts that came out of my *Inc.* 500 study was the value that inside directors can bring to the board of directors. This was not a totally new revelation, however, because as I have stated previously, Stan Vance has been making the same point since the 1950s. The key factors I attribute to the value of insiders are that they are readily available and that they are intimately familiar with the details of the firm.

Being an inside director does have its drawbacks, however. Insiders must wear two hats, the hat of their insider attribute (manager of marketing, comptroller, lawyer son, housewife spouse, etc.) and the hat of board member. Although board memberships are often thought of as representing some sort of constituency, this is primarily done to achieve a good balance of talent. Once in the board room, however, every board member should become a generalist. Each individual's background and technical expertise become the foundation for his or her thinking and contributions, however, the perspective needed by each board member is that of the company as a whole.

Keeping a top–down, strategic perspective is much easier for outsiders than insiders, because they are not dealing with some specific, functional area of the firm on a day-to-day basis. It is vital, however, that inside directors work to develop a strategic perspective to allow them to be the most effective directors possible. Sometimes this creates conflicts for insiders who feel torn between being an advocate of their own department and doing what is best for the firm as a whole. Common sense, however, dictates that if the firm as a whole is not put first, then eventually there may not be any departmental issues to worry about.

Serving Two Masters

Similar to the pressure insiders face in wearing two hats is the pressure outsiders face by serving two masters. A board directorship is not a full-time duty, nor does it provide a full-time paycheck. Nearly all outside directors have full-time employment elsewhere, perhaps as an officer or president of another firm. Balancing these multiple responsibilities can be quite a juggling act.

Nomination committees like to ask busy people to serve on boards because they have a record of success and a reputation for getting things done. Everyone, however, has a saturation point beyond which no more activities can be handled without a serious decline in quality, probably in all of his or her undertakings. A directorship is a serious responsibility and should not be accepted unless the candidate really has the time to devote to it. Further, the amount of time it takes is frequently much more than anticipated.

When considering a directorship, it is a good idea to ask "what can I give up" in order to devote the necessary time and energy to the undertaking? Companies do not need directors who frequently miss, arrive late, or leave meetings early. Nor do they need directors who are not able to concentrate at meetings because they are so preoccupied with other matters. I must confess to being guilty of these sins. I like to be busy in many things and have trouble saying no to new challenges. But everyone needs to be honest with themselves and be sure that you are not doing a disservice to a company by agreeing to serve, or staying on when you do not really have the time and energy to contribute.

From a company perspective, a nominating committee should consider whether they should restrict the number of other directorships or outside duties they would be comfortable with their directors (both outside and inside) having. I am not suggesting a hard and fast litmus test, but simply that availability and possible conflict of interest be considered when deciding whom to nominate. I currently hold four business directorships and can state categorically that I should not be allowed to serve on any other board unless I give up something else (even if the offer attracts me and I foolishly believe I could handle it). Everyone has a limit of how many masters they can serve. The needs of the company should be foremost in anyone's decision as to whether to accept or decline a directorship.

DEALING WITH CRISES

Occasionally, a director is forced to deal with a very extreme situation, such as a bankruptcy, hostile takeover, death or incapacitation of the owner/manager, or even removal and replacement of the president/CEO. These are not the sorts of issues bargained for when a board member nominee contemplates and accepts the invitation to serve. Nevertheless, it is in dealing with situations at the highest level of corporate governance that board members make their greatest contributions. These are the toughest business decisions of all. No one likes to make them, but they have to be made. Rather than speculate on a number of theoretical crises scenarios, I will attempt to relate the reality of how a crisis affects the firm and its people through a single, detailed case. Although this account represents an actual situation, the company and persons involved are left nameless at the request of the various parties who conveyed the information to me.

The case involved a situation where the board was forced to counsel the president of the company to resign. The firm was a small manufacturer that had been experiencing rapid growth and all the difficulties that typically accompany growth, including labor unrest and cash flow problems. The board consisted of the president, vice president, and three outsiders, two of whom were shareholders. The third outsider was an officer of a large manufacturing firm who had only attended one or two board meetings that were held nearly 2 years prior to the onset of the crisis (the last meeting called by the president).

The trouble began when the president fired the vice president over a labor policy disagreement. The vice president, who was corporate secretary, immediately notified the two shareholder outsiders of the situation. The vice president had been with the company since its founding and had always perceived himself more as a partner than a subordinate (as did many others within the organization).

The firing brought out a number of other organizational problems, all of which were related to the overall lack of trust and confidence inspired by the president, both within and outside of the business. The two shareholder outsiders interviewed a number of related parties for information and insights, and in the process began to question the president's ability to continue leading the company. Any potential action by the board, however, was complicated by the fact that the president controlled over one-third of the company stock. A solid agreement of all other shareholders would be required, therefore, to back up any challenge of the president's authority. According to one of the shareholder outsiders:

I had been involved with the company since its formation, and considered both the president and vice president friends. When the president took action, however [terminating the vice president], I was alarmed. I told the president that he had broken a vital partnership, and forced me to question which half of the broken partnership was better qualified to lead as a solo act. It wasn't a question, to me anyway, of supporting the president's action without question. After considering all the information before me, I became convinced that the vice president without the president was better for the business than the president without the vice president. I felt that the vice president was more on top of the product, the customers, and the attitudes of the employees than the president. These three factors are vital to the success of the organization.

Making a decision of this magnitude often has a hidden cost in terms of stress, or even guilt, even if no one is to blame. Managing crises often involves making the best selection from a set of less-than-perfect alternatives. As the outsider continued:

Anyway, I felt confident that changing the president was the best solution, and didn't think it would bother me. Sure, we were all friends, but, as a director, I had the long run health of the business as my first priority. I discovered the night before the emergency board meeting [called by the outside directors] that the ordeal was bothering me more than I realized. I woke up in the middle of the night from a bad dream where I was a spy. In the dream I didn't know whose side I was on, but I had a machine gun, and every few minutes I came upon a group of people and knew I had to kill them; it was a matter of survival. I opened fire and just shot blindly into the crowds. When I awoke, I realized just how much the board matter was bothering me.

The situation was resolved peacefully at the meeting when, after a tense, but respectful, discussion, the president agreed to resign in return for a generous compensation package, and an offer to help sell off his stock in the firm. The vice president was appointed president at the same meeting, and additional board controls were established to try and monitor the firm better in the future. The outside board member added:

The situation might have been avoided had the old president done a better job keeping us informed about the company overall, and the tension between the two officers. We hadn't had a board meeting in two years, and all assumed that no news was good news, so to speak. In a way, the president orchestrated his own demise by isolating himself within the business and alienating himself from the rest of the team that he depended on for support.

This outsider was probably as well equipped to deal with the crisis as possible. He had years of experience with the firm, as well as experience with several other boards to draw from. The nonshareholder outsider, however, was in a different situation. Although a seasoned and experienced businessman in his own right, his knowledge of the firm having the leadership crisis was limited to only a couple of meetings. He had been recruited to fill out the fifth board seat due to his manufacturing knowledge and experience with big companies. His call to the emergency meeting of the board was completely unexpected, and he found himself forced to deal with a situation for which he was poorly prepared, at best. According to this outsider:

I was fairly new to the company, and, as a nonowner outside director, I felt a little bit on the outside, compared to the others, who all had some vested interest in the firm. It makes you feel different. So, while I believe that I am capable of giving advice from my applicable experiences, I count the others' votes a lot higher, since they had been involved longer, and all had a financial stake. Regardless, I think I can still be a useful director, and believe I was during the crisis.

When interviewed a month after the company shakeup, he had this to say about the aftermath of the incident:

In light of the strong personalities involved, it was clearly the right course of action. No compromise could have been made which would have kept them [the former president and vice president] both there and kept the company running smoothly. I am left wondering, however, will the entrepreneurial spirit that was applied by [the former president] still be there under the new president? We still don't know what type of a leader he will be.

The key to stabilizing the situation following the board's action was the leadership of the former vice president who was appointed president. When asked for his reflections a month after his appointment as president, he stated that as time goes on, he finds a number of different ways to view the event:

Initially [at the time he was fired] my main focus was personal fear; naturally I had obligations, and I was personally obligated for a portion of the company's debt—yet I had lost my window into what was going on in the company. A couple days later, my concern became saving the company as I realized that the situation was out of control. I knew we were in serious trouble months before I was fired. I had asked several times for a full board meeting to get the issues out on the table and discuss the pros, cons, and the company direction.

Unfortunately, the board meeting never came until one was forced by the termination of the vice president. Fortunately, he was close to most of the staff, who kept him informed on the developments during the week that he was deposed from his office. This gave him the necessary resolve to work with the outside directors to bring about the leadership change.

After the dust had settled and he had time to assess the change from the distance of time he stated:

I have no reservations that [the action] wasn't the right thing to do. The only cloud over us is that the current economic slowdown is concealing just how good we are really doing now. Our productivity is way up, and morale is high. We are getting our financials in order, and our bankers seem very happy. Our customers are also satisfied, and we are recognized as a preferred vendor by many of them.

The happy ending to this story may be altered somewhat over time, but, at least for the moment, it is an excellent example of how a board can rally in a time of crisis. In this case, the insiders and outsiders pooled their talents and energy to resolve a very difficult situation. Although it certainly was not a pleasant exercise, the board functioned as it should have, and each party contributed as required.

BENEFITS OF SERVING AS A DIRECTOR

As has been said previously, there are many directors of privately owned businesses who serve without compensation. This should prove that there are other benefits of serving as a director, and there certainly are. This section briefly discusses the major benefits that the director might anticipate when trying to decide whether or not to serve.

Experience

Probably the single most valuable benefit one gets from serving on a board of directors is experience. No matter how successful someone might be in his own career, there is always much more to learn. The top-management level of a board is a wonderful place to observe and learn about strategy, competition, people, new technologies, and, of course, a different industry.

This benefit is more significant to younger directors, but it is frequently mentioned as a big plus by older, more experienced board members as well. Interesting, capable directors are turned on by new experiences and the opportunity to grow. Serving on the board of some other firm is one of the best places to do this.

Prestige

I almost would rather not discuss this point, because I think it is a terrible reason to accept a board position, at least by itself. Nevertheless, prestige is probably one of the major reasons that board seats are accepted, and often coveted. It goes without saying that directorships on big, well-known corporations like Ford, Exxon, and IBM are prestigious appointments. The prestige of a directorship of a smaller firm is not as significant, but in Anytown, USA, it is still a big deal.

Being asked to sit on boards of directors is a way of saying that "I've arrived" in the local business community. Anyone interested in building a career and making a name in the local community realizes the prestige value of a directorship, and will take this into consideration when attempting to decide whether to accept or decline the position.

Opportunity to Make a Difference

I like to watch things grow, and, whenever possible, play a role in the growth process. I think the opportunity to help another business succeed is a tremendous turn-on, and perhaps the most significant benefit of director service. When someone is asked to join a board, this is in fact a group of people asking another person for help. A board is not a social club. It is a governing or advisory body trying to lead a real business enterprise successfully into the future. The opportunity to play a role in this process is exciting.

More importantly, helping the success of America's small businesses is significant work. As discussed in Chapter 1, the small business sector is the heart of the U.S. economy, leading the way in job creation, new product and industry development, and innovation. Any service to help the small businesses of America is important work, and directors should appropriately be proud of their contributions to rebuilding our economy and improving our ability to compete in the global marketplace.

Fun

Although it should be clear by now that board service is mostly work, it can also be a lot of fun. A dynamic, hard working board will let its hair down occasionally, either officially (at a board social occasion) or unofficially (perhaps led by the board "comedian," who brings the house down with an occasional wise crack or joke). Over months and years of working together, boards can develop into tight, effective groups with a high degree of esprit de corps. Granted, most of the group's time together will be hard work, but work itself can be fun, as long as the people get along and like each other, and the work is productive and successful.

Compensation

I doubt if many directors receive monetary compensation that in any way matches their board efforts. The periodic $50, $100, or even $500 checks that directors may receive for their service rarely equal what they could make doing other things, or the value they place on free time.

Stock options, however, can occasionally make board service financially rewarding. Everyone has heard stories about company secretaries who accepted stock for pay during the early years of the business, and later retired as multi-millionaires. Some of these stories are true, and some exaggerations, but the possibility is real. No one should base his or her retirement plans on cashing in a few founder's or stock option shares of an entrepreneurial company. Many will never be worth much, and more will be hard to sell, because they are minority shares of a closely held company. However, the total package of compensation, regardless of whether it rates with the director's market worth, can certainly take the sting out of all the time invested, and sometimes can even result in a healthy payoff.

HOW TO BE AN EFFECTIVE DIRECTOR

This final section offers a few general tips for directors to help them become effective, contributing members of the board. Any director who seriously tries to apply the following five simple steps should become a more than successful director.

Know Your Role

Many readers have no doubt wondered about the quote from the book of Proverbs that appears at the beginning of the chapter, and is then ignored. "Plans fail for lack of counsel, but with many advisors they succeed" (Proverbs, 15:22, NIV). I think the quote helps put each director's role into context, and, therefore, felt it an appropriate, if unofficial, theme for the entire chapter. The purpose of the board, in a broad sense, is to provide the counsel that a leader needs to ensure the success of his plans. Essentially, each director needs to see himself or herself as one part of the whole advisory group. A director is not a solo act. He or she is an important act, perhaps, but not complete without the other directors and the board's leadership. The board is most effective when the ideas and perspectives from each member is voiced, heard, and put into the thinking process.

This group aspect of board counsel is hard for some dynamic, entrepreneurial types to deal with. These types are used to solo performances, and find participating in a group process to be very difficult and frustrating. It can be a very helpful growth process for entrepreneurial types, however, and may teach them a few things about teamwork, delegation, and the like, which they may take back to their own businesses.

Be Professional

Part of being on a team is knowing how to respect and treat others. This means being on time and not missing meetings, being prepared by having read the advance material, dressing in a way appropriate for the group (this doesn't necessarily mean wearing a suit), avoiding off-color jokes and locker room language, and otherwise being sensitive to the feelings and attitudes of the group. The style, formality, and such of a board is usually set by the leader, or management, so this can easily be picked up by the little cues sent out during interview and orientation meetings. This advice may seem like little more than common sense (which it is for most people), but inevitably some board member will always fail to "fit in" by stepping on someone else's toes by behavior, language, or other insensitivities. Generally, however, people with extreme unprofessional behavior will be identified during the nominating process and, hopefully, avoided.

Participate

A director may be the most talented, brightest person in the community, but if he or she fails to participate, the talent is of no use to the firm. Effective participation involves listening to others, relating your views and ideas, bringing in similar experiences when relevant, summarizing (to help clarify ideas), and, especially, brevity. Effective participators neither dominate nor stay out of discussions and debates.

Directors should periodically evaluate their own participation by asking questions such as "why did I seem to dominate that discussion (or meeting)?" or, "why did I fail to speak up on that point when I felt so strongly about it?" or "why can't I remember much about what went on between 3:00 and adjournment?" Good participation from everyone in a new board will not come automatically, but over time, and with a little effort, it will develop. The important thing is for each director to see this as a key part of his or her job.

Allow for an Orientation Period

Whether joining a new or established board, some orientation period will be necessary before a new member feels comfortable, at home, and accepted. When joining an established board a new director may even experience a period of ritualistic hazing by some of the old timers. This may consist of nothing more than being expected to refill the coffee cups, listen to tired old jokes and war stories, and be referred to as the new kid or greenhorn, but nevertheless it may be an awkward and uncomfortable time for the newcomer. The good news is that this will pass; it just requires a little patience.

The orientation period will go a little smoother if the new director takes it all in stride and with good humor. When being told to get the coffee, remember that it is better to serve than to be served. Almost everyone is impressed by the chairman who takes time to pour the coffee and otherwise show care and respect for the other directors, so why should a new director expect to do otherwise? In fact, the new director will quickly win respect by showing a little humility toward the others who certainly have more experience and seniority.

The new director also needs to avoid coming into a board with a loaded agenda and an attitude that says "I'm here to save you and correct all the mistakes you have made." Granted, the new director was recruited to bring ideas and help to the firm, but no one should come into a new situation and try to make changes the first day, or even the first several meetings.

Seek Feedback

Unlike many regular jobs, board positions do not typically have a formal performance evaluation process. Directors are recruited who are believed to be professionals, and then left to fend for themselves. The absence of a formal review, however, makes it important that directors seek feedback and evaluation to help them grow and be more effective. Because board leaders recognize that their directors are undercompensated in many ways, they are often hesitant to offer suggestions for fear of upsetting or losing directors who, overall, they are pleased with. This is no reason for the directors themselves, however, to settle for a personal performance of a "C" when they could be giving an "A" with a little coaching.

Feedback can and should come from several sources. First of all, it should be self-evaluated. As mentioned in the section on participation, one can usually evaluate how he or she is being received if that person is willing to do so. Also, feedback should be sought from the board leader. Simple questions such as "how am I doing as a director?" or "what can I do differently?" or "what can I do to help you more?" are really appreciated by board leaders who otherwise may be afraid to open the door of director evaluation. Believe me, the honesty of a director who is earnestly trying to be more effective will be greatly appreciated by management.

Finally, feedback should be sought by other directors. Ask them how you are doing, and for tips on how to be a more effective director. They too will appreciate the honesty, and you may start an avalanche of director self-improvement. The directors as a group may also suggest some sort of formal evaluation process as part of an ongoing director development activity.

SUMMARY

This chapter has attempted to address many of the key questions and concerns of directors and prospective directors. Serving on a board is a serious and time-consuming task, and should not be entered into lightly. There are, of course, pros and cons of board service, and with a little analysis, each director or nominee should be able to make the appropriate decision concerning board service.

Overall, I believe that serving on boards is a wonderful and rewarding experience. As a director, I know I have learned and experienced many things that I would not have otherwise. There are, of course, real costs and risks of board membership, and for many, the negatives outweigh the benefits. If a director enters into a board situation with a positive attitude, willing to contribute and work hard, then the benefits will usually pile up. Doors will open, contacts will be made, good times will be had, and, most importantly, you will be able to look back and see where you have made a difference that you can be proud of.

9

Summary of the *Inc.* 500 Study

As has been mentioned throughout the book, my formal study of the use of boards of directors by privately owned firms began as a dissertation topic. This study was a nearly full-time effort for approximately 2 years. Each step into the process seemed to lead to the need for further steps, as a question answered always led to more questions. When the study was completed, I realized that although I had learned a great deal about boards and how they operate, my most significant realization was how little we (both business academics and practitioners) knew about developing and using boards effectively. Hence, my interest in the topic was not satisfied, but had just begun.

The widespread interest in my study was a quite a surprise to me (although a pleasant one), and was probably the result of several factors. Most notably, I believe, was the unexpected results I found, which questioned the almost blind faith in outside directors demonstrated in the writings of many consultants and theorists. Another reason for the interest in the study was the corresponding (chronologically speaking) surge in interest in entrepreneurial firms, and how to help them. Finally, this study simply helped to fill a gap in the business literature, because it represented the first major empirical study on the subject.

In order to help clarify what my study was and was not, this chapter presents an executive summary of the research process and findings. This will help answer questions the reader may have about how and what was learned from this study. This section should also be of use to other researchers interested in exploring the board topic. The actual surveys used for the first two parts of the research are also reproduced.

PROBLEM STATEMENT

A growing body of normative literature asserts the need for successful privately owned firms to have working boards of directors or advisory boards to assist management in a wide range of areas. These boards are supposed to advise and assist management in determining objectives and strategies, reviewing policies and management actions, helping develop succession plans, and provide specialized expertise, among other duties.

It has been claimed that the presence of a number of outside directors is essential in order for the board to be optimally successful. Danco insists that an effective board: "requires outside directors who can stand up to the business owner's flak long enough to give him the advice, support, and help he needs" (1981, p. 27). The need for outsiders by privately owned firms has lacked research support, however, and some research on large, publicly owned firms has questioned the value of outsiders. Some theorists have suggested that inside directors are superior to outside directors. Danco, however, discredits this view (that insiders are superior to outsiders) stating "rarely are they [the insiders] in the position to start challenging the owner's judgments. They work for him, after all. Their livelihood depends on his funds, his goodwill, and his continued blessing" (1981, p. 39).

Stanley Vance, a pioneering researcher on boards, takes the opposing position regarding the value of outsiders by stating "What nonsense—no one would hire a plumber to perform surgery or a barber to build a bridge! . . . Coming from all sectors of society, many [of the outside directors] have not even mastered the business alphabet" (1983, p. 258).

The problem, then, for the entrepreneur or small business owner about to set up or reorganize the firm's board is to decide which school of thought to believe. The normative prescriptions hail the advantages of a board packed with outsiders. On the other side is empirical work led by Vance that advocates the superiority of inside directors. What are the facts? Do outside boards and directors really make a difference in privately owned companies, or is the issue more myth than reality?

A review of the literature helps to clarify both sides of the argument, but, unfortunately, does not yield a definitive conclusion. The issue is too important, however, to be left in the current state of uncertainty. The contribution of privately owned and entrepreneurial firms to our economy cannot be overstated. These firms are leading the current economic recovery and creating millions of net new jobs, whereas the *Fortune* 500 firms are falling behind in job creation. Boards of directors and advisory boards may be an important variable to enhance the privately owned sector of the economy and might improve the success of entrepreneurs. Many distinguished theorists believe this is true, including Harvard Business School's C. Roland Christensen, who has stated, "Outside directors are the most underappreciated and underutilized asset available to any business" (Posner, 1983, p. 74). The purpose of this study was to examine closely the role of boards in one of the most dynamic groups of privately owned firms, the *Inc.* 500.

RESEARCH METHOD

The *Inc.* 500 is an annual listing of rapidly growing, privately owned entrepreneurial firms as reported by *Inc.* magazine. The research was conducted using survey and interview techniques to gain data from owners and board members of the 1982, 1983, and 1984 firm listings. Because *Inc.* would not provide information on the firms, a database was constructed by telephoning to obtain all the names and addresses of the CEOs for each firm listed in the magazine. The names and addresses of board members were obtained in a similar manner, by asking for the information from the responding CEOs. In all, surveys were sent to 579 *Inc.* 500 chief executives and to 124 board members (all which could be identified). Three hundred twenty-five CEO surveys (56%) and 91 board member surveys (73%), representing 35 companies, were returned. Follow-up interviews were also conducted with owners and board members of seven firms.

Inc. 500 Board Profile

Of the 325 total CEO surveys, 111 (34%) responded that they had no board, and therefore were not considered for further statistical tests. Of those with a board, slightly over 70% consisted of between three to six members. One hundred eight firms (50.9%) had no outside members. For firms with outside directors one, two, or three (10.8%, 11.8%, and 11.3%, respectively) was the most common number of outsiders. Table 9.1 gives the board composition for the 214 firms in the sample that had boards.

Survey Design

The surveys were designed and pretested using Likert-type scales to measure primarily the respondents' perception of the influence or importance of the board as a unit for a variety of functions and activities traditionally believed to be in the board's domain. Four-point scales were used, with highly influential at the low end (1) and not influential at the other (4). Influence was used as the primary question in order to attempt to establish whether or not the boards actually have some level of influence or power over the owners and decision makers of these firms. Mintzberg has noted that where firms are owned by an individual or small group of owners the board may be powerless and simply a facade (1983, pp. 91–92).

A number of specific hypotheses were generated from the prescriptive literature designed to test the relationship between the percentage of outsiders on the board and the level of perceived influence and/or importance of the board for a variety

Table 9.1
Composition of 214 Boards

NUMBER OF MEMBERS	FREQUENCY	CUM. PERCENT
1	6	2.9
2	16	10.7
3	43	31.6
4	31	46.6
5	53	72.3
6	24	84.0
7	13	90.3
8	6	93.2
9	7	96.6
10	1	97.1
11	3	98.5
15	2	99.5
22	1	100.0
MISSING	8	----

NUMBER OF OUTSIDERS	FREQUENCY	CUM. PERCENT
0	108	50.9
1	23	61.8
2	25	73.6
3	25	84.9
4	11	90.1
5	9	94.3
6	9	98.6
7	1	99.1
15	1	99.5
21	1	100.0
MISSING	2	----

Figure 9.1
Normative Model of Outside Directors' Influence on the Boards of Privately Owned Firms

```
BOARD COMPOSITION ----------> BOARD INFLUENCE & IMPORTANCE

Greater numbers and/or        yields higher levels of
percentages of outside        influence in traditional
members on the board          areas of board domain
```

of activities and functions. In general, it was predicted that the greater the percentage of outside directors, the greater would be the board's influence for a given activity as reported by the respondent. The proposition is illustrated in Figure 9.1.

Hypotheses Tested

H1:   The greater the percentage of outside directors, the greater will be the board's influence in the firm's strategic planning process.

H2:   The greater the percentage of outside directors, the greater will be the board's influence in the firm's budget process.

H3:   The greater the percentage of outside directors, the greater will be the board's influence in the firm's management succession process.

H4:   The greater the percentage of outside directors, the greater will be the board's influence in the process of filling vacancies on the board and in top management.

H5:   The greater the percentage of outside directors, the greater will be the board's influence in reviewing management's policies.

H6:   The greater the percentage of outside directors, the greater will be the board's influence in crisis management.

H7:   The greater the percentage of outside directors, the greater will be the board's influence in new venture development.

H8:   The greater the percentage of outside directors, the greater the board will be relied upon as a source of technological, financial, or other specialized expertise.

H9:   The greater the percentage of outside directors, the less the chief executive officer will rely on outside advisors or consultants who are not board members.

H10:   The greater the percentage of outside directors, the greater will be the chief executive officer's confidence in the board's ability to assist in operating the firm in the event of the chief executive officer's temporary disability.

H11:   The greater the percentage of outside directors, the greater will be the chief executive officer's confidence in the board's ability to choose a successor in the event of the chief executive officer's permanent disability.

H12:   The greater the percentage of outside directors, the greater will be the chief executive officer's assessment of the importance of the board to the overall success of the firm.

In addition to the hypotheses, a number of more general questions were also probed by the surveys, as well as explored deeper during the interview phase

Table 9.2
T-Test for Inside vs. Mixed Boards (Mixed 1; Outsiders GE 1)*

VARIABLE	Inside N	Mean	Mixed 1 N	Mean	Level
Strategic Planning	58	1.8966	95	2.2632	.038
Budget Process	55	2.0909	96	2.7500	.000
Management Succession	49	2.1020	91	2.3297	.230
Filling Bd & Mgt Vac.	49	2.1429	91	2.4176	.170
Reviewing Mgt Policies	53	2.0189	95	2.3579	.052
Crisis Management	51	2.1569	93	2.6667	.009
New Venture Development	52	2.0000	90	2.1444	.438
Board Relied for Expert.	78	2.5513	102	2.6275	.603
Rely on Outside Advisors	81	2.8395	102	2.9118	.536
Bd's Ability if Disabled	81	2.4074	100	2.6400	.127
Bd's Ability Choose Suc.	81	2.3704	100	2.1900	.215
Bd's Overall Import	84	2.2500	101	2.4554	.168

*The Inside group consists of all firms having boards comprised totally of inside board members. Mixed 1 firms are those whose boards have some insiders and at least one outside member. (GE = greater than or equal to.)

of the study. These questions are shown as Q1 through Q7 on the Interview Guide reproduced following the surveys at the end of the chapter. Much of the findings from these questions have already been discussed in the earlier chapters of this book.

RESULTS

In order to test the hypotheses, the data were partitioned into two groups—those with boards comprised totally of insiders, and those with boards with outside members. T-tests were used to measure differences between means. (Recall that approximately one-third of the firms responded that they had no board, and these were excluded from the statistics.)

Table 9.2 shows the results for T-tests comparing the totally inside boards with the boards for all firms that had one or more outside member. As the table indicates, several of the mean differences were significant at 0.05 or 0.10 levels. However, eleven of the questions pertaining to the twelve hypotheses showed

Table 9.3
T-Test for Inside vs. Mixed Boards (Mixed 2; Outsiders GE 2)*

VARIABLE	Inside N	Mean	Mixed 2 N	Mean	Level
Strategic Planning	58	1.8966	74	2.2838	.033
Budget Process	55	2.0909	75	2.8000	.000
Management Succession	49	2.1020	71	2.2958	.325
Filling Bd. & Mgt. Vac.	49	2.1429	71	2.3944	.224
Reviewing Mgt. Policies	53	2.0189	74	2.3378	.082
Crisis Management	51	2.1569	72	2.7830	.008
New Venture Development	52	2.0000	69	2.1014	.607
Board Relied for Expert.	78	2.5513	80	2.6250	.633
Rely on Outside Advisors	81	2.8395	80	2.9250	.492
Bd's Ability if Disabled	81	2.4074	79	2.7215	.052
Bd's Ability Choose Suc.	81	2.3704	79	2.1519	.157
Bd's Overall Import	84	2.2500	79	2.4557	.197

*The Inside group consists of all firms having boards comprised totally of inside board members. Mixed 2 firms are those whose boards have some insiders and at least two outside members.

differences in the opposite direction from that predicted. That is, although the hypotheses suggested that the presence of outside board members would lead to greater influence or importance of the board, the reverse was discovered by this test. For example, for the issues of strategic planning, the budget process, and crisis management, inside boards were found to be more influential than mixed boards at the 0.05 significance level.

The only variable that produced a mean difference in the predicted direction was the issue concerning confidence in the board's ability to help choose a successor in the event of the CEO's permanent disability. This mean difference, however, was not statistically significant.

Tables 9.3 and 9.4 indicate the results when the tests were repeated after dropping firms with only one, or two or less, respectively, outsiders from the test. The rationale for these tests was the concern that some firms might have one or two outside members who were perhaps honorific or only nominally involved or informed in the activities of the firm.

As the tables indicate, roughly the same results occurred in these later tests. The variables budget process and crisis management (for both tests) and strategic

Table 9.4
T-Test for Inside vs. Mixed Boards (Mixed 3; Outsiders GE 3)*

VARIABLE	Inside N	Mean	Mixed 3 N	Mean	Level
Strategic Planning	58	1.8966	50	2.1800	.133
Budget Process	55	2.0909	51	2.8235	.000
Management Succession	49	2.1020	48	2.2083	.605
Filling Bd. & Mgt. Vac.	49	2.1429	48	2.3542	.355
Reviewing Mgt. Policies	53	2.0189	51	2.2941	.183
Crisis Management	51	2.1569	49	2.7347	.013
New Venture Development	52	2.0000	48	2.1250	.556
Board Relied for Expert.	78	2.5513	56	2.6429	.594
Rely on Outside Advisors	81	2.8395	56	2.8929	.695
Bd's Ability if Disabled	81	2.4074	55	2.6727	.148
Bd's Ability Choose Suc.	81	2.3704	55	2.0909	.103
Bd's Overall Import	84	2.2500	55	2.3818	.451

*The Inside group consists of all firms having boards comprised totally of inside board members. Mixed 3 firms are those whose boards have some insiders and at least three outside members.

planning (for the second test) showed mean differences at the 0.05 level in the opposite direction than was predicted. Only the variable concerning confidence in the board's ability to help choose the CEO's successor had a mean difference in the predicted direction.

Additional tests were conducted comparing means of inside boards with firms with exactly one, exactly two, or exactly three or more outsiders. Tests were also conducted comparing inside boards to boards with certain percentages of outsiders. Tests were performed for boards with less than 25% outsiders, 25% to 50% outsiders, and greater than 50% outsiders. The results for these tests were very similar to the results given for the Mixed Boards tests.

For example, Table 9.5 shows the results for a test for firms with boards that had at least one outsider, but a proportion of outsiders not greater than 25%. Only one variable, the budget process, showed a mean difference significant at the 0.05 level. It should be noted, however, that the cell sizes for the outside boards (Pro 25) were very small, only eleven or twelve per variable. The direction of the difference for the budget process and most other variables was opposite of the prediction, which was consistent with the previous tests run. The only

Table 9.5
T-Test for Inside vs. Proportional Boards (Pro 25; Outsiders LE 25%)*

VARIABLE	Inside N	Mean	Pro 25 N	Mean	Level
Strategic Planning	58	1.8966	12	2.3333	.214
Budget Process	55	2.0909	12	2.8333	.033
Management Succession	49	2.1020	11	2.4545	.330
Filling Bd. & Mgt. Vac.	49	2.1429	11	2.4545	.414
Reviewing Mgt. Policies	53	2.0189	12	2.5000	.152
Crisis Management	51	2.1569	12	2.5000	.359
New Venture Development	52	2.0000	12	2.3333	.359
Board Relied for Expert.	78	2.5513	13	2.6154	.834
Rely on Outside Advisors	81	2.8395	13	2.8462	.977
Bd's Ability if Disabled	81	2.4074	12	2.1667	.453
Bd's Ability Choose Suc.	81	2.3704	12	2.4167	.882
Bd's Overall Import	84	2.2500	13	2.3077	.853

*Pro 25 are those firms with no more than 25% outside board members. (LE = less than or equal to.)

exception to this was the variable confidence of the board's ability to help operate the firm in the event CEO becomes disabled, where the Pro 25 group mean was smaller than the inside group, but this difference was not statistically significant.

The test for the next group showed several significant differences. This test, shown in Table 9.6, is for boards with an outside proportion greater than 25%, and less than or equal to 50% (Pro 50). The variables budget process and reviewing management policies were both significant at the 0.05 level. Strategic planning, crisis management, and the board's overall importance to the firm were significant at the 0.10 level. The direction of the difference in each case was, again, opposite from the predictions, suggesting that the influence or importance of the boards is greater for firms without outsiders than for firms with 25–50% outside members for these variables. Only the variable confidence in the board to help choose the CEO's successor showed a difference in means in the direction predicted (more confidence in outside boards than inside boards). The inside group mean was 2.2704, versus 2.200 for the Pro 50 group. The difference showed a significance, however, of only 0.364.

The final test for proportional boards examined outside boards with greater

Table 9.6
T-Test for Inside vs. Proportional Boards (Pro 50; 50% LE Outsiders > 25%)

VARIABLE	Inside N	Mean	Pro 50 N	Mean	Level
Strategic Planning	58	1.8966	40	2.3250	.055
Budget Process	55	2.0909	40	2.5750	.024
Management Succession	49	2.1020	39	2.3590	.283
Filling Bd. & Mgt. Vac.	49	2.1429	39	2.4872	.152
Reviewing Mgt. Policies	53	2.0189	39	2.5128	.021
Crisis Management	51	2.1569	39	2.6154	.068
New Venture Development	52	2.0000	36	2.1667	.500
Board Relied for Expert.	78	2.5513	40	2.7500	.315
Rely on Outside Advisors	81	2.8395	40	3.0250	.206
Bd's Ability if Disabled	81	2.4074	40	2.7000	.141
Bd's Ability Choose Suc.	81	2.3704	40	2.2000	.364
Bd's Overall Import	84	2.2500	40	2.6250	.058

than 50% outside members (Pro 75). Table 9.7 gives the results of this test. The variables budget process and crisis management showed significant differences at the 0.05 level, with the inside group being rated as the most influential. The variable concerning confidence in the board to help choose the CEO's successor, however, showed an increase in the difference between means, with the outside group being the more influential. The significance level, however, remained fairly weak at 0.179.

These tests considered differences in group means for boards with differing proportions of outside members. The same variables continue to stand out as in the previous tests. Specifically, the variables strategic planning, the budget process, reviewing management policies, crisis management, and the board's overall importance tend to reveal a pattern of greater influence or importance for inside boards than for boards with varying levels of outside members. Often, the mean differences for these variables is statistically significant at the 0.05 level. One variable, confidence in the board to choose the CEO's successor, indicates a possible pattern of greater influence for boards with increasing levels of outside members. However, this pattern or difference has not been supported by a strong statistical significance.

Table 9.7
T-Test for Inside vs. Proportional Boards (Pro 75; Outsiders > 50%)

VARIABLE	Inside N	Mean	Pro 75 N	Mean	Level
Strategic Planning	58	1.8966	43	2.1860	.141
Budget Process	55	2.0909	44	2.8864	.000
Management Succession	49	2.1020	41	2.2683	.446
Filling Bd. & Mgt. Vac.	49	2.1429	41	2.3415	.410
Reviewing Mgt. Policies	53	2.0189	44	2.1818	.455
Crisis Management	51	2.1569	42	2.7619	.013
New Venture Development	52	2.0000	42	2.0714	.752
Board Relied for Expert.	78	2.5513	49	2.5306	.907
Rely on Outside Advisors	81	2.8395	49	2.8367	.985
Bd's Ability if Disabled	81	2.4074	48	2.7083	.117
Bd's Ability Choose Suc.	81	2.3704	48	2.1250	.179
Bd's Overall Import	84	2.2500	48	2.3542	.576

Other Findings

It should be noted that the surveys were designed to allow the respondents to add other issues that they felt were important to the quantitative rankings they were completing. (See Questions 5 and 6 on the CEO survey and Questions 9 and 10 on the Board Member survey.) Several issues were mentioned by a number of respondents, including External Financing (65 responses), Management and Personnel Issues (52 responses), Marketing and Sales (25 responses), and others. Of these, only the issue External Financing showed a significant mean difference favoring the outside group. For this issue, some evidence was found that boards with outside directors may be more influential than strictly inside boards, although the level of statistical significance was only 0.17. The validity of this question is also suspect because the question was volunteered by some of the respondents, rather than asked by the surveys themselves. It does support the notion, however, that outsiders may be very beneficial for at least some board issues. Further, evidence was found in several of the interviews to support the notion that outsiders can be extremely helpful when it comes to obtaining outside financing.

DISCUSSION

This study was designed to test a general model that suggests that the presence of outside board members on a board of directors increases the level of influence and importance of the board in traditional areas of board domain. In addition to rejecting the hypotheses, this study produced data that suggest that the opposite may be true. Instead of demonstrating that boards of directors with greater numbers of outsiders are related to greater influence and importance to the firms, these boards had statistically significant less influence or importance for a number of variables.

Data from the Board Member Survey, the open-ended questions from both surveys, and the follow-up interviews, although less conclusive, also supported the general finding that inside boards may be more influential or important to the firms than their mixed or outside board counterparts. Information from the interviews also suggested a number of theories as to why the outside board members may be less effective than insiders, and why they appear to reduce the effectiveness of the board.

The interview portion of the research consisted of case studies of seven of the firms that had previously responded to the surveys. The firms chosen for the interviews had previously participated in the survey portion of the study. The cases included a wide variety of firm and board types, including primarily outside boards, primarily inside boards, and variations in between. In one case, an interview was conducted with a company owner who had completely disbanded his board after concluding that it was ineffective and not worth the effort required to maintain it.

The case studies involved interviews with the chief executive officer and board members, and, in some cases, included nonparticipant observation of the actual boards during regular board meetings. The interviews were guided by a standardized set of questions that are reproduced following the surveys at the end of this chapter.

Two primary reasons for the findings that outside directors seem to be of less value than their inside director counterparts may be

1. lack of knowledge about the firm and its environment and,
2. lack of availability to the firm.

Although there were a few exceptions discovered to these generalities, a broad consensus emerged during the interviews that these two points were key in explaining the difference between inside and outside directors. Lack of knowledge means simply that a solid background and up-to-date information on the internal affairs of the firm are essential for a board member to be an effective participant in the major issues the board faces. Insiders naturally are in a superior position to have this information, whereas outsiders may find it difficult to obtain.

Monthly, quarterly, or semiannual briefings, supplemented with periodic reports, cannot be as effective as daily involvement in keeping up with the affairs of the firm. This point was made repeatedly as a criticism of outsiders, by CEOs, inside board members, and the outsiders themselves.

The availability point was observed in the need for decision makers to seek the advice and counsel of others (such as board members) when making plans and decisions for the business. The outside board members are typically un- available to serve in this capacity except for periodic meetings or occasional telephone calls. This appears especially true for the most talented outsiders, such as presidents of other companies, who are extremely busy with their own firms and other activities. The availability issue also refers to the legal requirement for a notification period when calling special board meetings. Some CEOs get around this requirement by having the board members sign "waiver of notice" forms, but it still is a source of frustration and delay that is especially trying during a crisis period. Effectively, what often occurs is that the outsiders are left out of the decision process until after the fact, when they are informed of what took place.

SUMMARY AND IMPLICATIONS

The results of this study raise some serious doubts about the popular notion that entrepreneurs and owners of smaller firms need a working board of directors complete with a number of outside board members in order to prosper and survive. The study failed in its attempt to provide empirical support showing that boards of directors with outsiders were more influential than their strictly insider counterparts, and, instead, found evidence to suggest that the opposite may be true. The seriousness of this issue is magnified by recent published reports by *Inc.* and Peat Marwick indicating that a majority of small- to medium- size firms are now staffing their boards with people from outside the firm.

The absence of empirical evidence supporting the value of outside directors and boards should concern business owners and researchers alike. The findings of this study would indicate that theorists and practitioners should concentrate more of their energy on what it takes to create a successful board, and, more importantly, when are they actually needed. The case study portion of this research discovered a few examples of very well run boards, with CEOs that were very pleased with the performances of their board members—both inside and outside. More importantly, several firms were studied with no outsiders, or perhaps no board at all, yet they all had received the significant mark of distinction for a growing firm—membership in the *Inc.* 500 listing.

As in most research, more questions appear to have been raised than answered. Much more research is needed. This study explored the general question of influence and importance—based on the perceptions of the CEO and board member respondents. Future studies could explore other performance measures, such as finances, as they relate to board composition. Another approach would be to look at the board from the view of other constituencies, such as nonboard member managers, customers, or members of the financial community. Finally, board members could be classified as to the type of board member (i.e., outside: financial expertise; outside: legal; inside: marketing expertise, etc.) and studied for more specific types of contributions. Clearly, the research on this important issue has just begun, and the final evaluation of the use of boards of directors for privately owned firms needs to wait until much more study occurs.

SURVEYS

The next several pages contain exact reproductions of the two survey instruments designed and used for the *Inc*. 500 study. They are included here for the benefit of researchers and other curious readers who wish to understand how the data were collected.

CHIEF EXECUTIVE
OFFICER SURVEY

Please respond to the following questions.

1. How would you classify the firm?
   _____ Corporation
   _____ Sub chapter S corporation
   _____ Sole proprietorship
   _____ Partnership
   _____ Joint Venture
   _____ Other (Please specify _____)

2. Do you have a board of directors or an advisory board?
   _____ Yes
   _____ No

   If no, please stop and return the survey. Be sure to include your name at the end of this questionnaire if you wish to be included on our mailing list.

   If yes, which type?
   _____ Board of directors
   _____ Advisory board

   If both types exist, please specify which type is more actively involved in the operation of the firm.
   _____ Board of directors
   _____ Advisory board

   If you have both types of boards, please respond to the following questions as they pertain to your more active board.

3. How many members currently serve on the board?

   _____

   Board members may be categorized as inside members or outside members:

   Inside directors are present, former, or retired officers or managers of the firm, and their spouses and children.

   Outside directors are all other members of the board. This group frequently includes, but is not limited to, representatives of financial institutions or investor groups, various professionals and academics, and officers of other privately-owned businesses.

4. Based on the definitions above, how would you classify each of your members? (Please classify each member into only one group).
   _____ outside members   _____ inside members

5. To what degree are the board overall, inside members, outside members, and you personally influential in the areas listed below? (Please leave blank any columns or rows which do not apply)

	BOARD				INSIDE MEMBERS				OUTSIDE MEMBERS				YOU PERSONALLY			
	HIGHLY INFLUENTIAL	MODERATELY INFLUENTIAL	SLIGHTLY INFLUENTIAL	NOT INFLUENTIAL	HIGHLY INFLUENTIAL	MODERATELY INFLUENTIAL	SLIGHTLY INFLUENTIAL	NOT INFLUENTIAL	HIGHLY INFLUENTIAL	MODERATELY INFLUENTIAL	SLIGHTLY INFLUENTIAL	NOT INFLUENTIAL	HIGHLY INFLUENTIAL	MODERATELY INFLUENTIAL	SLIGHTLY INFLUENTIAL	NOT INFLUENTIAL
Strategic Planning	( )	( )	( )	( )	( )	( )	( )	( )	( )	( )	( )	( )	( )	( )	( )	( )
Budget Process	( )	( )	( )	( )	( )	( )	( )	( )	( )	( )	( )	( )	( )	( )	( )	( )
Management Succession	( )	( )	( )	( )	( )	( )	( )	( )	( )	( )	( )	( )	( )	( )	( )	( )
Filling Board & Top Management Vacancies	( )	( )	( )	( )	( )	( )	( )	( )	( )	( )	( )	( )	( )	( )	( )	( )
Reviewing Management Policies	( )	( )	( )	( )	( )	( )	( )	( )	( )	( )	( )	( )	( )	( )	( )	( )
Crisis Management	( )	( )	( )	( )	( )	( )	( )	( )	( )	( )	( )	( )	( )	( )	( )	( )
New Venture Development	( )	( )	( )	( )	( )	( )	( )	( )	( )	( )	( )	( )	( )	( )	( )	( )
Other (Please specify)	( )	( )	( )	( )	( )	( )	( )	( )	( )	( )	( )	( )	( )	( )	( )	( )
Other (Please specify)	( )	( )	( )	( )	( )	( )	( )	( )	( )	( )	( )	( )	( )	( )	( )	( )

6. What are the major issues or problems currently facing the firm, and how much influence does the board have in dealing with these issues? (Please leave blank any columns or rows which do not apply)

	BOARD				INSIDE MEMBERS				OUTSIDE MEMBERS				YOU PERSONALLY			
	HIGHLY INFLUENTIAL	MODERATELY INFLUENTIAL	SLIGHTLY INFLUENTIAL	NOT INFLUENTIAL	HIGHLY INFLUENTIAL	MODERATELY INFLUENTIAL	SLIGHTLY INFLUENTIAL	NOT INFLUENTIAL	HIGHLY INFLUENTIAL	MODERATELY INFLUENTIAL	SLIGHTLY INFLUENTIAL	NOT INFLUENTIAL	HIGHLY INFLUENTIAL	MODERATELY INFLUENTIAL	SLIGHTLY INFLUENTIAL	NOT INFLUENTIAL
Issue (Please specify) _____	( )	( )	( )	( )	( )	( )	( )	( )	( )	( )	( )	( )	( )	( )	( )	( )
Issue (Please specify) _____	( )	( )	( )	( )	( )	( )	( )	( )	( )	( )	( )	( )	( )	( )	( )	( )
Issue (Please specify) _____	( )	( )	( )	( )	( )	( )	( )	( )	( )	( )	( )	( )	( )	( )	( )	( )
Issue (Please specify) _____	( )	( )	( )	( )	( )	( )	( )	( )	( )	( )	( )	( )	( )	( )	( )	( )

135

7. How would you rate the relative influence of the typical inside member versus the typical outside member in terms of meeting the overall purpose and objectives of the board? (If you do not have any outside members, please skip this question).

Insider Much More Influential	Insider Somewhat More Influential	Insider and Outsider Equally Influential	Outsider Somewhat More Influential	Outsider Much More Influential
_____	_____	_____	_____	_____

8. How often do outside board members influence your day-to-day decision making?

Almost Always	Often	Sometimes	Almost Never	Do not have outside board members
_____	_____	_____	_____	_____

9. To what extent is the board relied on for technological, financial, or other specialized expertise by your firm?

Almost Always	Often	Sometimes	Almost Never	Not Sure
_____	_____	_____	_____	_____

10. To what extent do you rely on outside advisors or consultants who are not members of the board?

Almost Always	Often	Sometimes	Almost Never	Not Sure
_____	_____	_____	_____	_____

11. How confident are you of the board's ability to help operate the firm in the event of your temporary disability?

Very Confident	Confident	Somewhat Confident	Not Confident	Not Sure
_____	_____	_____	_____	_____

12. How confident are you of the board's ability to help choose your successor in the event of permanent disability?

Very Confident	Confident	Somewhat Confident	Not Confident	Not Sure
_____	_____	_____	_____	____

13. How confident are you of your management team's ability to operate the firm in your absence?

Very Confident	Confident	Somewhat Confident	Not Confident	Not Sure
_____	_____	_____	_____	_____

14. In your opinion, how important is the board to the overall success of your firm?

Very Important	Important	Somewhat Important	Not Important	Not Sure
_____	_____	_____	_____	_____

15. Briefly, what characteristics do you look for in potential candidates when seeking new board members?

I would like to take the opportunity to thank you again for your cooperation. Please remember to include a mailing address when returning your completed questionnaire if you would like to receive a summary of the findings of the study, and copies of future articles published from the data collected.

Name _____

Address _____

_____

Questionnaire is numbered for statistical purposes only. All responses will be handled on an anonymous basis and complete confidentiality will be maintained.

Please feel free to give any comments or insights concerning your board in the space remaining. Attach additional pages as needed.

BOARD MEMBER
SURVEY

Please respond to the following questions.

1. How would you classify the firm?
   _____ Corporation
   _____ Sub chapter S corporation
   _____ Sole proprietorship
   _____ Partnership
   _____ Joint Venture
   _____ Other (Please specify _____)

2. Is the firm's board that you serve on an advisory board or a board of directors?
   _____ Advisory board
   _____ Board of directors

3. How many times did the board meet during the last 12 months?
   _____

4. How many times did you have contact with the chief executive officer outside of board meetings during the last 12 months? _____

5. How long have you served on the board? _____

6. How many members currently serve on the board? _____
   Board members may be categorized as inside members or outside members:

   Inside directors are present, former, or retired officers or managers of the firm, and their spouses and children.

   Outside directors are all other members of the board. This group frequently includes, but is not limited to, representatives of financial institutions or investor groups, various professionals and academics, and officers of other privately-owned businesses.

7. Based on the definitions above, how would you classify each of the members? (Please classify each member into only one group).
   _____ Outside members   _____ Inside members

8. How would you classify yourself?
   _____ Inside member   _____ Outside member

9. To what degree are the board overall, inside members, outside members, and you personally influential in the areas listed below? (Please leave blank any columns or rows which do not apply)

	BOARD				INSIDE MEMBERS				OUTSIDE MEMBERS				YOU PERSONALLY			
	HIGHLY INFLUENTIAL	MODERATELY INFLUENTIAL	SLIGHTLY INFLUENTIAL	NOT INFLUENTIAL	HIGHLY INFLUENTIAL	MODERATELY INFLUENTIAL	SLIGHTLY INFLUENTIAL	NOT INFLUENTIAL	HIGHLY INFLUENTIAL	MODERATELY INFLUENTIAL	SLIGHTLY INFLUENTIAL	NOT INFLUENTIAL	HIGHLY INFLUENTIAL	MODERATELY INFLUENTIAL	SLIGHTLY INFLUENTIAL	NOT INFLUENTIAL
Strategic Planning	( )	( )	( )	( )	( )	( )	( )	( )	( )	( )	( )	( )	( )	( )	( )	( )
Budget Process	( )	( )	( )	( )	( )	( )	( )	( )	( )	( )	( )	( )	( )	( )	( )	( )
Management Succession	( )	( )	( )	( )	( )	( )	( )	( )	( )	( )	( )	( )	( )	( )	( )	( )
Filling Board & Top Management Vacancies	( )	( )	( )	( )	( )	( )	( )	( )	( )	( )	( )	( )	( )	( )	( )	( )
Reviewing Management Policies	( )	( )	( )	( )	( )	( )	( )	( )	( )	( )	( )	( )	( )	( )	( )	( )
Crisis Management	( )	( )	( )	( )	( )	( )	( )	( )	( )	( )	( )	( )	( )	( )	( )	( )
New Venture Development	( )	( )	( )	( )	( )	( )	( )	( )	( )	( )	( )	( )	( )	( )	( )	( )
Other (Please specify)	( )	( )	( )	( )	( )	( )	( )	( )	( )	( )	( )	( )	( )	( )	( )	( )
Other (Please specify)	( )	( )	( )	( )	( )	( )	( )	( )	( )	( )	( )	( )	( )	( )	( )	( )

10. What are the major issues or problems currently facing the firm, and how much influence does the board have in dealing with these issues? (Please leave blank any columns or rows which do not apply)

	BOARD				INSIDE MEMBERS				OUTSIDE MEMBERS				YOU PERSONALLY			
	HIGHLY INFLUENTIAL	MODERATELY INFLUENTIAL	SLIGHTLY INFLUENTIAL	NOT INFLUENTIAL	HIGHLY INFLUENTIAL	MODERATELY INFLUENTIAL	SLIGHTLY INFLUENTIAL	NOT INFLUENTIAL	HIGHLY INFLUENTIAL	MODERATELY INFLUENTIAL	SLIGHTLY INFLUENTIAL	NOT INFLUENTIAL	HIGHLY INFLUENTIAL	MODERATELY INFLUENTIAL	SLIGHTLY INFLUENTIAL	NOT INFLUENTIAL
Issue (Please specify)	( )	( )	( )	( )	( )	( )	( )	( )	( )	( )	( )	( )	( )	( )	( )	( )
Issue (Please specify)	( )	( )	( )	( )	( )	( )	( )	( )	( )	( )	( )	( )	( )	( )	( )	( )
Issue (Please specify)	( )	( )	( )	( )	( )	( )	( )	( )	( )	( )	( )	( )	( )	( )	( )	( )
Issue (Please specify)	( )	( )	( )	( )	( )	( )	( )	( )	( )	( )	( )	( )	( )	( )	( )	( )

11. How would you rate the relative influence of the typical inside member versus the typical outside member in terms of meeting the overall purpose and objectives of the board? (If the board does not have any outside members, please skip this question).

Insider Much More Influential	Insider Somewhat More Influential	Insider and Outsider Equally Influential	Outsider Somewhat More Influential	Outsider Much More Influential
_____	_____	_____	_____	_____

12. How often do outside board members influence the CEO's day-to-day decision making?

Almost Always	Often	Sometimes	Almost Never	Do not have outside board members
_____	_____	_____	_____	_____

13. To what extent is the board relied on for technological, financial, or other specialized expertise by the firm?

Almost Always	Often	Sometimes	Almost Never	Not Sure
_____	_____	_____	_____	_____

14. How confident are you of the board's ability to help operate the firm in the event of the CEO's temporary disability?

Very Confident	Confident	Somewhat Confident	Not Confident	Not Sure
_____	_____	_____	_____	_____

15. How confident are you of the board's ability to help choose the CEO's successor in the event of his/her permanent disability?

Very Confident	Confident	Somewhat Confident	Not Confident	Not Sure
_____	_____	_____	_____	_____

16. How confident are you of the firm's management team's ability to operate the firm in the CEO's absence?

Very Confident	Confident	Somewhat Confident	Not Confident	Not Sure
_____	_____	_____	_____	_____

17. In your opinion, how important is the board to the overall success of the firm?

Very Important	Important	Somewhat Important	Not Important	Not Sure
_____	_____	_____	_____	_____

18. In your opinion, why were you selected to serve on the board?

I would like to take the opportunity to thank you again for your cooperation. Please remember to include a mailing address when returning your completed questionnaire if you would like to receive a summary of the findings of the study, and copies of future articles published from the data collected.

Name   _____

Address   _____

            _____

            _____

Questionnaire is numbered for statistical purposes only. All responses will be handled on an anonymous basis and complete confidentiality will be maintained.

Please feel free to give any comments or insights concerning the board in the space remaining. Attach additional pages as needed.

INTERVIEW GUIDE

QUESTIONS PROBED DURING CASE STUDIES

Opening Question

Privately owned firms are not required to have or utilize a board of directors other than for some minimal duties specified by your corporate charter. You have a board that is doing [much more] than this. I'd like to know why the board was established, that is, what were the owner/manager objectives for the board? (Follow up with how? Finding members, setting parameters, getting started.)

Follow-up Question

Has the board evolved from what it was originally intended to be? And if so, how is it different now?

Specific Research Questions

Q1:   What are some of the areas (in addition to those suggested by the literature) in which the board and/or outside members are active with the firms? (What does the board do?)

Q2:   To what extent is the board influential in dealing with the major issues facing the firm?

Q3:   Are the outside members (for firms that have them) more, less, or equally influential as inside members in dealing with these major issues?

Q4:   What is the relative influence of typical inside members versus typical outside members (in firms that have outside members) in meeting the overall purpose and objectives of the board, in the opinion of the chief executive officer? (Also in the opinion of board members.)

Q5:   What characteristics do chief executive officers look for in potential board candidates?

Q6:   To what reasons do board members attribute their selection to the board?

Q7:   How often do outside board members influence the CEO's day-to-day decision making? (Examples/anecdotes.)

10

Case Histories

INTRODUCTION

I am greatly indebted to three friends and colleagues for this chapter. Nearly two years ago when I was first discussing the possibility of a board of directors project with Quorum editor Tom Gannon, he suggested that a couple of detailed "real life" cases would strengthen book. At this suggestion, I asked three individuals whom I knew to have excellent board contacts, insight, and writing skills if they each would be willing to prepare a case for the book. Happily, each agreed, and the following is the result. By reading through these cases, the reader will gain knowledge of the many of the strategies and details of board management, director contributions and problems, as well as the longitudinal perspective of observers and participants who have spent years following their respective firms.

The first case history is about ComSonics, a company in the cable television industry, written by company founder and Chairman of the Board, Mr. Warren L. Braun, P.E. Mr. Braun takes the reader from the formation of a consulting business in 1957 through expansion into manufacturing, *Inc.* 500 membership, and transformation into an Employee Stock Ownership Plan (ESOP) company. Throughout the case, author Braun focuses clearly on the evolution, composition, and function of his board of directors.

Warren L. Braun holds a BSEE degree from Valparaiso Technical Institute in Indiana. He became a registered professional engineer in 1957, and received an Honorary Doctor of Science degree from Shenandoah College in 1987. Braun is a board member and past president of the Employees Stock Ownership Council of America, past president of the Virginia Association of Professions, and past vice president of the Virginia State Chamber of Commerce. He has also held numerous other government and private memberships, directorships, and offices. He also is the author of numerous papers and two books, the holder of three patents, and the recipient of several professional awards and honors. Braun resides in Harrisonburg with his wife Lillian (Dickie) and they have a daughter who lives in Detroit.

The second case is about Technopaints (a disguised name to conceal the identity of the company and its people) and was provided by professor William Q. Judge, Ph.D. Technopaints shows how a board functions during a crisis period, where the board must play a key role in a difficult succession and turnaround situation. Judge obtained the information on this case while doing his doctoral research at the University of North Carolina at Chapel Hill.

Dr. Judge is an assistant professor in the Strategic Management department of the School of Business at the University of Tennessee at Knoxville. He teaches courses in the areas of Strategic Management and Business and Society. He has done extensive research on the board's involvement in the strategic decision process. Based on personal interviews with over 114 directors from over 42 organizations, he has tried to better understand the board's strategic role in a wide variety of contexts. In addition, he has studied top and middle managers' involvement in that same process. Judge welcomes comments and ideas from interested managers and directors. Correspondence should be sent to him at the University of Tennessee, Knoxville, TN 37996–0545. Judge resides in Knoxville with his wife Diane.

The third case concerns Dallas-based TDIndustries, a firm that began as a small heating, ventilating, and air conditioning business and grew to over $100 million in sales in just over 40 years. The case, provided by professor Joseph Rosenstein, Ph.D., paints a picture of a relatively inactive, primarily inside board. The author shows how this firm has survived and prospered ''in spite'' of having only an insider dominated, minimally functioning board. He suggests, however, that a serious test may come in the next CEO succession process.

Dr. Joseph Rosenstein is an Associate Professor at the University of Texas at Arlington. He completed undergraduate and graduate studies in the social sciences at the University of Chicago. Following 5 years of military service in World War II, he resumed his studies at Chicago and completed his Ph.D. in 1950. He then spent 30 years in various management positions in the packaging products industry before taking an early retirement to begin an academic career. Dr. Rosenstein's recent research interests have focused on boards of directors and employee ownership. He has published numerous articles, professional papers, and book contributions. He resides in Dallas with his wife Maryanne.

ComSonics Corporate History:
A Focus on the Board of Directors

Warren L. Braun

In 1972 ComSonics, Inc., was formed out of an existing business, Warren L. Braun Consulting Engineers, with the consulting firm continuing to operate in its own marketing sphere.

The consulting firm was started in 1957 as a part-time endeavor, providing technical support for various Broadcast–Communications firms while I was a full-time broadcasting executive: designing, installing, and managing a variety of AM–FM and TV broadcast facilities. None of these activities provided me an opportunity for equity participation. Therefore, in 1965, I decided to develop the consulting firm, expanding its scope of service to include CATV and acoustics. Although the consulting firm was a moderately successful proprietorship, the "services" aspect of the consulting activities were growing more rapidly than the "pure" consultancy activities of the firm.

The consultancy was envisioned as a full-time, limited personal activity, housed in the 2500 sq. ft. basement of my personal home. As described, the firm's activities grew more rapidly than the service activities, leading to a support staff of three after five years of operation. By this time it became evident that the services aspect could grow more rapidly with some deliberate marketing effort. The then existing laws of the State of Virginia prohibited a consulting engineering firm from engaging in the type of promotion and marketing that would be necessary to promote the service offerings of the firm. After two years of marketing effort *within* the constraints of the state law, the services demand required a staff of 16, still operating out of the home basement. In the third year, the staffing had grown to 22. The zoning administrator sent a letter that this business enterprise, although licensed as a profession, was clearly out of character for a quiet residential street. Adequate, but hardly suitable, lease quarters were located quickly while a full steam ahead effort was made to locate suitable property for construction of a facility geared to the firm's special needs. This property was located in 1971 with the construction of a shell commencing in the same year. The staffing had now grown to 26 with most of the employees now full-time instead of part-time as had been the case previously.

Since the services aspects of the business were quite different from the consulting activity and since the state law restricted the promotion of such services to the degree that they needed to provide for full development of this activity, I decided to incorporate the services arm of the consulting firm in a separate organization as ComSonics. With the corporate charter in hand, this transition was made in July of 1972. Capital funding for the corporation was deliberately limited since the future of the business development for CATV field vis-à-vis our firm was not clear. To provide for the corporation's startup expenses, personal loans were provided to the corporation to meet the cash flow requirements, with the building and equipment being leased to the corporation on an "industry comparable" basis. Business development for the corporation grew slowly for the first three years, averaging roughly 8% per year.

I had determined that whenever and however possible, the employees would share in the ownership of the firm, with the final objective for them to own all of the company. Most of the employees were very young and had no resources to purchase the stock. Further, the stock sharing concepts available during those years did not appear to offer much benefit to either the employees, or to the corporation.

Dr. Louis Kelso's concept of an Employee Stock Ownership Plan met our requirements but it was not yet law. In 1974, Senator Russell Long guided this legislation through the Congress and ComSonics adopted an "ESOP" plan the following year. The narrative of ComSonics corporate growth following this event is available in *On the Way to Successful Stock Ownership*, which volume also discusses the corporate challenges and rewards associated with an ESOP implementation.

From 1975 forward (after the ESOP installation) the corporate growth rate increased to an average of 20% per year with the addition of participatory management, ComSonics grew at an annual rate of 31% in a few years. The firm became an *Inc*. 500 growth company in 1982, receiving the U.S. Senate Productivity Medal in 1985, along with many other awards for achievement. All these developments are reflected to some extent in the board membership selection and its role in the development of the corporation. I will also comment on what I believe the role of a board should be in such an environment.

The rest of this chapter is a chronological recitation of the board composition, with a narrative indicating the board role and major accomplishments in each fiscal year.

FISCAL YEAR 1972/1973

ComSonics was founded in 1972 with receipt of the corporate charter on July 25th of that year. Transfer of pertinent operations from the consulting firm took place on August 1, 1972. To this day we have kept the same fiscal year.

The initial board of directors was as follows:

Warren L. Braun, President and Treasurer

Lillian C. Braun, Vice President and Secretary

Ruby Garber, Assistant Secretary/Treasurer

I personally owned all of the corporate stock and provided the initial funds for capitalization, legal fees, and accounting fees to set up the corporation. My wife, Lillian, had always supervised the accounting of the consulting firm with part-time assistance, usually doing most of the work herself. Ruby Garber became the first full-time accountant of the new firm. Although 5,000 shares were authorized only 240 shares were issued by the corporation to me.

During the first year of operation, the retained cash earnings were so small, that I had to endorse my salary checks to meet the payroll in addition to lending the corporation additional funds needed for operations. Had the ongoing consulting firm's income not been available, the corporation could have capsized.

Our legal advisor, George S. Aldhizer, II, was both a friend and our personal attorney. During the first fiscal year the board met when needed to pass resolutions and other housekeeping matters always with George Aldhizer sitting with the initial board members and advising them. Policy was not a function of the board nor was there any advice given or received except on an informal basis.

It is probably important here to describe my philosophy of a board of directors. I believe that the members should meet all legal requirements, plus providing additional insight into the broader business world while also providing appropriate guidance where they felt that the information might be received constructively. I did not feel that frequent, i.e., monthly, board meetings were necessary or appropriate in this concept of a board of directors. The gross sales for the first year of operation were $325,000 and the net profit was $10,000. Our new facility had been completed during the year and was then leased to the corporation at a rate determined to be comparable to other facilities in the area. Also, a substantial amount of technical equipment was necessary, which was purchased personally and leased back to the corporation on a five year industrial lease rate.

FISCAL YEAR 1973/1974

The board of directors membership this year was as follows:

Warren L. Braun, President

Lillian C. Braun, Secretary/Treasurer

George S. Aldhizer, II, Vice President

George R. Aldhizer, Jr.

Ruby Garber, Assistant Secretary/Treasurer

George Aldhizer, II, our corporate attorney, had provided invaluable advice during the first year of operation. George was a very successful businessman as well as a second ranking (seniority) Senator in the Virginia General Assembly. His business advice during the initial year of operation had been so valuable that I asked him to join the board. As in our first year of operation the board meetings were held as necessary to conduct the affairs of the corporation that could not be accomplished by the president alone. I had also asked George R. Aldhizer, Jr., a cousin of George S. Aldhizer, to join us on our board during the year. Both men were from the same legal firm, however, each had quite different corporate practice experience. This was especially important since I was preparing to set up an ESOP Trust in the following fiscal year in which effort we were plowing new legal ground.

During the second fiscal year retained earnings were still not enough to fully fund the corporate cash needs, so I continued to lend the corporation the proceeds of my earnings plus any additional cash that was necessary. Obviously, a line of credit could have been established with the firm's bank, however, this would have required personal endorsement, so one way or the other, I had to lend or guarantee the operating cash of the corporation.

The earnings for fiscal year 73/74 were as follows: gross sales of $325,000 and a net profit of $10,000. The board adopted a $50 fee for all full board meetings, which was composed of an annual meeting in November of 1973.

FISCAL YEAR 1974/1975

It became clear to me that our business insight was limited to a regional perspective, and since we wanted it to grow to a national firm it was important to add board members that could provide us that vision. Since my brother Carlton was a Senior Executive of Motorola I asked him to serve on the board and he agreed. His insight and guidance have been of enormous help in moving the goals of the corporation forward into the future.

The board composition in 74/75 was

Warren L. Braun, President

Lillian C. Braun, Secretary/Treasurer

George S. Aldhizer, Vice President

Carlton R. Braun, Second Vice President

Donald Suter, Assistant Secretary/Treasurer

Early in the fiscal year our accountant, Ruby Garber, asked to leave the position of bookkeeper of the corporation as the workload was becoming burdensome within the confines of her expertise. Donald Suter was hired to replace her. His experience included data processing, which was sorely needed at this point in the corporate development.

Near the end of the fiscal year on July 25, 1975, the board executed the ESOP Trust Agreement and simultaneously agreed to fund the Trust with 25 shares of newly issued stock. Our ESOP Trust lawyer was Charles Webb of the McQuire, Woods, and Battle firm. Gross sales for the fiscal year 74/75 were $406,000 and a net profit of $14,000.

FISCAL YEAR 1975/1976

The board composition was as follows:

Warren L. Braun, President
Lillian C. Braun, Secretary/Treasurer
George S. Aldhizer, II, Vice President
Dikki Carol Braun
Carlton R. Braun
James Zirk

During this year the board was enlarged to accommodate the reality of a growing business environment. Our daughter, who was living in Detroit, had indicated an interest in joining the firm at some point in the future. This never materialized but we put her on the board of directors so that she would have the opportunity to be familiar with the corporate activity.

As stated previously, I had always felt that the board members should be active in the corporate life, short of "running the corporation." During the year, one of our senior employees, James Zirk, was promoted to Operations Manager and asked to serve on the Board.

During the year it became evident that personal funding of the corporation was not in the best interest of either the company or my personal finances. Therefore, we went "public" internally, selling 72 shares of newly issued stock to the ESOP Trust for $54,000, which funding was obtained by "leveraging" the ESOP. This provided much needed operating capital and increased the employee shares such that they now owned approximately 18% of the corporation, reducing my holdings in the corporation to 82%.

FISCAL YEAR 1976/1977

The board's composition was as follows:

Warren L. Braun, President
Lillian C. Braun, Secretary/Treasurer
George S. Aldhizer, II, Vice President
Carlton R. Braun, 2nd Vice President
Dikki Carol Braun
James Zirk
Donald Suter, Assistant Secretary/Treasurer

The fiscal year saw the establishment of a separate in-house sales and marketing effort. In the prior years this had been contracted through an independent agent.

Although the independent agent had continued for over a year, it was found to be highly unsatisfactory, with the decision at the end of the year to terminate this agreement, and to establish our internal corporate/sales and marketing staff. In future years this turned out to be a very important, positive decision. Late in this same year after some discussion with a member of the board of directors, I determined that we should put into place a more formal method of training our employees in the salient aspects of the ESOP. Since the ESOP had been in place since July of 1975 the motivational effort of this participation did not appear to be what I felt it could be although there had been an improvement in the overall corporate productivity. To my dismay, I found that the majority of the employees did not understand stock generally, and certainly did not understand the specifics of ComSonics' stock ownership, even after a number of training sessions. I realized that this was a problem that required *considerable effort* and should be accomplished by retaining a consultant/specialist. After interviewing a number of individuals I found a man who I believed to have the appropriate background, i.e., employee training, developing employee skills in the participation process, and to work on the successor management development, since I wanted the staff of the firm to be able to manage the company effectively when the transfer of ownership had been completed.

After outlining the scope of these objectives to a Consultant, John Dickie, I asked if he felt he could accomplish all of these objectives. He averred that he felt that he had the qualifications and experience and was retained effective as of March of 1977. After three years of consulting to this end the end goal had been accomplished, and a very effective staff had been developed. I doubt that this level of organizational development could take place without the very skilled and competent and corporate consultant such as John Dickie. At the time that John Dickie was retained some board members felt that this training process could be done by individuals within the company, however, I felt that a greater effectiveness in training could be accomplished by someone who was experienced in this field and understood what we were trying to do. The gross sales for the fiscal year 1976/77 were $714,000 with a net income of $28,000.

FISCAL YEAR 1977/1978

The board composition was as follows:

Warren L. Braun, President
Lillian C. Braun, Secretary/Treasurer
George S. Aldhizer, II, Vice President
Carlton R. Braun, 2nd Vice President
Donald Suter, Assistant Secretary/Treasurer

With the ESOP Trust in place for more than a year it became clearly evident that fractional share ownership was not a good accounting method for a given employee's account and was quite confusing to the employees when they examined their employee reporting forms.

George Aldhizer recommended that we have a 1000–1 stock split, which changed the employee's ownership to 92,000 and my personal holdings to 245,000, leaving the balance of percentage of ownership the same between the employees and myself. Although the substance of this change was not material, the effect on the ESOP participants was favorable. Since our ESOP Trust did not have any vesting prior to five years, this did not affect any employee's account. Also, 100% vesting did not occur until 15 years of service, therefore, there would be very little account activity until later years.

In this year, James Zirk, our business manager, decided to return to his family farm management activities. Although he was a well-trained physicist, he did not find the corporate world to his liking. When he left the corporation he asked to be relieved of his responsibility as a board member and was removed from the board at that time.

Due to the well-coordinated marketing effort by our newly organized internal sales and marketing staff the gross sales for the period were substantially improved over the prior year, rising to a new height for the corporation. Gross sales for fiscal year 77/78 were $923,000 with a net income of $78,000.

During this fiscal year the consulting firm began to purchase its staff supporting services directly from ComSonics on a contractual basis. This resulted in a gross revenue contribution of $18,000, which total is included in the previous gross sales figure. The terms for such purchases were on the basis of "most favorable client" basis, i.e., subject to the same discount.

FISCAL YEAR 1978/1979

The board composition was as follows:

Warren L. Braun, President
Lillian C. Braun, Secretary/Treasurer
George S. Aldhizer, II, Sr. Vice President
Carlton R. Braun, Vice President
Donald Suter, Assistant Secretary/Treasurer
John Dickie

The employee training was well underway, commencing with "Financial Management for Non-Financial Managers" and "Principles of Managing by Personal MBOs" with a heavy emphasis on consensus building. John Dickie, our corporate consultant, joined the board at my request after six months of very successful training activities with the employees. At that time I also asked him to serve as Chairman of the ESOP Administrative Committee, a board function that he has filled very effectively even to this day in the corporation.

Our annual board meeting was held in November of 1978 with several called meetings during the year as needed. The gross sales during the year rose to $1,234,000 with net income of $113,000. The consulting income, which is included in the gross income, was $130,000.

FISCAL YEAR 1979/1980

The board composition was as follows:

Warren L. Braun, President
Lillian C. Braun, Secretary/Treasurer
George S. Aldhizer, II, Sr. Vice President
Carlton R. Braun, Vice President
John Dickie, Vice President
Donald Suter, Assistant Secretary/Treasurer

The training of the executive group was now well underway with peer group decision making introduced into the training schematic. John Dickie, by now filling a role of an outside corporate facilitator, was somewhat hesitant to introduce this concept earlier in the fiscal year but I felt it was imperative if the corporation was to develop a good understanding of true participative management. The first few meetings, ocurring at weekly intervals, were rough, but soon the concept of consensus building was understood and the executives were able to relate to each other in a true participative mode. This same effort had begun at the supervisory level with somewhat less success, but this effort nevertheless was continued. Productivity was moving ahead at a rapid pace as was the utilization of the facility with 7,200 sq. ft. of space and 63 employees. Gross sales for fiscal year 1979/80 were $1,901,000 with a net income of $168,000. Consulting income contribution was $384,000.

FISCAL YEAR 1980/1981

The board members were as follows:

Warren L. Braun, President
Lillian C. Braun, Secretary/Treasurer
George S. Aldhizer, II, Sr. Vice President
Carlton R. Braun, Vice President
John Dickie, Vice President of Financial Affairs
Donald Suter, Assistant Secretary/Treasurer

In a thrust to enhance the sense of ownership, three executives of the firm were appointed as vice presidents in charge of specific areas of operation, with the added responsibility to report the results of their operations to the board of directors at the annual board meeting.

The corporate facilitator was assigned the task of providing the additional training for the executives, tailored to each individual by weekly counseling/ project review sessions. This process seemed to work quite well, with accelerated executive development ensuing. The executive's subjects to the special training were:

Carl H. Hensley, Vice President of International Operations

Richard Shimp, Vice President of Research and Corporate Development

Dennis Zimmerman, Vice President of System Services

Although these men were appointed vice presidents, they did not have a board vote nor did they participate in the board discussions except relevant to their individual reports.

With the substantial growth in sales it became obvious that the corporate quarters were too small, and planning was begun to enlarge the existing facility. A major obstacle was soon uncovered, that being the area zoning as R–1, residential property! Unfortunately, the 1972 area rezoning process was of such a nature that we were not notified that our property had been zoned R–2 in August of 1972 when it had been A–1 (agricultural) at the time of the original building permit issuance in May 1972. The plan was set in motion to have the property rezoned M–2 (manufacturing) in the next fiscal year.

Near the close of our fiscal year, I was appointed by Governor John Dalton to join an official Virginia Trade Mission to Japan, Taiwan, and Hong Kong. The mission covered the time period of April 11–30, 1981. I arranged the return trip to permit a two-day lecture in Ohau and Maui in the Hawaiian Islands since a substantial number of cable operators were in this part of the world. Following this I returned to the mainland of the United States on April 30th. The lectures in Hawaii were oriented to the topic of cable television system leakage and resulted in direct product sales. A report of the entire trip was made to the board of directors on May 12, 1981. I had served on two prior missions to the Far East for each of two other governors and had developed a number of business contacts in the Far East, which contacts are still utilized today. The gross sales in 80/81 were $2,594,000. The consulting firm contribution was $401,550 and the net income was $167,700.

FISCAL YEAR 1981/1982

The board members were

Warren L. Braun, President

Lillian C. Braun, Secretary/Treasurer

George S. Aldhizer, II, Senior Vice President

Carlton R. Braun, Vice President

John Dickie, Vice President of Financial Affairs

Donald Suter, Assistant Secretary/Treasurer

Nondirector officers were

Carl H. Hensley, Vice President of Internal Affairs

Richard Shimp, Vice President of Research and Corporate

Dennis Zimmerman, Vice President of System Services

Glen K. Shomo, Vice President of Product Development and Production

The property rezoning requests, started in the prior fiscal year, were continued, going before a joint meeting of the Planning Commission and County Board of Supervisors on August 11, 1981. On September 2, 1981, by a 5/2 affirmative vote the Planning Commission agreed to the rezoning of the property. On September 15, 1981, the Board of Supervisors, on recommendation of the Planning Commission, rezoned the property to M–2. On October 7, 1981, the adjacent property owners sued the Board of Supervisors and ComSonics citing "inconsistency" of the rezoning act. Although the City of Harrisonburg had no official status in this rezoning, the City Manager, Marvin Milam, publicly stated his opposition to this act since the City was contemplating annexation of a good deal of the property around the City, which included this property. The court set the rezoning case for trial on election day, November 3, 1981, which normally was a vacation date for the court. However, Judge Robinson recognized the need for a prompt decision since this was holding up the sorely needed expansion of the facility. During this entire process the board was kept advised of the rezoning activities, however, since the property was personally owned by me, there was no need for action on the part of the board. All of the ongoing legal costs were paid by me personally. After several legal maneuvers by the City of Harrisonburg to be included in the suit, these were excluded and the trial took place as scheduled on November 3, 1981. After a 9-1/2 hour trial, Judge Robinson upheld the rezoning.

During these proceedings, plans had been prepared to delineate the expansion by a local architect, John Sease. Since the expansion was to be financed by industrial revenue bonds, the existing building and land had to be sold to the corporation at the then appraised value of the property on December of 1981. This process went forward quite smoothly with unanimous board approval in the November 1981 annual board meeting.

The remainder of the fiscal year was devoted primarily to the design, ground breaking, and construction of the addition to our existing facilities. Since this new construction surrounded the existing structure and continued operation of the existing facility was required, a rather substantial hardship was imposed on the staff. However, the excitement of the construction helped all employees to bear this was borne well with very minor problems.

As a measure of our determination to continue to be good neighbors, adjacent householders were involved in the selection of appropriate screening shrubs or trees and landscaping.

It was also a memorable year personally as I served my last day as a member and Chairman of the State Water Control Board, having originally been appointed in 1972. In seven years prior to that I had served on the State Air Pollution Control Board as a board member. I had also served on the eight state, Ohio River Sanitation Commission, serving as chairman of that body for two years. Many activities were closing and new doors of opportunity were opening.

The increased complexity of the accounting system required for the enlarged operations was beyond the skills of our Assistant Secretary/Treasurer, Don Suter. This was made very clear to him, and with his agreement, we set out to find an individual who could head the financial functions of the organization in the future. A local individual, Thomas Robinson, who had a good background in banking, finance, and manufacturing was brought on board to serve in this position. Gross sales for fiscal year 1981/82 were $3,372,000. Consulting engineering contribution was $314,000 and the net income was $218,000.

FISCAL YEAR 1982/1983

The board members were

Warren L. Braun, President/CEO
Lillian C. Braun, Secretary/Treasurer
George S. Aldhizer, II, Senior Vice President
Carlton R. Braun, Vice President of Operations
John Dickie, Vice President of Financial Affairs
Donald Suter, Assistant Secretary/Treasurer

Nonboard member officers were

Carl H. Hensley, Vice President of Internal Operations
Richard Shimp, Vice President of Research and Corporate Development
Dennis Zimmerman, Vice President of System Services
Glen K. Shomo, Vice President of Product Development and Production
Thomas Robinson, Vice President of Finance

In September of 1982, I was invited to join the Governor's delegation to meet with the Japanese delegates at the Euro-joint meeting of the Japanese/American Meeting in Nashville, TN. The proceedings of the meeting were reported informally to the board of directors. Just prior to the board meeting I was invited to view the first operational flight of the space shuttle Columbia and its launch of two satellites.

Also, just prior to the board meeting in November of 1982, we were notified by *Inc.* magazine that we had been selected as one of the "500 fastest growing, privately held corporations." This was truly an exciting time for the employees and the board of directors.

In the spring of 1983, we had a visit from Senator Russell Long, the legislative "Father" of ESOP legislation. On April 23rd Senator Long included his observations of the "ComSonics' ESOP" in the Congressional Record.

The State of Kentucky hosted the *Inc.* 500 formal award ceremonies in Lexington, Kentucky, on April 3–6, 1983. Approximately 100 of the "500" were represented at the formal proceedings.

Since the inception of our ESOP, I have been active in the founding organization, both in supporting the concept and serving on the Board of the ESOP Association virtually since its inception. In this year I served as Vice President and keynote speaker at the New Orleans, Louisiana, convention on May 11–14, 1983. The ESOP organization was beginning to develop some muscle thanks to Senator Long's prestigious support.

On June 19, 1983, after completing our expansion of our facility, we had opening ceremonies and a ribbon cutting with our keynote as Senator Paul Trible, with the actual ribbon cutting done by Harrisonburg Mayor, Roy Erickson, and Rockingham County Board of Supervisors Chairman, Glenn D. Heatwole, serving at the opening ceremonies. By this time I recognized that we needed to expand our board of directors membership from the "outside world" preferably from the electronics field. Dr. Louis T. Rader, Professor Emeritus of the Darden Graduate School of Business, of the University of Virginia, then a member of the National Academy of Engineering, was asked to serve on our board of directors. In the past he had also been a senior corporate officer of the Sperry Univac Corporation, IT&T, and General Electric. He remains a faithful and contributing board member to this day. He has provided us exemplary counsel and advice.

I believe the boards of directors need to grow and expand to the needs of the corporation. There is little question that the expansion of our board membership over time had greatly benefitted the corporation in its insight and guidance, which has been gratefully received by me as well as the other executives of the firm.

Fiscal 82/83 gross revenue was $3,829,000. Consulting contribution included in this figure was $101,000 and a net income of $176,000.

FISCAL YEAR 1983/1984

The board members were

Warren L. Braun, President/CEO
Lillian C. Braun, Secretary/Treasurer
Carlton R. Braun, Vice President of Operations
Donald Myers, Trustee Dominion Trust
Dr. Louis T. Rader
George Aldhizer, II, Senior Vice President
John W. Dickie, Vice President of Financial Planning
Donald Suter, Assistant Secretary/Treasurer

Nondirector officers were as follows:

Richard Shimp, Vice President of Advanced Concepts and System Services
Dennis Zimmerman, Vice President of Sales and Marketing
Glen K. Shomo, Vice President of Product Development and Production
Carl H. Hensley, Vice President of Internal Operations
Thomas H. Robinson, Vice President of Finance

In April of 1984 I was invited to lecture to the senior students in the School of Business at James Madison University in addition to a public forum on the topic of "Participatory Management and Ownership." This was a two-day affair.

For several years I had invited the Trustee of our ESOP to be a member of our board, but the rules of the bank would not allow him to join us. This year the rules changed and we were happy to appoint Don Myers, of Dominion Trust Company, to the board.

During this fiscal year we attempted a new accounting system, increasing the "contribution margin" (profit) of each product and activity of the corporation based upon the "strategic business unit accounting system." Although our Vice President of Finance made a heroic effort to establish the concept, it became evident that he did not have a good command of the accounting methodology required for this task. It was eventually decided that he would leave the firm, with replacement recruiting commencing upon his leaving the firm. After culling through over 100 applications, all of whom were well qualified, three candidates appeared better qualified. One individual, Bill McIntyre, stood out above the others, with an excellent academic and experience background, and who had participated in successfully setting up the desired accounting system in another corporation. He was hired.

Gross sales for the year were $4,507,000 with the consulting income contributing $164,000 of that amount. Net profit for fiscal 83/84 was $160,000. At the end of the fiscal year, I set my retirement for fiscal 89/90 at which time I would have appointed a corporate successor making such changes in the top management of the corporation as was appropriate to this end. It was also my intent to sell my remaining personal stock interest to the ESOP Trust prior to my retirement, however, I had not set a date for this action. To select the successor executives, I structured a comprehensive performance analysis system for all executives who wished to compete in the quest for the top position, which analysis critique was confidential to each executive.

FISCAL YEAR 1984/1985

The board members were

Warren L. Braun, President/CEO

Lillian C. Braun, Secretary/Treasurer

Carlton R. Braun, Vice President of Operations

Donald Myers, Trustee Officer

Dr. Louis T. Rader

George Aldhizer, II, Senior Vice President

John W. Dickie, Vice President of Corporate Planning

Donald Suter, Assistant Secretary/Treasurer

Nonboard member officers were as follows:

Richard Shimp, Vice President of Advanced Concepts and System Services

Dennis Zimmerman, Vice President of Sales and Marketing

Mark Barber, Vice President of Repair Services and Corporate Development

On August 26, 1984, Carl Hensley, Vice President of Sales and Internal Operations suffered a fatal heart attack. Dennis Zimmerman was promoted to the position that Carl Hensley had been filling. Although Carl's demise was totally unexpected, the peer circle decision making process facilitated an unusually smooth transition of management roles. The value of participatory management continued to demonstrate its worth. This was also the year in which I decided to sell the remainder of my personal stock, represented by 51.5% of the total corporate shares into the ESOP Trust. This was facilitated by structuring the sale in the form of a leveraged buyout, however, the bank required that I place the proceeds of the loan in escrow for five years. Upon meeting certain terms of corporate growth by 1990, the escrow could be lifted. In early February of 1985 I was interviewed by Connie Chung of NBC News on the "Today Show" to discuss the role of ESOPs generally and our corporation specifically. This was with only one day's notice before the interview.

On January 18, 1985, I gave the commencement address at my alma mater, the Valparaiso Technical Institute. The theme of the address was "We Stand on the Shoulders of Greatness." It was interesting to meet my former instructors who were still living as well as the widow of the dean of the school, Nettie Hershman.

Also this year, I testified before the Senate Finance Committee on the topic of the productivity gains to be made through Employee Stock Ownership.

The most interesting part of the day was a private breakfast with Senator Long and his Legislative Aide, Jeff Gates, during which Senator Long stated that he would not run for reelection since in his words, "the Senate has lost its role as a deliberative body." The pro-ESOP legislation passed the Senate in late 1985.

On April 16, 1985, ComSonics was awarded the prestigious bronze medal for first place in the U.S. Senate productivity competition. This was quite an accolade for the employees and management of the firm.

As the fiscal year closed our good friend, George S. Aldhizer, II, who was our Senior Vice President, passed away after an extended illness. His wise counsel has been sorely missed. With his passing it became necessary to recruit another board member with the appropriate legal background. This individual was located after several months of recruiting, James R. Sipe, the senior partner of the firm Litten, Sipe and Miller. Jim has been a trusted friend, confidant, and advisor for many years, and it was certainly very pleasing to me that Jim accepted the invitation to join our board of directors. At the close of the fiscal year we completed the transaction, transferring my ownership of the corporation to the Trust and completing the acquisition of the consulting firm at the same time.

Gross sales for the year were $5,383,000.00 inclusive of $43,000 of consulting revenue. A net profit of $168,000 was realized on this income stream.

FISCAL YEAR 1985/1986

The board members were

Warren L. Braun, President/CEO
Lillian C. Braun, Secretary/Treasurer
Carlton R. Braun, Vice President of Operations
Donald Myers, Vice President of Capital Funding
Dr. Louis T. Rader, Vice President of New Ventures
G. William McIntyre, Assistant Secretary
John W. Dickie, Vice President of Financial Planning
Dennis Zimmerman, Chairman of the ESOP Advisory Committee

This is the year I announced my retirement, setting the date as July 31, 1990. Since the ESOP Advisory Committee was functioning well, its chairman elected by the committee was asked to serve on the board of directors. In this fiscal year, that individual was Dennis Zimmerman.

We also moved Bill McIntyre into the role of Assistant Secretary/Treasurer, replacing Don Suter. It seemed inappropriate to keep Don in this position on the board while his boss was not privileged to attend the board meetings. For past services to the company and the board by Don Suter, I asked and got board approval for his continued attendance any time he wished.

Continuing our past practice nondirector/nonboard member officers were appointed as follows:

Richard Shimp, Vice President of Field Services

Glen K. Shomo, Vice President of Manufacturing

Mark E. Barber, Vice President of Repair Services and Corporate Development

Donald L. Suter, Controller

In October of 1985 I was asked to chair the National District Export Council meeting. Over 400 participants met in the D.C. area to discuss export marketing. Many useful contacts were made at this meeting.

In February of 1986 I testified before Congress in support of the District Export Council's activity along with two other industry representatives. The Export Council's funding was not diminished as a consequence of the testimony and the committee's decision.

The gross sales for the corporation were $5,797,000 with a net profit of $24,000. Extraordinary legal fees associated with new industrial bond financing, special appraisals and associated activities depressed this fiscal year's profit. There was no separate consulting revenue for this year, since the consulting firm had been acquired in the prior year.

FISCAL YEAR 1986/1987

The board members were

Warren L. Braun, President/CEO

Lillian C. Braun, Secretary/Treasurer

Carlton R. Braun, Vice President of Operations

John W. Dickie, Vice President of Financial Planning

G. William McIntyre, Assistant Secretary/Treasurer

Donald L. Myers, Vice President of Capital Funding

Dr. Louis T. Rader, Vice President of New Ventures

James R. Sipe

Mark E. Barber, Chairman of the ESOP Advisory Committee

Nondirector officers were

Richard Shimp, Vice President of Field Services

Dennis Zimmerman, Vice President of Repair Services

Donald L. Suter, Controller

It was a very busy year selecting finalists/successors from within the company for my position as well as serving as President of the ESOP Association. By the end of the fiscal year two successor candidates remained for my position, Dennis Zimmerman and Mark Barber, both of whom were qualified, but required special training for the new responsibility. On April 1, 1987, my wife and co-worker Lillian Braun resigned her post as Director of Accounts Receivable. She continued as Secretary/Treasurer of the corporation. No few words can ever express my gratitude for her support and help in the operation of the corporation. I am indeed grateful as was the board for her long and hard working contribution to the success of the corporation.

On April 26, 1987, I received an Honorary Doctor of Science Degree from Shenandoah College and Conservatory, based on contributions to the Science and Technology of Communications. (I had been a staff instructor at Shenandoah during the period 1942 through 1945.)

This was the year in which we had a great deal of difficulty in launching the "Window I" project. The manufacturing implementation of this project was so poorly done that we had nearly 50% of the product returned for repair within warranty. It became obvious that some decisive steps would need to be taken so we implemented immediately a program to improve the product, removing the difficulties that were associated with its design. In what became the "Window II" product, new features and a corresponding two year warranty were added to overcome the difficulty associated with the launching of the product as "Window I." Needless to say, this was an expensive effort, which depressed the end of year's sales somewhat and certainly reduced the net profit sharply. The fiscal 86/87 sales were $6,344,000 with a net profit of $100,000.

FISCAL YEAR 1987/1988

The board members were

Warren L. Braun, President /CEO

Lillian C. Braun, Secretary/Treasurer

Carlton R. Braun, Vice President of Operations

John W. Dickie, Vice President of Financial Planning

G. William McIntyre, Assistant Secretary/Treasurer

Donald L. Myers, Trustee and Vice President of Capital Funding

Dr. Louis T. Rader, Vice President of New Ventures

James R. Sipe
Donn Meyerhoeffer, Chairman of the ESOP Advisory Committee

Nondirector officers were

Richard Shimp, Vice President of Field Services
Dennis Zimmerman, Vice President of Sales
Donald L. Suter, Controller

During this fiscal year the concept of nondirector officers was terminated as it interfered with the appropriate actions and control of the board officers.

The process of selecting a successor was completed in this fiscal year, and the successful candidate, Dennis Zimmerman, was exposed to additional specialized training to determine his ability to absorb new concepts and additional responsibility while also serving as the Vice President of Sales.

Tentative selection of a successor was not communicated to the board until after the annual board meeting. Further, the staff was not notified of this change during the fiscal year. The other contender, Mark Barber, was advised that he was not meeting the demands expected of his position and he resigned.

The corporate debt retirement continued on schedule during the year, largely due to the efforts of Bill McIntyre, who carefully scheduled the accounts payable without damaging the prompt payment record of the company. This adroit handling of the corporate finances resulted in greater freedom to fund much needed R&D on the Window II project. By the end of this fiscal year, the major problems of the Window II had been solved.

FISCAL YEAR 1988/1989

The board members were

Warren L. Braun, President/CEO
Lillian C. Braun, Secretary/Treasurer
Carlton R. Braun, Vice President of Operations
John W. Dickie, Vice President of Financial Planning
G. William McIntyre, Assistant Secretary/Treasurer
Donald L. Myers, Vice President of Capital Funding
Dr. Louis T. Rader, Vice President of New Ventures
James R. Sipe
E. Lee Chattin, Chairman of the ESOP Advisory Committee
Dennis Zimmerman, Executive Vice President/Chief Operating Officer

By this fiscal year, Dennis had emerged as my choice as successor, and with my recommendation, he was elected to the position of Executive Vice President and Chief Operating Officer. His performance continued to improve with the responsibility to replace himself with a suitable candidate for the Director of Sales. Also, during the year the Director of R&D resigned to start his own business, and it was necessary to replace him as well. Candidates selected appeared eminently qualified to fill their positions. It also appeared that the personal retirement I had targeted for fiscal 89/90 would be a reality. The year was spent in organizing events for the retirement phase this coming fiscal year.

Our gross sales for the year were $9,637,000 and a net income of $402,700.

FISCAL YEAR 1989/1990

Board membership was as follows:

Warren L. Braun, President/CEO

Lillian C. Braun, Secretary/Treasurer

Carlton R. Braun, Vice President of Operations

John W. Dickie, Vice President of Financial Affairs

G. William McIntyre, Assistant Secretary/Treasurer

Dr. Louis T. Rader, Vice President of New Ventures

James R. Sipe

Jerry Cummings, Chairman of the ESOP Advisory Committee

Dennis Zimmerman, Executive Vice President and COO

Dominion Trust Company, with whom we had our ESOP Trust, again changed its rules and Don Myers resigned from our board. He still attends the Stockholders' Meetings, and we have appreciated his ongoing involvement in that capacity.

This year was spent in active decoupling from the corporation's day-to-day affairs. During the first three months of the fiscal year, I deliberately spent most of my time away from the office, either in pertinent seminars or on planned business trips. In 1990 I reduced my work week even further, concentrating on development of the future plans and opportunities for the corporation. The final quarter of the year, I defined my continuing role with the corporation as chairman, leaving adequate time and space to work on a strategic plan for the future of the corporation. As I leave the active management of the corporation I find many things to be pleased about, particularly the development of the understanding of the employees' role as owners. I am especially proud of the executive team that is in control of the corporation today and I know they will carry it on into the future without any hesitancy or pause in the growth of the company.

SUMMARY

The chronology of the ComSonics' board development does not do justice to the many hours of consultation provided by our individual board members, particularly those falling in the "outside" board member classification.

As early as the first two years of our corporate development this pattern of consulting the board members was firmly established, providing me insight into corporate matters I would not have otherwise been fully aware of. For instance, George Aldhizer gave much wise counsel on the development of the ESOP before it was established and through the process of early implementation. Further, after it was in place, he provided a great deal of insight into the human relations aspect of this major corporate thrust. George's wise counsel often came forward with simple but wise statements, e.g., "don't fix something that is working well," "make sure you really *need* the corporate change," and "keep your corporate payroll as lean as possible at all times so you can manage your cash in tough corporate times." This has been a very excellent lesson learned well during the early corporate years.

After Carlton Braun came on the board he would send books, articles, and periodicals pertinent to operation problems he knew we were experiencing. Fortunately his corporate contacts were such that his experience was directly relevant to our corporate life. His input was much more frequent than the board meetings, as was true of input received from Dr. Rader. Even though he was retired, Dr. Rader was still a very active participant in the engineering/management field also serving as Professor Emeritus of the McIntyre School of Business at the University of Virginia. His almost daily contact with the Business School professors provided us insight into activities we were about to embark on. This kind of special expertise coming from a man of Dr. Rader's stature certainly provided us much needed and very excellent insight into the management of the corporation.

Too many executives managing closely held corporations regard the outside board members as adversaries or potential adversaries. This unfortunately leads to confrontation rather than an expanded horizon for the CEO of the corporation. I have found both our outside and our inside directors' opinions and observations to be particularly helpful in developing the successful corporation we have today. My advice is use your directors as fully and frequently as they are willing to serve. You may be surprised how much easier your task becomes.

Technopaints: A Board in a Crisis Situation

William Q. Judge

INTRODUCTORY COMMENTS

Due to the sensitive nature of the following situation, the case has been disguised so that the readers cannot identify the actual board and company under scrutiny. However, the description of the role of the board in a closely held firm facing an actual crisis is essentially unaltered. Furthermore, the case data are based on actual observations and quotations obtained by the author in conducting another research study of corporate governance.

Part of what makes this case sensitive is that the company in question underwent a very painful transfer of power due to the unexpected death of the CEO. In the process, many employees were dismissed (including the new CEO, who was a member of the family with the controlling interest) and a lot of money was lost. Nevertheless, this case documents how the board belatedly galvanized into an effective and involved decision-making group during a period of adversity.

In the interest of anonymity, the names of the executives and the company have been changed to disguise their actual identities. Furthermore, the location of the firm and its financial performance have also been disguised. For the remainder of the discussion, this firm will be referred to as Technopaints.

TECHNOPAINTS' BACKGROUND

The company develops, manufactures, and markets high-performance coatings worldwide. While these coatings were used in a wide variety of applications, the firm's strongest market was in specialized coatings for nuclear power plants. The distinctive feature of these coatings was their high-temperature and radiation resistance. Using esoteric technologies from chemical and nuclear engineering, the firm specialized in several high-technology niches throughout the world. Due to the very specialized and highly technical nature of the firm's products, most of its customers were other commercial firms.

The company's principal offices are located in New England. It was founded in 1968 by Bill Smith, a chemical engineer trained at M.I.T. In the early 1970s, the firm had sales of only $3 million and a three-member board of directors— all of whom were members of the Smith family. Under Bill Smith's leadership, the company grew gradually through the internal development of new product markets and relatively small acquisitions. According to one executive who was with the company throughout the 1980s, "We were a sleepy little New England company that found a high-technology niche that the big boys didn't want to trouble themselves with. The founder and CEO was a technical wizard and

Table 10.1
Ownership Structure at Technopaints

FAMILY OWNER	1983	1985	1987	1989
Peter W. Smith	26.9%	24.3%	24.7%	24.4%
William C. Smith (Trust)	23.5%	22.0%	9.5%	9.4%
James R. Smith	16.2%	21.0%	5.2%	4.4%
Total family control:	66.6%	67.3%	39.4%	38.2%

respected by all the employees. It was a comfortable, conservatively managed business.''

Although the firm went public in 1983, the Smith family still exercised considerable influence over company affairs. Table 10.1 reveals that family control has been diluted since going public; however, the Smith family still owned a substantial portion (nearly 40%) of the company.

THE DEATH AND SUCCESSION OF THE FOUNDER

Then the event that changed Technopaints' destiny occurred: the very technically skilled and well-respected CEO, Bill Smith, died in a small-plane accident in 1981. According to one outside director, ''Due to his relatively young age (45), little thought or effort had been directed toward succession planning by Bill or the board of directors.''

Since the majority stockholder, Peter Smith, was also the brother of the deceased CEO, the board asked him to manage the succession process. One outside director reasoned, ''Normally, it is the board's responsibility to manage the succession process. However, our situation was unique—the Smith family not only controlled a majority of the stock, but Peter was also a savvy businessman. We felt that he was the one most suited to handle the delicate transfer of power so that both shareholder and family interests were most thoughtfully addressed.''

Peter was a highly successful chief executive of a diversified, high-technology firm in Texas. At first, he was reluctant to take the responsibility due to his already full schedule. However, when the widow of Bill Smith approached him and asked him to help, he stated, ''I couldn't decline; I had to protect the family's financial future by getting involved.''

After reviewing some potential successors, Peter decided that the youngest of the three brothers, Jim Smith, would be the most suitable successor. Jim had minimal business experience and had never worked at Technopaints before, but he had served on the board of directors and he confided to Peter that he would love to assume the responsibility of CEO. Although Jim was a relatively inexperienced manager, the board quickly confirmed his appointment. Jim assured the board that he would emulate his successful brother's style and Peter's backing made his confirmation a quickly determined matter.

According to one outside director, "The board recognized that Jim was not as technically or interpersonally skilled as his two older brothers, but he would have a team of talented and dedicated managers under him. And while the firm was struggling some with the current recession, the balance sheet was strong and signals that the recession would soon end were appearing." As such, the board of directors hoped that he would grow into the job.

However, not all of the employees were pleased with the decision. While nonfamily members working at Technopaints recognized that they would never be CEO because "they did not have the right surname," several of the most respected and experienced managers "doubted that Jim had the will or the ability to manage the firm." Thus, after the succession decision was announced on November 1, 1981, the chief financial officer and chief operating officer, both long-term employees in good standing, resigned from the firm over the next two months. In addition, several other managers questioned the wisdom of the board's decision and began "dusting off and mailing out their résumés."

Unfortunately, the doubters' worst fears materialized over the next few years. According to current and former employees, Jim became more dictatorial and egoistic as the firm grew. A former vice president stated, "Jim became the CEO just as we were beginning to pull out of a pretty severe recession. Although he had little or nothing to do with the company's growth in 1982, he took that as a sign that he had what it takes to lead. He was dead wrong."

Two years after Jim Smith took control, some of the company's problems started to fester. One manager describes it as follows: "Some managers started challenging this guy and he immediately fired them. All they had to do was question the wisdom of his perspective on a matter and they were gone. That started a revolving door in key positions. Three new vice presidents were hired and fired over a period of four years! There was total turmoil in our markets—disarray in our field sales operation, morale was low, service problems were ignored. On top of that, we hired a CFO who was green and his only qualification was that he was enamoured with Jim! On top of not fixing existing problems, he even made matters worse—he completely botched up our financial reporting system. Eventually, some pretty patient customers who had been with us for ten or more years started leaving us."

Although Technopaints was very conservatively managed and possessed a strong balance sheet, the company began gradually developing serious financial problems. Sensing oncoming disaster, one loyal executive director, Carl Largent, talked to the outside directors between board meetings and asked them to challenge the current CEO or remove him. Each one of them listened to Carl, but refused to get involved. According to several directors and Carl, the board chose to not get involved because they thought that "this was primarily a family matter, not an issue for board members.'' They had great respect for the majority stockholder and family leader, Peter Smith, and felt that he would act on the situation when it was appropriate.

Frustrated with the reluctance of the board to act, Largent took a risk and approached Peter Smith directly and tried to convince him of the need for a new CEO. Peter was caught because he saw the firm quickly heading for bankruptcy, but he was reluctant to remove his brother from the CEO's job and he kept hoping for things to turn around. As he ''wrestled with his head and heart,'' the firm's results continued to decline. Eventually, he took an intermediate step by asking a young venture capitalist, whom he respected, to join the board and help get a handle on the firm's financial status.

The new director's name was Don Montaine. In the course of Peter Smith's own business dealings, he had worked with Don and was impressed with his financial acumen and strong interpersonal skills. He met with Don and persuaded him to join the board at Technopaints. Don accepted the challenge as a favor to Peter and as an opportunity to learn about another business.

DON'S FIRST BOARD MEETING

Don joined the board in July of 1985. In that meeting, he learned that the company was in serious financial problem and some drastic actions would be necessary (see Tables 10.2 and 10.3). Despite a strengthening economy and growing market for Technopaints' products, the firm's sales and net income had dropped 10.8% and 195%, respectively, over the previous year. Furthermore, long-term debt had ballooned to 46% of equity and the firm had decreased its working capital by $1.4 million. To make matters worse, no one knew exactly how bad things were and all the new managers were still trying to learn their new jobs. As Don recalled, ''It was quite simply a mess.''

As more and more bad news rolled in over the next two months, Peter Smith eventually was convinced that the firm would go bankrupt if some drastic changes were not made. Regretfully, he approached his brother, Jim, and asked him to step down as chief executive. Jim acquiesced to Peter's request and Peter immediately approached Don to see if he would serve as interim CEO while he conducted a proper search for a new successor. Due to the immediacy of the situation, he gave Don 24 hours to make up his mind.

TURNAROUND EFFORTS

Don accepted the challenge over the telephone the next day. Leaving his wife and children to pack up the house, he flew from the West coast to Technopaints the following day. Recognizing the crisis at hand, he went straight to headquarters before even checking into a hotel.

Montaine was brought in with a mandate to fix things and there were plenty of things to fix. Immediately, he studied its cost and asset structure and decided

Table 10.2
Technopaints' Financial History

	1981	1982	1983	1984	1985	1986
Quick Ratio	0.88	0.79	0.56	0.44	0.32	0.45
Current Ratio	2.23	1.91	1.67	1.32	1.23	1.00
Receivables Turnover	10.52	9.63	8.99	8.42	8.93	4.86
Inventory Turnover	11.78	8.58	7.71	7.60	4.94	4.79
Return on Sales	-2.0%	1.5%	4.1%	5.4%	0.2%	-21.9%
Return on Assets	-3.4%	2.2%	5.8%	6.2%	0.2%	-17.6%
Return on Equity	-5.6%	4.7%	9.6%	15.7%	0.5%	-61.8%
Times Interest Earned	24.7	20.5	21.1	21.8	-1.0	-3.5
Current Debt/Equity	0.01	0.02	0.03	0.04	0.02	0.03
Long Term Debt/Equity	0.05	0.11	0.26	0.48	0.46	1.04
Net Income ($ Millions)	-0.4	0.3	1.1	2.0	0.1	-5.1
Net Sales ($ Millions)	20.00	22.70	27.00	37.10	33.10	23.00
Total Assets ($ Millions)	11.90	13.60	18.90	32.60	32.70	28.80
Employees	220	238	264	365	360	237

that it had to cut back operations and "stop the bleeding." He established an executive committee and it met weekly to discuss the cutbacks. The committee was comprised of himself, Peter Smith, and Carl Largent, the only remaining senior manager who was knowledgeable about the firm and its markets. The mission of this committee was to cut out unnecessary expenses fast without killing the business. Cash was reviewed daily. Extensive work was done to delay payments and speed collections. The executive committee met daily and the full board met weekly during the crisis.

During this period, the executive committee had all the decision-making power. Everyone recognized that the firm's survival was at stake and that action needed to be taken immediately. Thus, all recommendations to the board were ratified immediately over the telephone or in person.

After two weeks into the job, Montaine had cut out nearly one-third of the company's assets in order to remain in business. "It was a difficult job laying off all those people," Don said, "But it had to be done . . . the only alternative was to declare bankruptcy." Reflecting on why the board waited so long, Largent stated: "The Smith family owns 50% (sic) of this company. Most of the other outside directors told me privately that they had to take a different approach to

Table 10.3
Sources and Uses of Funds at Technopaints

	6/30/84	6/30/85	6/30/86
SOURCES:			
Net Income	2,013	67	(5,057)
Depreciation & Depletion	1,049	1,479	1,356
Deferred Income Taxes	135	907	(1,222)
Minority Interest/Subsidiaries	NA	(324)	186
Issue Long Term Debt	6,300	NA	2,700
Sale of Stock	4,452	128	78
Other Sources of Funds	62	NA	NA
TOTAL SOURCES OF FUNDS	14,011	3,721	(1,959)
USES:			
Capital Expenditures	10,336	2,962	699
Decrease Long-Term Debt	696	202	178
Other Uses of Funds	413	557	(13)
TOTAL USES OF FUNDS	11,445	3,721	864
INCR/DEC IN WORKING CAPITAL	2,566	(1,464)	(2,823)

their responsibility since it really is still a family business. I think that that was a mistake, but that was the rationale that they used.''

CHANGES IN THE BOARD'S COMPOSITION

Throughout this ordeal the board's composition changed significantly. Table 10.4 reveals the board's composition in 1983. During that year, the board was comprised of nine members. Compared to other boards in the *Fortune* 500, Technopaints' board was relatively young (average age was 47.2 years old) and the insiders dominated the membership (66.7%). The board had a wide blend of skills ranging from general management, technology, marketing, finance, and legal expertise.

Over the intervening four years, however, the board's composition changed dramatically (see Table 10.5). The board's size shrunk from nine to seven members; Peter Smith became the chairman of the board; all but one of the inside directors left the board; and all but one of the "outside" directors also left the board. (Although Peter Smith is technically an outside director, he is

Table 10.4
Technopaints' Board of Directors in 1983

Name	Age	Position	Background
William Smith	38	Chairman; CEO	Director since 1976; became CEO in 1981
Carl Largent	42	Executive VP	Director since 1977; joined as VP in 1978; was CEO of Furniture Co.
James Englander	49	VP - Technology	Joined in 1978; was R&D manager at DuPont
Paul Handle	33	VP - Finance	Joined firm in 1980; was outside auditor for firm
Edward Enders	50	Vice President	Joined firm in 1968; marketing manager in Europe
James Marshall	59	Vice President	Joined firm in 1979 due to acquisition of his firm
Peter Smith	59	Outside Director	Director since 1976; CEO of high-technology firm
James Spindle	46	Outside Director	Director since 1983; senior VP of large bank
James Wilson	49	Outside Director	Director since 1968; attorney at law

not an independent overseer as the term implies.) In addition, the proportion of inside directors dropped from 66.7% to 28.6% and the CEO no longer held the chairman's position. Although the average age remained at 47 years, this was clearly a very different board.

Because access to the actual participants in this drama was restricted, we can only speculate why the board's composition changed so dramatically over the crisis period. Possible explanations for the high board turnover include burnout due to the higher demands of a turnaround situation, fear of suits due to potential charges of poor business judgment, or plain old guilt over all the hardship created. My best judgment is that the previous board members felt that they were in a situation where they could not operate properly. The members recognized the importance of an involved board and they seemed to have confidence in them-

Table 10.5
Technopaints' Board of Directors in 1987

Name	Age	Position	Background
Don Montaine	38	CEO; President	Director since 1985; was a venture capitalist
Carl Largent	46	COO; Exec. VP	Director since 1977; became COO in 1986
Peter Smith	63	Outside Director; Chairman of Board	Director since 1976; became Chairman in 1985
William Smith	42	Outside Director	Director since 1976; resigned as CEO in 1985
James Spindle	50	Outside Director	Director since 1983; senior VP of large bank.
Sherry Worrell	49	Outside Director	Director since 1984; professor at M.I.T.
Roger Calender	42	Outside Director	Director since 1984; CEO of high-tech. firm

selves; however, the dominating influence of the Smith family precluded effective action because it was not politically feasible.

If this speculation is correct, then effective board composition must be much more than insider/outsider considerations or judgments about the balance of skills and experiences of prospective board members. Rather, effective boards are composed of people who are committed to the organization's survival and mission. Furthermore, effective board members have the courage to act in politically delicate situations. Clearly, these qualities are much more subtle than traditional considerations about boards such as functional expertise.

EPILOGUE

Using Montaine's metaphor, the harsh medicine worked and the patient survived. In 1986, the firm's slide continued, but in 1987 the financial situation stabilized, and in 1988, the firm started to grow and actually strengthen. Due to Don Montaine's quick and successful actions, Peter Smith asked him to stay on as chief executive and Don accepted.

In 1988, Don reflected on his strategic leadership, "Over the past two years, the company has largely been putting out fires. Its time horizon has been monthly and sometimes even weekly in length. It is largely an informal process. It would have been inappropriate to look long-term. You have to get out of the hospital before you go to work." As the company has worked its way out of its difficulties, Don anticipated installing a more formal and long-term planning system. However, he added, "We always expect a dynamic environment so we don't want to be married to a myopic direction."

Regarding the future role of the board, Montaine stated, "We have an excellent board of directors now and clearly they must have more input in strategic decisions than they did during our crisis period, but I'm not exactly sure how much they can get involved because the outsiders don't know as much about the firm and the industry as management does. Board involvement in strategy is a complex issue that has no simple answers or clear guidelines."

COMMENT ON THE BOARD'S ROLE

Picking up where Don Montaine left off, there are no simple answers or clear guidelines for board involvement in strategic decision making. However, what is clear is that the board at Technopaints is an example of what not to do in a crisis situation.

Clearly, the passive board described in this case is not uncommon and, in fact, may be appropriate for many well-managed firms. However, Technopaints was clearly not being well-managed after Jim Smith's untimely death and the deferral of responsibility to Peter Smith was an abdication of responsibility, in the opinion of this author.

One of the greatest virtues of a strategically active board is objectivity. Even if the CEO has a consensual style and a capable group of top managers, the board still needs to be informed of the firm's direction and constantly evaluating the top management team, especially the CEO. In this situation, the board repeatedly refused to acknowledge what was going on or hold top management accountable. Only when the firm was close to bankruptcy did one of the board members, Peter Smith, reluctantly act. And in retrospect, Peter indicated that his "only regret was that he did not act sooner."

Strategic management can be thought of as a learning process. Learning can be conceived as a process whereby dysfunctional habits are broken and replaced with more functional behaviors. In this context, the board can be viewed as a group of individuals responsible for the learning process so that the multiple constituencies of the firm (e.g., stockholders, employees, customers, and society in general) are best served.

At Technopaints, some formerly functional habits (i.e., passive governance) became dysfunctional when conditions changed (e.g., Bill Smith's death, Jim

Smith's lack of experience/talent, and a worldwide recession). From this stand-point, the board failed to unlearn previous habits and that failure cost many employees their jobs and nearly bankrupted the firm.

Although there is no model board for all occasions, the trend is clearly for greater board involvement across all industries. This trend is caused mainly by legal action by stakeholders of the firm (especially shareholders), but some exceptional firms have proactively recognized the importance of an involved board and have made their boards a more informed and active participants in the strategic decision-making process. My research in this area indicates that the most involved boards appear to be in industries where the industry norms em-phasize the pursuit of multiple goals, such as in nonprofit hospitals (e.g., prof-itability and patient care) and in new, biotechnology firms (e.g., fast-growth, new technologies, and flexible working condictions for highly skilled employees).

Therefore, despite the information asymmetry between management and out-side directors, the board has a fundamental and growing responsibility to become more active and involved in the major strategic decisions of the firm. Further-more, they must learn to recognize the limits of their knowledge and know when to defer to management and when to challenge management. Boards of the future may ''learn'' to do this reactively, or they may choose to proactively develop these habits before a crisis is at hand.

TDIndustries: Corporate Governance

Joseph Rosenstein

"As a legal right, the Board of Directors has the authority to do anything it chooses in directing the affairs of the corporation provided, of course, the Board stays within the law. In the past, however, the Board has chosen a relatively inactive role. We recommend that, under normal conditions, the TD Board should stay relatively inactive. It would have one transcendent power—the power to hire, fire and set compensation of the CEO and other officers. Otherwise, we suggest that the Board normally be expected to fulfill only those formal responsibilities that are required by law, plus major decisions that are brought to the Board for official approval."

This paragraph comes from a statement representing the consensus of 82 employee-owners of Texas Distributors, Inc. (now TDIndustries, Inc.) in 1980 and still reflects accurately the function of the board in this company. The role of the board in TDIndustries under Jack Lowe, Sr., during its period of rapid growth and prosperity, and under his successor, Jack Lowe, Jr., during a time when prosperity was followed by adversity, is particularly interesting because the company is employee-owned. Indeed, the situation which occasioned the drafting of this paragraph and the formal document from which it comes followed the granting of full voting rights to stock which, over a period of years, had been issued to a very high percentage of employees under an employee stock ownership plan.

The size and composition of the board has changed over the years—from a three person, family type board in the early years to the current insider board of eight (more information on size and composition at several key points in the firm's history is provided in Table 10.6). Throughout all its history, however, the board has met infrequently, generally only once a year and at its meetings has formally ratified decisions already reached. The role and function of the board in TDIndustries must, therefore, be explained in the context of the firm's history and its processes of decision making and governance. The case will first present the important elements in the history and development of the firm. Next will come an analysis of governance and decision making, with attention to some of the issues related to the firm's employee ownership plans; because of the minimal functions assumed by the board, it is necessary to understand how major decisions have been, and are being, made outside the board framework. Finally, we will focus on a few of the major problems and issues of governance confronting a company that has had this kind of insider, inactive board.

THE FOUNDER: TEXAS DISTRIBUTORS UNDER
JACK LOWE, SR.

Jack Lowe, Sr., who founded Texas Distributors and was its chief executive until his death in 1980, returned to Dallas in 1946 after receiving his discharge

Table 10.6
Board Size and Composition at Key Points in the Company History

Year	Event	Board Size	Composition
1946	Company Founded	3	CEO+2 Family Mentors
1954	Serious illness of CEO	5	CEO+3 Vice Presidents + 2 "outsiders"
1979	Voting rights granted	13	CEO+10 other officers + 1 retired officer + 1 "outsider"
1989	Termination of pension plan; change to ESOP	8	CEO + other officers + 1 retired officer

from the Army. Before his wartime service, he had been an engineer in the Air Conditioning Department of General Electric, one of the pioneering firms in climate control. He wanted to start a business of his own and, in view of the promising growth prospects in air conditioning and his own experience in that field, chose air conditioning as the field for the new firm. In the beginning, it was financed by funds of his own and money provided by his mother and aunt. Although called Texas Distributors, the company for about a year had no equipment to distribute, not having yet established an arrangement with a supplier; its first activities were confined to repair work. About a year after founding, the company signed on as a distributor for the Worthington Corporation. With the help of additional money from family, friends, and employees (who bought nonvoting stock), the new company was well on its way. Becoming the North Texas distributor for General Electric in 1950 was a major step forward, and by that time Jack Lowe had assembled a talented and dedicated group of associates.

The company was growing and prospering in the early 1950s, but beginning in 1954 a serious illness suffered by Jack Lowe threatened the viability of the firm. The diagnosis was tuberculosis, and the treatment involved very extended isolation and rest, with only minimal contact with the business, and included surgery. One of the results of this long period of illness and isolation was a kind of spiritual transformation which in later years would make him one of the most courageous civic leaders in Dallas. This experience was not a conversion (he already had a definite religious interest and affiliation) but rather an impetus that led him to act out his faith in various forms of civic leadership. He went on to play a prominent role in the Greater Dallas Community of Churches, in the Citizens Council (a business establishment group that reputedly "ran" Dallas and was instrumental in the handling of a transition toward racial integration in the city), and in the Dallas Alliance (which shepherded the desegregation of Dallas schools). In the later portion of this case, which deals with governance and decision making, we shall see that this strong spiritual orientation also had a profound effect within the firm he founded.

In 1956, after a year in which Texas Distributors recorded a loss (this was during the time of the illness and also at a time when GE equipment developed very serious quality problems), the company resumed its pattern of rapid growth and prosperity. The expanding population of North Texas, especially Dallas, and growing dependence on air conditioning (in a climate where it came to be regarded almost as a necessity), fueled the growth of Texas Distributors. The strains of financing that growth led in 1956 to a special arrangement with General Electric. That company provided $200,000, in return for which it took out some preferred stock in Texas Distributors on a temporary basis. Although profitable operations made it possible to retire that obligation, Jack Lowe looked for a new source of funds for expansion that would avoid dependence on outside sources. The solution was to transform what had been a conventional employee profit-sharing plan into a new plan. The new PS-S-SP (Profit Sharing-Stock-Savings Plan) was a pioneering approach toward giving employees a financial stake in their company and was a particularly bold step for a company to take in the late 1950s. Under the plan, employees were encouraged to set aside 3%, 4%, or 5% of their pay for purchase of stock, with their contributions to the pool being augmented by company contributions set as a high percentage of pretax profits. Each year the employee payments and the tax-sheltered company contributions were used to purchase newly issued stock, a process that was an important source of funds for company growth. At this time, the stock issued to employees did not carry any voting rights.

The year 1957 also marked a significant turning point in the business of the company. That was the year when Texas Distributors became a subcontractor of Trammell Crow's huge Dallas Furniture Mart. Trammell Crow, already one of the leading builder-developers in Dallas and later to become one of the top builders in the United States (Sobel, 1988) had known Jack Lowe since 1948 and had used Texas Distributors as subcontractor for his HVAC (Heating, Ventilating, and Air Conditioning) requirements. The Furniture Mart was far larger than any of Crow's earlier projects and strained his own financial resources and those of Texas Distributors as well. Texas Distributors' gamble in participating in this large project cemented the company's relationship with Crow and also marked a significant shift from earlier reliance on distributing air conditioning equipment to dealers (the "Wholesale" part of the business) toward an increasing emphasis on design and installation of HVAC systems in large-scale projects (the "Contract" part of the business).

Texas Distributors' ties with Crow led to the development of another important part of the company's business, installation of HVAC and plumbing in large apartment projects. At that time, Crow was a partner in RCLP (Rockefeller, Crow, Lyle, Pogue), which was an in-house entity of Lincoln Property Co., a very large apartment developer, and which did the HVAC, plumbing, and electrical work for Lincoln. Texas Distributors was asked to take over the HVAC and plumbing business of RCLP; this entity was renamed Tempo and ultimately was owned outright by Texas Distributors. Tempo proceeded to take on this same kind of work also for projects where Crow and his associates were not involved.

By 1968, the first year for which figures broken down by division are available, total revenues had grown to $9 million, of which only $2.7 million (about 30%) were from Wholesale, with the balance coming mostly from Contract and Tempo. In the 1970s, all of the divisions of the company grew. The decade was marked by strong economic development of the North Texas area, especially Dallas–Fort Worth; population for that SMSA (Standard Metropolitan Statistical Area) increased from 2,377,623 in 1970 to 2,974,805 in 1980.

Construction activity was especially high in large office and commercial buildings and in multifamily residential construction. With its Tempo division, Texas Distributors was well positioned to participate in the multifamily market, achieving a 24% market share in Dallas. In the Contract Division (now renamed TDMechanical), the company had several strengths, which became more evident with changes in the Dallas market. TDMechanical concentrated on very large HVAC and plumbing jobs. The company was nonunion; although Dallas unions were never as powerful as in most other major cities, they had a preferred position in some large-scale projects, especially tall buildings in the downtown area. Texas Distributors had been excluded from direct participation in actual construction work on such buildings, although obtaining some work for providing design, engineering, and supervision (but not actual construction work with the company's own labor force). By the end of the 1970s, the barriers to use of nonunion labor on tall buildings in Dallas had been greatly reduced, permitting the company to participate more fully in this fast growing sector of the Dallas construction market. Total Texas Distributor sales in this decade increased from $10,565,000 in 1970 to $56,160,000 in 1980. Of that 1980 total, only about half was in the original Wholesale and Service segments. Profits had increased from $84,000 in 1970 to $963,000 in 1980.

1980 was the year that I became acquainted with Jack Lowe, Sr. I met with him several times to explore doing a research project within the company to evaluate the effects of employee ownership. He was most gracious and open, and quickly gave the green light to proceed with the research. Along with Larry French, a colleague from the University of Texas at Arlington, I undertook a large-scale study that involved interviews with a substantial number of Texas Distributor employees, followed by a questionnaire survey that in time resulted in several articles on employee ownership in academic journals (French and Rosenstein, 1984; Rosenstein and French, 1985; Rosenstein, 1987). This direct experience gave us a first-hand "feel" for the company's culture. It was marked by an unusually high degree of trust between top management and others in the company, by openness in communication, and by a very high esprit de corps. Much of what we witnessed seemed attributable to the personal qualities, ethical values, and business philosophy of the founder. It was therefore a shock to us, as well as to the Texas Distributor employees, when Jack Lowe died unexpectedly of heart failure on Thanksgiving Day, 1980.

THE SUCCESSOR: YEARS OF PROSPERITY AND ADVERSITY UNDER JACK LOWE, JR.

Jack Lowe, Jr., who followed his father as CEO, had a strong background and training for this position. Like his father, he held an engineering degree from Rice, a fine Texas school. Since joining Texas Distributors in 1964, he had worked in all of the divisions of the company; he had, in turn, been in charge of Tempo, the Wholesale, the Contract (later TDMechanical), and the Service divisions. In several of these, he had taken action to reverse short-term losses or improve operating results. He was sympathetic with, and shared, his father's values regarding the company's leadership style, culture, and philosophy. Although there was no formal succession plan, he was the expected and logical successor to his father.

The first three years under the new CEO were years of continued growth and prosperity. Sales increased from $56 million in 1980 to $115 million in 1983. Net income increased by 57% in the same period. In 1982, the company name was changed from Texas Distributors to TDIndustries, recognizing that distribution was no longer the major activity of the firm. During this period, the company also expanded into construction work outside the North Texas area, undertaking major projects in other large Texas cities and also outside the state.

Beginning in 1984, TDIndustries started to encounter a series of problems. Many of these were related to the decline, and later the collapse, of the Texas real estate market, a phenomenon that by the late 1980s was to capture national attention. As early as 1984, one of TDIndustries' main competitors fell into bankruptcy, but not before demoralizing pricing levels in the industry. Declining profit margins on bids brought into focus the weaknesses of some of the company's control systems in estimating and construction. Movement into the Houston market proved to be very poorly timed, almost coinciding with the real estate "bust" in that city, which was the first to bear the brunt of what later became a statewide collapse in construction activity. The company also suffered from a problem of another kind: General Electric, the company's basic equipment supplier since 1950, sold that business to Trane (later acquired by American Standard). This new relationship was not working out well for either party, so in 1984 TDIndustries shifted to a relatively new company, Snyder General. That changeover did not go smoothly.

In the same year, serious problems with the employee stock ownership plan surfaced and affected the overall financial situation of the company. This plan—called the PS-S-SP (Profit Sharing-Stock-Savings Plan)—was based on voluntary decisions of employees to participate by contributing 3%, 4%, or 5% of their earnings; the company in turn contributed a high percentage of pretax earnings, making participation very attractive to employees during the extended period of prosperity of the firm. The value of the stock, computed by a formula related to earnings over a five-year period, rose from $15.84 in 1980 to $36.45 in 1984. In these favorable circumstances, a very high percentage of employees—usually above 85%—signed up to participate as soon as eligible. A severe drop in profits in 1985 cut back the company contribution and diminished the attractiveness of the plan. At about the same time, a number of long-time employees with heavy shareholdings were ready to retire and cash in their holdings. Also, in 1985 company contributions to the PS-S-SP for the first time fell below employee contributions. These developments led to requests to sell stock back to the company in very high amounts. These requests, if fully met, would have exceeded the company's ability to buy without impairment of capital and violation of Texas statutes. (The extent of these redemptions at this time and in later years, together with other information on the PS-S-SP, is shown in Table 10.7.) Under these very adverse circumstances, Jack Lowe, Jr., spearheaded a plan that in effect rationed the stock buybacks and offered employees the opportunity to participate in the plan beyond the 5% level. The response was surprisingly favorable: out of 740 employees in the plan, 284 (38%) moved to the new maximum of 7%.

The last half of the 1980s was a period of retrenchment. The Distribution business, the heart of the company in its early years, was sold in 1988. The major buildings occupied by the company were sold or placed on the market. Strenuous efforts were made in a number of other ways to protect the financial soundness of the business. Despite all of these steps, 1989 proved to be a near disaster. With the collapse of large construction activity in Texas, TDIndustries, especially the TDMechanical Division, had taken on a large percentage of its contract volume outside the state—for example, in Georgia, North Carolina, and Virginia. The company had also bid low on complex projects outside its area of experience and expertise. The result of taking on this kind of work, some of it based on poor estimating, was a heavy loss in the TDMechanical Division. The year 1989 was marked by extensive use of ill-qualified temporary help, high overtime, and other problems which led to cost overruns and heavy losses. As the year ended, the company took corrective action by (1) reducing its volume and focusing on simpler buildings with less geographic dispersion, (2) improving

Table 10.7
Contributions, Redemptions, and Price per Share: PS-S-SP, 1985–89 (All Figures in $000 Except Price per Share)

Year	Employee	Company	Bought Back	Price per Share
1985	$912	$520	$4,462	$38.55
1986	948	415	2,428	34.05
1987	770	142	2,036	32.73
1988	774	173	868	34.53
1989	377	0	881	19.22

the estimating and the prejob planning procedures, and (3) increasing management at job sites and providing training in management systems to control costs.

These operating steps alone were not considered sufficient to assure the survival of the company. With the pension fund overfunded by about $1,100,000, the company decided to terminate the pension plan completely and distribute the money due to the employees; this step permitted the company to take prompt advantage of the overfunding and provided the company with over $1 million.

Further, at about the same time the company took two steps on the PS-S-SP (the employee stock ownership program). First, it changed the formula used to compute the share price of stock bought back from employees, thereby reducing at least for a while the cash drain caused by redemptions. Second, the company announced that contributions to the PS-S-SP by employees and the company would be halted at the end of the year. To replace the PS-S-SP, the company set up an ESOP (a conventional Employee Stock Ownership Plan), a form utilized rather broadly in the United States (Rosen, Klein, and Young, 1985; U.S. General Accounting Office, 1987). At this point, employees were strongly encouraged to take part of the money received from the pension plan liquidation and invest it in the ESOP. The response was amazingly positive; the employees invested $1,118,000, roughly one-quarter of the pension plan money they had received. When the company used this money from the ESOP to purchase stock held by the company, that amount was added to the cash available for operations. In 1990 and later years, the company is committed to contribute 20% of its pretax operating income to the ESOP, and the plan permits employees to contribute up to 10% of their annual compensation, up to a rather modest dollar limit, in order to share in the benefits of the ESOP.

At midyear 1990, Jack Lowe, Jr., is optimistic that the drastic, and sometimes dramatic, steps taken in the final years of the 1980s will have served to protect the future of TDIndustries and put it back on the path to good profitability. With indications that Texas construction activity shows signs of revival, this optimism may receive further support.

GOVERNANCE AT TEXAS INDUSTRIES: 1946–1980

Having looked at the company's history in terms of significant events and developments under two CEOs, we are ready now to analyze the context of corporate governance within which the CEOs have operated. The paragraph quoted at the head of this case study clearly indicates that the board of directors has played a rather minimal role. Under these circumstances, what have been the significant decision-making groups and processes?

For the earliest years of the company, it is difficult to find much material to answer that question. The funds to start the company came from the savings of Jack Lowe, Sr., and his wife and from his mother and aunt, who served with him on the first board of directors. From his associates during his time with General Electric's Air Conditioning Division and from other sources, he soon assembled a small but talented group of fellow managers. There are indications that, even in these early years, Jack Lowe, Sr., approached major decisions on the basis of consensus building within the firm. That approach became more conscious and deliberate as the company grew and is clearly articulated in a 1980 company document which will be analyzed later.

In the company's first ten years, the board of directors included "outsiders" (nonmanagement members)—first, two older family members; later, friends and business acquaintances of Jack Lowe, Sr., who invested money and sometimes offered advice and "contacts." It was one of these who introduced him to Trammell Crow, whom we have seen was by far the company's most important customer. As the circle of stockholders widened, including stock sales to other employees, Jack Lowe began to take the precaution of issuing nonvoting, rather than voting, stock.

By 1954, when his serious illness began, the board included Jack Lowe himself, his three vice presidents, and two outside directors. The year or more of Lowe's illness in the mid–1950s was the first big test of corporate governance. With the CEO seriously ill, isolated, and under instructions to distance himself from the business, the three vice presidents took on a large role in decision making. With minimal guidance, they made some major decisions and dealt with a significant crisis—serious mechanical failures in the General Electric equipment for which the company was a distributor. The Board as such in this period remained relatively inactive, meeting only once a year and meeting only the statutory requirements.

Jack Lowe, Sr.'s spiritual experience during his illness had effects that greatly affected his approach to life and business. His wife put it this way: " . . . it did make him think and reevaluate, and money, for one, became a very minor thing" (Cheshire, 1987, p. 63). In his account of these years, Cheshire comments: "In terms of the business he had founded, it meant that he began to look at Texas Distributors less as an instrument for the production of wealth than a device that could create well-being for the growing number of people who were part of it" (1987, p. 63).

In 1958, a decision that ultimately had important implications for governance was made—the decision to set up the PS-S-SP (Profit Sharing-Saving-Stock Purchase Plan), which encouraged employees to commit a percentage of their pay to purchase company stock under a plan which called for a generous share of company profits to the PS-S-SP. This replaced a conventional profit-sharing plan set up in the firm's first year. Lowe's motives for setting up this new plan were mixed—it provided a new and important source of capital funds but it also reflected his concern that employees should share not only in the current profits but also in the future prosperity of the firm, with a real stake in the success of the business.

Stock issued under the 1958 plan was nonvoting. As the years passed, Lowe's doubts about the wisdom of this feature increased. Although some technical–legal questions existed, his basic concern was that, in not providing voting rights to employees' stock, there was a serious contradiction to the fostering of confidence and trusting relationships between a leader and his followers. He had developed a philosophy close to that of Robert Greenleaf, whose book *Servant as Leader* was widely circulated among management in the company because of its congruence with the company's culture. In 1978, the contradiction was resolved, and the stock in the PS-S-SP was given voting rights, to begin in 1979.

That decision occasioned a far-reaching internal discussion on corporate governance and on the composition and function of the board of directors. In November 1979, Jack Lowe initiated the dialogue with a memorandum to his sixteen Senior Managers. It began:

My sense . . . is that most major decisions have evolved as a consensus of those who are best able to comprehend them and deal with them. Some of these consensus groups . . . have been very broad. A clear example was the original decision to change from a cash profit sharing plan to the PS-S-SP . . . other major decisions have evolved from very broad consensus groups involving up to hundreds. This happens, I believe, through innumerable conversations between individuals and within groups. . . . On the other hand, some consensus groups have probably been as small as two people—possibly what we now know as the Executive Committee being the most common. The most noticeable group that has been very handy as a consensus group is our Senior Managers group. . . .

I started by saying I believe most major decisions have been made by consensus. At the other end of the spectrum, I can remember some that I think were made by me without a consensus.

As I project ahead, given the extraordinary and unique character of TD, I believe the most effective and safest decision-making process for TD in the future is one modeled after and refined from the process that has worked for us in the past.

That part of the memorandum ended with a strong plea for continuing with a strong, capable, consensus-minded CEO. The memorandum went on to discuss the company's board of directors in terms of its traditional composition (largely insiders from top management) and limited activities (largely confined to complying with statutory requirements) and concluded that no real changes in the board should be made. The responses were generally in agreement. Jack Lowe, Jr., however, raised the issue of adding some nontraditional employee board members and presented some arguments both pro and con. He also proposed:

In the future, we should involve our middle managers/long term employees, as an identifiable group, more in this consensus process. We should also spend some effort in helping more people understand this process, that the process is working, and that they are really a part of this process.

In May 1980, based on a memorandum from the two Lowes, the senior managers looked at the arguments for and against including nontraditional board members and concluded: "It seems to be current consensus that outside directors will not be appropriate for our Board of Directors in the foreseeable future." Following the suggestion in Jack Lowe, Jr.'s memorandum as quoted before, a decision was made that a draft, based on Jack Lowe, Sr.'s original memorandum, would be submitted to a group of managers and long term employees to be convened for this discussion. Of the 130 invited, 82 attended. The group in effect ratified the consensus previously reached by the Senior Managers (later known as the Planning Committee). Some pertinent passages from the eight-page document are quoted in what follows. The document concluded with a recommendation that a similar group be convened from time to time to consider important matters.

The Board of Directors at Texas Distributors

(Excerpts from a 1980 Company Document)

If things are working well, the Board will usually be considering and approving decisions that have already been carefully studied and formulated somewhere on the spectrum between consensus and CEO—with heaviest weighting toward consensus. Yet, we must emphasize that the Board is the ultimate authority in the major decisions of the corporation and it does indeed have the power to disapprove or change any decision. It is a powerful entity.

The level of authority above the Board is the shareholders as a group. Authority is exercised over the Board by a vote of the shareholders who hold a majority of the stock. To carry out that authority, the shareholders could replace the Board with a new Board composed entirely or partly of new members. The new Board could then change some decisions or make new and different ones.

As long as things are going well, it doesn't make too much difference who is on the Board. But we will certainly face times of trial and, perhaps, peril in the future. In those times, our Board's composition could be crucial.

There are two main questions concerning the composition of the Board.

1. Who should be on the Board?
2. How should these people be selected?

In the past, the current Board has always nominated its successors and our tradition has been to choose members from among the company's officers adding one or two "outsiders" who were close to the company. The current outsiders are Ed Rose, our insurance agent and a longtime TD shareholder, and Art Durbin, retired Senior Vice President. Ed represents a tradition that we do not see being repeated. Because of TD's unique character and the normally inactive role we expect the Board to take, we do not generally envision "outside" directors in the future. One exception to that might be a retired employee who would be very valuable on the Board. Art Durbin is an example of that on our present Board. The central issue now is whether or not we should elect some non-traditional Board members.

It seems in keeping with the character of Texas Distributors and our philosophy of openness and involvement at all levels, to have a few nonofficer employee shareholders on our Board of Directors. In addition, it could help to generate trust between employees (especially new employees) and the company. That trust will be harder to get as we grow larger. A nontraditional Board member might have different perspectives on important company issues and input that would be healthy. Employees might also give comments to a nontraditional member that they would not make to an officer of the company.

There are some negatives to the idea. Since the role of the Board is normally official approval of decisions already formulated, adding nontraditional members to the Board could be perceived as tokenism. It might inappropriately put these nontraditional members in uncomfortable positions when they are asked to "endorse" or at least "go along with" major decisions in which they may not have been a part of the consensus in arriving at a decision.

The strongest negative argument was the concern that the nontraditional members would be thought of as especially representing the interest of the employees in general. This might imply that the officer Board members have abdicated or should abdicate their responsibility for representing the needs and desires of all employees. Even if this happened subconsciously, it would drastically change the character of our company since all Directors have the full responsibility of concern for the interests of all employees and shareholders.

In addition, the appropriateness of having nontraditional Board members is compromised by the difficulty in finding an effective method for selecting such members. The employees could nominate nonofficer members to the Board. That, however, opens wide the door of "politics" which we believe seriously endangers our company. We could negate the political effects by allowing the current Board to select both the traditional and nontraditional members. But, it is possible that nonofficer Board members nominated by the past Board could be perceived as "pawns." If so, the possible advantages would be nullified—and, in fact, we would be worse off than if the system had not been initiated.

At this time, having nontraditional members on the Board of Directors does not seem like an effective way to get more employee input in the decision-making process. Our consensus decision was to leave things pretty much as they are. The current Board will function as it has in the past and will nominate its successors in a traditional manner.

GOVERNANCE AT TDINDUSTRIES: 1980–1990

A few months after the document on decision making was put in its final form, Jack Lowe, Sr., died, and his son became the CEO. The board under his leadership has continued with the same composition and the same minimal functions all through the varied conditions of prosperity and adversity described earlier.

The group of 130 invited to consider the 1980 statement on decision making and the board has not met frequently. In a ten year period, it has met only about six times, notably during the 1984 crisis on restructuring the PS-S-SP and the 1988–89 decisions to terminate the pension plan and substitute a conventional ESOP for the PS-S-SP.

The Planning Committee group to which Jack Lowe, Sr., ascribed an important role in the decision-making process added a few members and continued to meet monthly until early 1989. During the period of most severe adversity, it fell into disuse but recently has resumed meeting on a schedule of twice each quarter.

Responsibility for considering major alternatives and making important decisions has rested primarily with a group of four—Jack Lowe, Jr., as the leader; Tommie Pierce, the long-time Chief Financial Officer, who was given the title of President several years before his retirement; Ben Houston and Bob Ferguson, heads of TDMechanical and Tempo Mechanical, respectively. After Tommie Pierce's retirement very early in 1990, his place was taken by Mike Fitzpatrick, the Chief Financial Officer, who was employed in 1984. As contrasted with the others, all of whom had been with TDIndustries for decades, he was a newcomer who brought with him a fresh point of view and some new approaches to dealing with the company's financial problems when the crunch became severe; his inclusion in this basic decision-making group, resisted at first, is now regarded as having been quite helpful. During the very troubled period of 1989, this group met frequently, often weekly. Basic decisions—such as the sale of the Distribution business, sale of real estate, changes in control and management systems, termination of the pension plan, the change to a conventional ESOP—were initiated in this small group.

All four of the men were on the board of directors and indeed constituted the executive committee of the board. However, the meetings of the board's executive committee were held only four times a year, and the decision-making sessions just described were not viewed in a board context. The board itself continued to meet only once a year and in effect only satisfied the statutory requirements.

The tradition of consensus, so strongly emphasized by Jack Lowe, Sr., was not discarded. Considerable attention was still given to communication with employees, and Jack Lowe, Jr., devoted a great deal of time and energy to meeting with employees from time to time in relatively small groups, even at locations distant from Dallas headquarters. This was done particularly at critical junctures, such as the alteration of the PS-S-SP, the termination of the pension plan, and the launching of the conventional ESOP. The efficacy of such meetings is evidenced by the additional commitments to the PS-S-SP in 1985, even at a time when the plan was in trouble because of high redemption requests from retiring employees and also by the fact that employees were willing to invest about one-fourth of the proceeds from the pension plan termination to the newly established ESOP. In connection with the latter, Jack Lowe, Jr., exercised a strong element of persuasion and leadership to induce commitments from all members of the planning committee; they were told that their participation was vital to their continued employment and to the survival of the company. However, there was also a good response from employees not in that category.

One new group came into existence in 1990. This group of 75 or so, including midlevel managers, meets once a quarter. The meetings begin with smaller numbers, broken down by divisional or profit-center categories, to be followed by a meeting of the entire group of 75. The primary purpose is business and financial review and revision of budget targets, thereby touching on decision making. This focus is consistent with the tighter systems of management control instituted in 1989. It also reflects the influence of consultants. Consultants have been used by the company from time to time in the past, but more broadly in recent years.

As the decade of the 1990s began, Jack Lowe, Jr., seemed generally satisfied with the system of governance at TDIndustries, though not unaware of some of the issues and problems that system may face in the future.

CORPORATE GOVERNANCE AT TDINDUSTRIES: THREE ISSUES

The board at TDIndustries includes only members of upper management, meets infrequently to take care of business matters in accordance with statutory requirements, and on problems involving basic policy or strategic decisions has merely ratified management decisions.

Under these circumstances, three pertinent issues may be raised:

1. How adequately does the board represent the interest of the stockholders?
2. Does the lack of "outsiders" on the board impair its effectiveness because diversity of expertise and points of view is lacking?
3. With a board of this kind, how will the problem of CEO succession be handled?

Guarding the Interests of Stockholders

With the development of the American corporation, particularly large enterprises, there has been rising public concern about the separation of management from ownership; the work of Berle and Means (1932) sounded an early warning. In the 1970s, when the Penn-Central debacle and similar financial disasters occurred, there was widespread criticism of management-dominated boards of directors that failed as guardians of stockholder interests. As a result, in large corporations there was a major move toward expanded use of "outsiders" as board members and toward the use of board committees (like audit) consisting of outside directors. Management dominance of the board, either by use of too many insiders or through CEO dominance of the selection process, was viewed as potentially undesirable (Mace, 1986). Some economists, who viewed the problems in terms of "agency" theory (Fama, 1980), pointed to the divergence of interest of stockholders as compared with management, and looked to the board of directors as arbiters responsible for safeguarding stockholder interests (Kosnik, 1987).

In this context, what can be said of the board at TDIndustries? First, the separation between ownership and management is much less than in those corporations, which led to the concerns of Berle and Means and of the agency theorists. Officers of the company owned about 29% of the company stock in 1990; if the ownership and life interest of Mrs. Jack Lowe, Sr., are included, the percentage would rise to 38%. Further, there is no evidence of the unduly high compensation, unreasonable "perks," or other phenomena which concern agency theorists.

Consideration must be given, however, to the fact that TDIndustries is virtually 100% employee-owned (again, including the holding of Mrs. Lowe, Sr.), with stockholding broadly dispersed among employees at all levels (French and Rosenstein, 1984). To what extent can the board be judged as adequately safeguarding the interests of stockholders other than upper management? Two factors seem pertinent, based on experience to date. First, the original CEO and his successor have both exhibited a keen sense of stewardship that appears to be shared by the other insider board members. Second, and perhaps more pointedly, the employees have demonstrated strong confidence in top management by their high degree of voluntary participation in the PS-S-SP over a long period of time and even under adverse circumstances in the crises of the late 1980s. During the last of these crises, many employees made commitments of substantial money from the pension-plan distribution to purchase stock under the ESOP. In this respect, the situation at TDIndustries differs from most conventional ESOPs, where the funds for stock purchases are not tied into voluntary employee participation.

The issue of having several nontraditional (nonofficer) board members to represent the rank and file employee stockholders was carefully considered in 1980, as described in the lengthy extract earlier. In the absence of a union, which might be able to lay formal claim to representation of some of the employee categories, the arguments against token members seems persuasive—particularly so since TDIndustries' board has exercised minimal functions.

Lack of "Outsider" Expertise and Viewpoints on the Board

The desirability of strong outsider presence on boards of large publicly held corporations is now generally accepted. The value of such outsiders for small companies is still a matter of debate. Since the arguments pro and con have been analyzed in earlier chapters, they will not be reviewed here. At TDIndustries, this issue of diversity is complicated by the fact that the top management group over the years has been highly inbred, with Mike Fitzpatrick being the only officer who has not grown up with the company.

In a portion of Jack Lowe's 1979 memo not previously quoted, he argued that—for an outside director to be of real value—the person would have to spend a great deal of time familiarizing himself with the company and its situation and keeping abreast of developments. For that effort, substantial compensation would be necessary. Lowe believed that better value for the company would be realized by use of consultants on specific matters. He followed that practice, and so has his son—increasingly so in recent years, when the company encountered rough going.

The Problem of CEO Succession

Constructive provision for CEO succession is critical. The important role that the board can play in that process in large corporations has been clearly described in a recent book by Vancil (1987). Succession can be no less critical in smaller companies (Ford, 1988; Levinson and Stone, 1990).

At TDIndustries, the only succession so far went well without board involvement: In a business with a strong family tradition, the father was succeeded by a son who was experienced in the business and who commanded respect because of his accomplishments in all of the divisions of the company. Jack Lowe, Jr., is now in his early fifties. Barring unexpected developments, such as a health problem, the next succession is likely to be many years away. However, when it comes, it may prove troublesome. There is no family member to be a likely candidate; the two senior officers, each a member of the executive committee, are almost the same age as Jack Lowe, Jr.; cross-training of managers between divisions has been minimal. The board, with its current composition and skeletal functions, is not well constituted to play a significant part in the succession process.

At the start of this case, TDIndustries' 1980 statement on the board stressed that the "transcendent power" of the board lies in its relationship to conditions of employment of the CEO, including his hiring.

Prudent exercise of this power at some future date may well require careful planning and an eventual rethinking of the composition and role of the board at TDIndustries.

REFERENCES

Berle, A. A., and Means, G. C. (1932). *The Modern Corporation and Private Property.* New York: Macmillan.

Cheshire, A. (1987). *A Partnership of the Spirit: The Story of Jack Lowe and TDIndustries.* Dallas: Taylor.

Fama, E. F. (1980). "Agency Problems and the Theory of the Firm." *Journal of Political Economy*, 88, 288–307.

Ford, R. H. (1988). "Outside Directors and the Privately-Owned Firm: Are They Necessary?" *Entrepreneurship Theory and Practice*, 13(1), 49–57.

French, J. L., and Rosenstein, J. (1984). "Employee Ownership, Work Attitudes, and Power Relationships." *Academy of Management Journal*, 27, 861–69.

Kosnik, R. D. (1987). "Greenmail: A Study of Board Performance in Corporate Governance." *Administrative Science Quarterly*, 32, 163–85.

Levinson, H., and Stone, N. (1990). "The Case of the Perplexing Promotion." *Harvard Business Review*, 68(1), 11–21.

Mace, M. L. (1986). *Directors: Myth and Reality*, Harvard Business School Classics Edition with a new preface. Boston: Harvard Business School Press.

Rosen, C. M., Klein, K. J., and Young, K. M. (1985). *Employee Ownership in America.* Lexington, MA. D. C. Heath.

Rosenstein, J. (1987). "TDIndustries: An Employee Owned Company." *Journal of Management Case Studies*, 3, 80–89.

Rosenstein, J., and French, J. L. (1985). "Attitudes Toward Unionization in an Employee-Owned Firm in the Southwest." *Work and Occupations*, 12, 464–78.

Sobel, R. (1988). *Trammell Crow, Master Builder: The Story of America's Largest Real Estate Empire.* New York: Wiley.

U.S. General Accounting Office (1987). *Employee Stock Ownership Plans: Little Evidence of Effects on Corporate Performance.* Washington, D.C.: U.S. Government Printing Office.

Vancil, R. F. (1987). *Passing the Baton: Managing the Process of CEO Succession.* Boston: Harvard Business School Press.

Important Contacts for Small Businesses

BOARD OF DIRECTORS-RELATED CONTACTS

The Conference Board: 845 Third Avenue, New York, NY 10022. (212) 759–0900. Fact-finding institution that conducts research and publishes studies on business economics and management experience. Publications: (1) *The Sommers Letter*, 30/year; (2) *Across the Board*, monthly; (3) *Consumer Attitudes and Buying Plans*, monthly; (4) *Management Briefing: Human Resources*, monthly; (5) *Statistical Bulletin*, monthly; (6) *Management Briefing: Business Finance*, bimonthly; (7) *Management Briefing: Marketing*, bimonthly; (8) *Business Executives' Expectations*, quarterly; (9) *Manufacturing Investment Report*, quarterly; (10) *Utility Investment Report*, quarterly; (11) *World Economic Monitor*, quarterly; (12) *Survey of Financial Indicators*, semiannual; (13) *Cumulative Index*, annual; (14) *Economic Road Maps*, periodic; it also publishes statistics, bulletins, and reports on continuing research in business and industry.

CT Corporation System: associated with the Corporation Trust Company, 1633 Broadway, New York, NY 10019. (212) 246–5070. CT's services are furnished to the legal market and they include statutory representation for corporations and other special services. CT's statutory representation service is available on a yearly basis and consists primarily of furnishing, under the direction and upon the instructions of lawyers, the statutory agent and/or office for receipt of service of process that corporations are required by statute to maintain in the state or jurisdiction where they are incorporated and in the other states or jurisdictions where they are licensed to engage in business.

National Association of Corporate Directors: 1707 L. Street, NW, Suite 560, Washington, D.C. 20036. (202) 775–0509. A not-for-profit organization concerned with the world of corporate directorship and boardroom activities.

Prentice Hall Legal & Financial Services (Paramount Communications, Inc.): 15 Columbus Circle, New York, NY 10023–7780. (212) 373–8000. Prentice Hall Legal & Financial Services supplies information search, retrieval, and filing services for corporations, law firms, and financial service companies (Charles E. Simon, Infosearch, Master Data Center, and PH Online). It also provides document filing and representation (Prentice Hall Corporate Services).

PUBLICATIONS: GENERAL

These publications are devoted exclusively or primarily to small and emerging private business interests.

Ace Action. Bimonthly publication of the Association of Collegiate Entrepreneurs (ACE). 1845 N. Fairmount, Wichita, KS 67208. (316) 689–3000.

Boardroom Reports. Semimonthly publication giving executives advice and ideas from the most knowledgeable experts, business innovators, and lawmakers. Boardroom Reports, Inc., 330 W. 42 Street, New York, NY 10036. (800) 234–3834.

BusinessWeek Newsletter for Family-Owned Business. Published biweekly with pertinent articles of particular interest for executives of family owned businesses. McGraw-Hill Inc., 1221 Avenue of the Americas, New York, NY 10020. (800) 445–9786 or (212) 512–2184. (Publication ceased operations in 1990.)

Entrepreneur. Monthly publication on business startup. 2392 Morse Ave., Irvine, CA 92714. (800) 421–2300.

Entrepreneurial Woman. Published bimonthly with pertinent information relating to women who own businesses. Entrepreneur, Inc., 2392 Morse Ave., Irvine, CA 92713–9440. (212) 682–6688.

Family Business. Monthly publication with management information and public policy in family businesses. 38 Mahaiwe St., Great Barrington, MA 01239. (413) 528–5160. (Publication ceased operations in 1991.)

Inc. Monthly publication on business startup and growth. 38 Commercial Wharf, Boston, MA 02118. (800) 234–0999.

Nation's Business. Monthly publication on business startup and operations. 1615 H. St. NW, Washington, D.C. 20062. (800) 525–0643.

Self Employed America. Published six times yearly as a benefit exclusively for members and affiliate members of the National Association for the Self-Employed. Subscriptions and single issues not available to the general public. NASE, 2328 Gravel Road, Fort Worth, TX 76118. (800) 232-NASE.

PUBLICATIONS: RESEARCH

These journals are devoted to, or with frequent coverage of, entrepreneurial, small, and private business concerns.

Entrepreneurship Theory and Practice. Quarterly publication that features current research on the creation of enterprises; management of small firms; issues on family business; and others. Baylor University, Hankamer School of Business, The John F. Baugh Center for Entrepreneurship, Speight Avenue at 5th St., Waco, TX 76798–8011. (817) 755–2265.

The Executive. An Academy of Management journal published quarterly whose goal is to provide practicing executives with relevant management tools and information based on recent advances in management theory and research. John P. Young, Editor, *The Executive*, University of Colorado, Campus Box 149, 1200 Larimer St., Denver, CO 80204–5300. (419) 772–1953–4.

Family Business Review. Quarterly publication that seeks articles on new research and theory about family firms; ideas about practical applications of research findings, frameworks, and methodologies for diagnosing and intervening in family firms. Jossey-Bass Inc., 350 Sansome St., San Francisco, CA 94104. (415) 433–1767.

Harvard Business Review. Journal published bimonthly for professional managers. It is a program in executive education of the Graduate School of Business Administration. The Editor, *Harvard Business Review*, Boston, MA 02163. (617) 495–9933.

Journal of Business & Entrepreneurship. Published biannually, it keeps readers abreast of current knowledge and research in small business and entrepreneurship. Northwestern State University, Natchitoches, LA 71497. (800) 368–5855.

Journal of Small Business Management. Published quarterly, it provides articles, notes, and other features on subjects of current professional interest in the fields of small business management and entrepreneurship. USABE, c/o Allen C. Filley, University of Wisconsin, 1155 Observation Drive, Madison, WI 53706.

Journal of Small Business Strategy. Published annually on applied research on topics related to entrepreneurship and small business operations. Stresses strategy in all functional areas. JSBS, Kepner 2090B, Department of Marketing, University of Northern Colorado, Greeley, CO 80639.

Small Business Economics. Quarterly publication whose purpose is to provide the first forum for the economic analysis of the role of small business. Publishes articles on the absolute, relative, and dynamic roles of small business. P.O. Box 358, Accord Station, Hingham, MA 02018–0358.

Small Business Forum. Published quarterly by the Association of Small Business Development Centers, University of Wisconsin, 432 North Lake Street, Madison, WI 53706.

Small Business Reports. Published monthly, addressing a variety of business topics, including finance, marketing, human resources, administration, productivity, management, and legal issues.

GENERAL CONTACTS

ACE (Association of Collegiate Entrepreneurs), 1845 N. Fairmount, Wichita, KS 67208. (316) 689–3000. Network for young entrepreneurs.

The ESOP Association, ESOP, 1100 17th St., NW, Suite 310, Washington, D.C. 20036. The Employee Stock Option Plan is a plan designed to give employees an ownership share in their company. This plan allows employees to benefit personally as the company profits and grows. It is a federally qualified employee benefit program designed to give employees a beneficial ownership stake in the company where they work.

International Franchise Association, 1350 New York Ave., NW, Suite 900, Washington, D.C. 20005. Publications on franchising.

IRS Tax Information. Contact your local IRS office for information about business tax returns. To get an IRS tax number or employer identification number, call (800) 424–1040 and ask for form SS–4.

National Association for the Cottage Industry, P.O. Box 14460, Chicago, IL 60614. (312) 472–8116. Information for home-based businesses.

National Association for Female Executives, 127 West 24th St., New York, NY 10011. (212) 645–0770.

National Association of Women Business Owners, 600 South Federal, Suite 400, Chicago, IL 60605. (312) 922–0465.

National Minority Business Directories, 65 22nd Ave., NE, Minneapolis, MN 55418. (612) 781–6819.

National Venture Capital Association, 1655 N. Ft. Myer Drive, Suite 700, Arlington, VA 22209. (703) 528–4370.

Office of Small and Disadvantaged Business Utilization, U.S. Department of Commerce, 14th and Constitution St., NW, Room 6411, Washington, D.C. 20230. (202) 377–2000.

SBA (U.S. Small Business Administration). Offers information, facts, assistance, and loans for starting a business. Local offices are located in every state. Consult your local telephone directory for SBA offices listed under U.S. Government Offices or call the SBA Answer Desk at (800) 827–5722 (UASKSBA).

SBDC (Small Business Development Centers). Located throughout the United States. Provide free consulting and information for both business startup and growth. Ask your local SBA office for the SBDC near you or call (202) 653–6881.

State Department of Commerce. Consult your local telephone directory under State Government Offices. Typically, for free or minimal cost, they provide information on needed federal, state, and local licenses needed for starting a business. Also contact your state's or city's chamber of commerce for nongovernmental support for new business. For incorporation information, contact the Secretary of State.

Directory of State Corporation Commissions

Alabama	Secretary of State; Corporation Division; 524, State Office Bldg.; Montgomery, AL 36130; (205) 261–5326
Alaska	State of Alaska; Dept. of Commerce and Economic Development; Corporations Section; P.O. Box D; Juneau, AK 99811; (907) 465–3521
Arizona	Incorporating Division; Corporation Commission; 1200 W. Washington; Phoenix, AZ 85007; (602) 542–3076
Arkansas	Corporations Supervisor; State Capitol; Room 58; Little Rock, AR 72201; (501) 371–5156
California	Secretary of State; 1230 J Street; Sacramento, CA 95814; (916) 324–1485
Colorado	Corporations Department; Department of State; 1560 Broadway, Suite 200; Denver, CO 80203; (303) 866–2311
Connecticut	Commercial Recording; 30 Trinity Street; Hartford, CT 06106; (203) 566–2448
Delaware	Corporation Division; Department of State; Townsend Bldg.; Dover, DE 19901; (302) 736–3073
Florida	Secretary of State; Division of Corporations; P.O. Box 6327; Tallahassee, FL 32301; (904) 487–6900
Georgia	Secretary of State; Business Services and Regulations 2; Martin Luther King Jr. Dr., SE; Suite 315 W. Tower; Atlanta, GA 30334; (404) 656–2817
Hawaii	Business Registration Division; 1010 Richards St.; Honolulu, HI 96813; (808) 548–6111
Idaho	Secretary of State; Room 203; Statehouse; Boise, ID 83720; (208) 334–2300
Illinois	Secretary of State; Corporations Department; 328 Centennial Bldg.; 2nd and Edwards; Springfield, IL 62756; (217) 782–6961

Indiana	Corporations Division; Room 155; Statehouse; Indianapolis, IN 46204; (317) 232–6587
Iowa	Corporation Division; Secretary of State; 2nd Floor, Hoover Bldg.; Des Moines, IA 50319; (515) 281–5204
Kansas	Secretary of State; 2nd Floor, State Capitol; Topeka, KS 66612; (913) 296–2236
Kentucky	Corporate Division; State Capitol Bldg.; Frankfort, KY 40601; (502) 564–3490
Louisiana	Corporation Division; P.O. Box 94125; Baton Rouge, LA 70804; (504) 925–4704
Maine	Secretary of State; Bureau of Corporations; State House Station #101; Augusta, ME 04333; (207) 289–4190
Maryland	Charter Division; 301 W. Preston St.; Room 809; Baltimore, MD 21201; (301) 225–1350
Massachusetts	Secretary of State; Corporations Division; 1 Ashburton Place; Room 1711; Boston, MA 02108; (617) 727–9640
Michigan	Corporations Division; Document Review Section; 6546 Mercantile Way; Lansing, MI 48910; (517) 334–6212
Minnesota	Secretary of State; ATTN: Business Services; 180 State Office Bldg.; St. Paul, MN 55155; (612) 296–2803
Mississippi	Secretary of State; Corporations Division; P.O. Box 136; Jackson MS 39201; (601) 359–1350
Missouri	Secretary of State; P.O. Box 778; Jefferson City, MO 65102; (314) 751–4153
Montana	Secretary of State; State Capitol; Helena, MT 59620; (406) 444–3665
Nebraska	Department of Corporations; Secretary of State; Room 2300, State Capitol; P.O. Box 94608; Lincoln, NE 68509; (402) 471–4079
Nevada	Secretary of State; Capitol Complex; ATTN: Corporations; Carson City, NV 89710; (702) 885–5203
New Hampshire	Secretary of State; State House; Room 204; Concord, NH 03301; (603) 271–3244
New Jersey	Division of Commercial Recording; CN 308; ATTN: Corporate Filing Section; Trenton, NJ 08625; (609) 530–6400
New Mexico	Corporation Commission; Corporation Department; P.O. Drawer 1269; Santa Fe, NM 87504–1269; (505) 827–4508
New York	Division of Corporations; Department of State; 162 Washington Ave.; Albany, NY 12231; (518) 474–4750
North Carolina	Secretary of State; Corporations Division; 300 N. Salisbury St.; Raleigh, NC 27603–5909; (919) 733–4201
North Dakota	Secretary of State; Main Capitol Bldg., 1st Floor; 600 E. Boulevard Ave.; Bismarck, ND 58505–0500; (701) 224–3669

Ohio	Secretary of State; 30 E. Broad St.; 14th Floor; Columbus, OH 43266–0418; (614) 466–8464
Oklahoma	Secretary of State; 101 State Capitol; Oklahoma City, OK 73105; (405) 521–3911
Oregon	Corporation Division; 158 12th Street, NE; Salem, OR 97310–0210; (503) 378–4383
Pennsylvania	Corporation Bureau; Department of State; 308 N. Office Bldg.; Harrisburg, PA 17120; (717) 787–1379
Rhode Island	Secretary of State; Corporations Division; 100 N. Main St.; Providence, RI 02903; (401) 277–3040
South Carolina	Corporations Division; P.O. Box 11350; Columbia, SC 29211; (803) 734–2155
South Dakota	Secretary of State; State Capitol Bldg.; Pierre, SD 57501; (605) 773–3537
Tennessee	Secretary of State; Suite 1800; James K. Polk Bldg.; Nashville, TN 37219; (615) 741–2286
Texas	Secretary of State; Corporation Section; Box 13697, Capitol Station; Austin, TX 78711; (512) 463–5586
Utah	Division of Corporations; Heber M. Wells Bldg.; 160 E. 300 S.; 2nd Floor; Salt Lake City, UT 84111; (801) 530–6016
Vermont	Secretary of State; Corporations Division; Pavilion Office Bldg.; Montpelier, VT 05602; (802) 828–2386
Virginia	State Corporation Commission; 13th Floor, Jefferson Bldg.; Richmond, VA 23219; (804) 786–3604
Washington	Secretary of State; Corporations Division; 2nd Floor, Republic Bldg.; 505 E. Union, M/S PM–21; Olympia, WA 98504–0419; (206) 753–7120
West Virginia	Secretary of State; State Capitol; ATTN: Corporations; Charleston, WV 25305; (304) 342–8000
Wisconsin	Secretary of State; Corporations Division; P.O. Box 7846; Madison, WI 53707; (608) 266–3590
Wyoming	Corporations Division; Office of Secretary of State; State Capitol; Cheyenne, WY 82002; (307) 777–7311
District of Columbia	Department of Consumer and Regulatory Affairs; 614 H Street, NW; Room 407; Washington, D.C. 20001; (202) 727–7278
Puerto Rico	Department of State; ATTN: Corporations Division; P.O. Box 3271; Old San Juan Station; San Juan, PR 00902–3271

References and Bibliography

Adkins, Lynn W. (1989). "An Ousted Father Goes To Work For His Son: Why The Story Has A Happy Ending." *The BusinessWeek Newsletter for Family-Owned Business*, 1(21), 5.

Alderfer, Clayton P. (1988). "Understanding and Consulting to Family Business Boards." *Family Business Review*, 1(3), 249–60.

Aldrich, H., and Zimmer, C. (1986). "Entrepreneurs through Social Networks." In *Art and Science of Entrepreneurship*, D. Sexton and R. W. Smilor, Editors. Cambridge, MA: Ballinger.

Andrews, Kenneth R. (1986). "Director's Responsibility for Corporate Strategy." In *Strategic Planning*, J. William Pfeiffer, Editor. San Diego: University Associates, 57–69.

Bacon, J., and Brown, J. K. (1977). *The Board of Directors: Perspectives and Practices in Nine Countries*. New York: The Conference Board.

Bank Directors Responsibilities. (1987). Richmond, VA: Division of Research and Structure, Bureau of Financial Institutions, State Corporation Commission.

Barnard, Chester I. (1976). *The Functions of the Executive*. Cambridge, MA: Harvard University Press.

Birch, David L. (1987). *Job Creation in America*. New York: The Free Press.

Bird, Barbara J. (1989). *Entrepreneurial Behavior*. Glenview, IL: Scott, Foresman.

"A Board of Directors Extends A Firm's Reach." (1990). *Nation's Business*, June, 10–12.

Brown, Buck. (1989) "Enterprise. Latest Board Advice Is Keep It in the Family." *The Wall Street Journal*, January, B–1.

Cabot, L. W. (1976). "On An effective Board." *Harvard Business Review*, 54(5), 40–46.

Castaldi, Richard, and Wortman, Max S., Jr. (1984). "Boards of Directors in Small Corporations: An Untapped Resource." *American Journal of Small Business*, 9(2), 1–10.

Chandler, Alfred D., Jr. (1978). *Strategy and Structure: Chapters in the History of the American Industrial Enterprise*. Cambridge, MA: The M.I.T. Press.

Cochran, Philip L., Wood, Robert A., and Jones, Thomas B. (1985). "The Composition of Boards of Directors and the Incidence of Golden Parachutes." *Academy of Management Journal*, 28(3), 664–71.

Danco, Leon A. (1975). "It's Your Business—Perpetuate or Liquidate." *Retail Control*, 44, 48–51.

Danco, Leon A., and Jonovic, Donald J. (1981). *Outside Directors in the Family Owned Business*. Cleveland: University Press.

Dooley, Michael, P. (1990). *A Practical Guide For The Corporate Director*. KPMG Peat Marwick. Charlottesville, VA: Center for Corporate Governance Education and Research.

Drexler, John A., and Nielsen, James F. (1988). "Corporate Leadership: Boards, Directors, and Strategy." *Family Business Review*, 1(3), 330–33.

Drucker, Peter E. (1989). "What Business Can Learn from Nonprofits." *Harvard Business Review*, 67(4), 88–93.

Fletcher, William Meade. (1990). *Fletcher Cyclopedia of the Law of Private Corporations*. Deerfield, IL: Callaghan & Company.

Ford, Roger H. (1986). *Outside Directors and the Privately-Owned Firm: A Study of the Inc. 500*. Ph.D. dissertation, Syracuse University.

Ford, Roger H. (1987). "The Value of Outside Directors: Myth or Reality?" *Business*, 37(4), 44–48.

Ford, Roger H. (1988). "Outside Directors and the Privately-Owned Firm: Are They Necessary?" *Entrepreneurship: Theory and Practice*, 13(1), 49–57.

Ford, Roger H. (1989a). "For Many Family Firms, Outside Directors Are a Hindrance Because They Don't Know the Business." *The BusinessWeek Newsletter for Family-Owned Business*, 1(6), 6.

Ford, Roger H. (1989b). "The Board of Directors: A Tool For The Future." In *Women Owned Businesses*, Oliver Hagan, Carol Rivchun, and Donald Sexton, Editors. New York: Praeger, 79–101.

Ford, Roger H. (1989c). "Establishing and Managing Boards of Directors: The Other View." *Family Business Review*, 2(2), 142–46.

Ford, Roger H. (1990). "A Board of Directors Extends A Firm's Reach." *Nation's Business*, June, 8, 10.

Ford, Roger H., and Priesmeyer, H. Richard. (1990). "Perceptions of Board Influence in Inc. 500 Firms: A Comparison of Inside and Outside Boards." *Journal of Management in Practice*, 2(1), 37–41.

Ford, Roger H., and Takas, Andrew. (1988). *Student Business Counselor's Handbook*. Harrisonburg, VA: James Madison University.

Garrett, Echo. M. (1989). "Venture's Decade: Up Like a Rocket, Down Like a Rock." *Venture*, 11(5), 46–55.

Geneen, Harold. (1984). *Managing*. New York: Doubleday.

Giardina, James A., and Tilghman, Thomas S. (1988). *Organization & Compensation of Boards of Directors*. New York: Arthur Young.

Gilbert, Betsy. (1984). "Playing for Time on Home Computers." *Advertising Age*, 55(31), 22–24.

Harris, Thomas B. (1989). "Some Comments on Family Firm Boards." *Family Business Review*, 2(2), 150–52.

Heidrick, Gardner W. (1984a). "Building a Stronger Board." *The President*, 20(3), 4–5.

———. (1984b). "An Attractive Alternative: The Board of Advisors." *The President*, 20(3), 5.

———. (1988). "Selecting Outside Directors." *Family Business Review*, 1(3), 271–77.

Hisrich, R. D., and Brush, C. (1984). "The Woman Entrepreneur: Management Skills and Business Problems." *Journal of Small Business Management*, January, 30–37.

"The *Inc.* 500." (1984). *Inc.*, December, 136.

Jacobs, Stanford L. (1985). "A Well-Chosen Outside Board Gives Owners Peace of Mind." *The Wall Street Journal*, January 21, 25.

"The Job Nobody Wants." (1986). *Business Week*, Sept. 8, 57–61.

Johnson, Elmer W. (1990). "An Insider's Call for Outside Direction." *Harvard Business Review*, 68(2), 46–55.

Khan, Arshad M., and Manopichetwattana, Veerachai. (1989). "Models For Distinguishing Innovative and Noninnovative Small Firms." *Journal of Business Venturing*, 4(3), 187–96.

Kesner, I. F., Victor, B., and Lamont, B. T. (1986). "Board Composition and the Commission of Illegal Acts: An Investigation of the Fortune 500 Companies." *Academy of Management Journal*, 29(4), 789.

Kuratko, Donald F., and Hodgetts, Richard M. 1989. *Entrepreneurship: A Contemporary Approach*. Chicago: The Dryden Press.

Lanser, Ross E. (1969). *Visible Traits of Board of Directors of New Enterprise*. Ph.D dissertation, Stanford University.

Lovdal, M., Naver, R. A., and Treverton, N. H. (1977). "Public Responsibility Committees." *Harvard Business Review*, May–June, 40–64, 178, 180–81.

Mace, Myles L. (1971). *Directors: Myth and Reality*. Boston: Harvard University Press.

Manual of Excellent Managements. (1955). New York: American Institute of Management, 23.

Mathile, Clayton L. (1988). "A Business Owner's Perspective on Outside Boards." *Family Business Review*, 1(3), 231–37.

Maturi, Richard J. (1989). "Small-Business Boardroom." *Entrepreneur*, 17(8), 128–32.

Mautz, R. K., and Neumann, F. L. (1970). "The Effective Corporate Audit Committee." *Harvard Business Review*, *Boards of Directors: Part I*, 83–91.

McCarthy, Charles, Jr. (1989). "The Chronicling of Corporate Minutes." *Board Practices Monograph*, 2(3), 1–4.

Mintzberg, Henry. (1983). *Power In and Around Organizations*. Englewood Cliffs, NJ: Prentice Hall.

Moskowitz, Daniel B. (1990). "CEOs Laud Outside Directors, But Only If They Are Used Right." *The BusinessWeek Newsletter for Family-Owned Business*, 2(11), 1 and 10.

Mueller, Robert Kirk. (1984). *Behind the Boardroom Door*. New York: Crown.

———. (1988). "Differential Directorship: Special Sensitivities and Roles for Serving the Family Business Board." *Family Business Review*, 1(3), 239–47.

———. (1990). *The Director's & Officers. Guide to Advisory Boards*. Westport, CT: Quorum.

Nash, John M. (1988). "Boards of Privately Held Companies: Their Responsibilities and Structure." *Family Business Review*, 1(3), 263–69.

———. (1990). *Board Tenure*, Board Practices Monograph. Washington, D.C.: National Association of Corporate Directors.

Nelson, G. W. (1987). "Information Needs of Female Entrepreneurs." *Journal of Small Business Management*, July, 38–44.

New York Insurance Laws. (1985). Chatsworth, CA: NILS Publishing Company.

Pfeffer, Jeffrey. (1972). "Size and Composition of Boards of Directors: The Organization and Its Environment." *Administrative Science Quarterly*, 2, 218–28.

Phillips, Bruce D. (1989). "Small Business Administration." Personal telephone interview with the author on November 3, 1989.

Pocket Guide for Directors and Guidelines for Financial Institution Directors. (1988). Washington, D.C.: Federal Deposit Insurance Corporation.

Posner, Bruce G. (1983). "A Board Even an Entrepreneur Could Love." *Inc.*, April, 73–87.

Revchun, Carol, Hagan, Oliver L., and Sexton, Donald L. (1989). "Your Board of Directors: A Tool for the Future." In *The Woman Entrepreneur: Reflections on the Future*. New York: Praeger.

Richard, J. E. (1990). *Director's Monthly. Compensation Committee Development Ideas*, 14(6), 1–5.

Robinson, Richard B., Jr., (1982). "The Importance of 'Outsiders' in Small Firm Strategic Planning." *Academy Of Management Journal*, 25(1), 80–93.

Ronstadt, Robert C. (1984). *Entrepreneurship: Text, Cases, and Notes*. Dover, MA: Lord Publishing.

Say, Jean Baptiste. (1816). *Catechism of Political Economy*. London: Sherwood, 28–29.

Schipani, Cindy A., and Siedel, George J. (1988). "Legal Liability: The Board of Directors." *Family Business Review*, 1(3), 279–85.

Schmidt, R. (1975). "Does Board Composition Really Make a Difference?" *The Conference Board Record*, 38–41.

Sexton, T. N., and Dahle, R. D. (1976). "Factors Affecting Long-Range Planning in the Small Business Firm." *Marquette Business Review*, 20(2), 158–65.

Sherman, S. P. (1988). "Pushing Corporate Boards to Be Better." *Fortune*, July, 58–67.

Solomon, Steven. (1986). *Small Business USA*. New York: Crown.

"Succession Planning in Closely Held Firms." (1984). *Small Business Report*, November, 52–58.

Swoboda, Frank. (1990). Empowering the Rank and File. *The Washington Post*, September 30, 1990, H3.

The State Of Small Business. (1983). A Report of The President. Washington, D.C.: U.S. Government Printing Office.

The State of Small Business. (1989). A Report of The President. Washington D.C.: U.S. Government Printing Office.

Tillman, Fred A. (1988). "Commentary on Legal Liability: Organizing the Advisory Council." *Family Business Review*, 1(3), 287–88.

Timmons, Jeffry A., Smollen, Leonard E., and Dingee, Alexander L. M., Jr. (1985). *New Venture Creation*, Second Edition. Homewood, IL: Irwin.

Twiss, Brian C. (1980). *Managing Technological Innovation*. London: Longman.

Vance, Stanley C. (1955). "Functional Directors and Corporate Performance." *Business Week*, November 26, 128–30.

———. (1964). *Boards of Directors: Structure and Performance*. Eugene, OR: University of Oregon Press.

————. (1983). *Corporate Leadership: Boards, Directors, and Strategy*. New York: McGraw-Hill.

Verschoor, Curtis C. (1989). "Building A More Effective Audit Committee." *Board Practices Monograph*, 2(4), 1–20.

Wallen, Eileen. (1989). "ESOPS May Be a Good Way to Keep the Company in the Family." *The BusinessWeek Newsletter for Family-Owned Business*, 1(13), 1.

Ward, John L. (1988). "The Active Board with Outside Directors and the Family Firm." *Family Business Review*, 1(3), 223–29.

————. (1989). "Defining and Researching Inside Versus Outside Directors: A Rebuttal to the Rebuttal." *Family Business Review*, 2(2), 147–50.

Ward, John L., and Handy, James L. (1988) "A Survey of Board Practices." *Family Business Review*, 1(3), 289–308.

Wasnak, Lynn. (1989). "Helping Hands." *Ohio Business*, 13(4), 21–25.

Whisler, Thomas L. (1988). "The Role of the Board in the Threshold Firm." *Family Business Review*, 1(3), 309–21.

"Who Needs Outside Directors?" (1989). *Strategic Direction*, (44), *June* 27–28.

Williams, Roy O. (1989). "How to Get Family Members Interested in the Business— And to Want to Run It." *The BusinessWeek Newsletter for Family Owned Business*, 1(9), 7.

Wollner, Kenneth S. (1991). "Preparing for Changes in the Directors and Officers Liability Insurance Market." *Director's Monthly*, 15(1), 10–11.

Wommack, W. W. (1979). "The Board's Most Important Function." *Harvard Business Review*, September–October, 48–62.

Wood, Robert W. (1989). "A Primer on the Ins and Outs of ESOPs: How to Decide If It's the Right Option for Your Firm." *The BusinessWeek Newsletter for Family Owned Business*, 1(25), 9.

Zahra, Shaker A., and Pearce, John A., II. (1989). "Boards of Directors and Corporate Financial Performance: A Review and Integrative Model." *Journal of Management*, 15(2), 291–334.

Name Index

Subject Index

About the Author

ROGER H. FORD is the Zane D. Showker Professor of Entrepreneurship and the Director of the Center for Entrepreneurship at James Madison University. Prior to his career in higher education, he founded and operated a number of businesses in the real estate, retail, and food service industries. Currently, he serves on the boards of directors for four businesses and as a consultant to several others.